'Of course one cannot write a book about Leopardi or Byron without bearing in mind that they were poets; nor about Francesco Datini without referring to trade in the 14th. century . . . But unless what comes out of the book is a living person, whom you feel you might meet in the street tomorrow, it will not be a good biography. . . . In the case of Francesco Datini, for instance, his personality was so tightly bound up with his possessions and his trade that it was necessary to put together a very detailed mosaic of small facts before a man appeared.'

Iris Origo, *Images and Shadows* John Murray, London, 1970.

GEORGE WICKES

1698–1761

ROYAL GOLDSMITH

Elaine Barr

RIZZOLI
NEW YORK

IN ASSOCIATION WITH CHRISTIE'S

To R.A.B.

ENDPAPERS: illustration commissioned by the
Goldsmiths' Company in 1707. This was intended to depict
every process of goldsmithing rather than a workshop
of the day. *Courtesy of the Worshipful Company of Goldsmiths*

TITLE PAGE: *Portrait of George Wickes*, 29½ × 24½ in (74.9 × 62.2 cm)
attributed to John Vanderbank. Formerly in the
possession of Robert Garrard. An inscription on the back
of the portrait reads: 'Portrait of Master George Wickes at
ye King's Arms, property of Robert Garrard, Gold
and Silversmith, 31 Panton Street, Haymarket'.
Private Collection

Published in the United States of America by:

*R*IZZOLI INTERNATIONAL PUBLICATIONS, INC.
712 Fifth Avenue/New York 10019

in association with Christie's.

Copyright © Elaine Barr 1980

First published in 1980 by Studio Vista,
a division of Cassell Ltd. in association with Christie's

LCC NO. 80-5472
ISBN 0-8478-0326-0

Manufactured in Great Britain

Contents

1

The Discovery of the Garrard Ledgers

In 1952 the business of the Crown Jewellers and Goldsmiths, Garrards, was acquired by the Goldsmiths' and Silversmiths' Company of Regent Street. The premises in Albemarle Street to which the former firm had moved in the coronation year of George V, 1911, from the original premises in Panton Street, were disposed of and an auction sale was held of the fittings, furniture and books in Albemarle Street. Thinking that there might be items of interest to Christie's, I obtained a catalogue and thought to go and view the sale. Before I was able to do so, however, my friend Norman Penzer, author of the definitive work on Paul Storr, over lunch told me he was going to the view. I declined to join him from pressure of work.

At about 3 p.m. the same day he rang me up in great excitement saying that he had stumbled on the most unexpected find, no less than the ledgers of the firm going back to George Wickes' start in Panton Street in 1735. He told me that he had, perforce, to return to Sussex, but pleaded with me to do all possible to save them as otherwise they were destined for pulping. His story was that he had already viewed the sale, in which were copies of the Royal plate inventories of both William IV (which he already had) and George V (which he hoped to buy) and had then gone diagonally across the road to his booksellers, Sawyer's in Grafton Street, to leave a commission with them to buy the latter. While he was discussing this another man in the shop turned round and introduced himself as Sulmann, the secretary of Garrard's. He said that if Penzer was so interested, since he already had the William IV inventory, he, Sulmann, would like to present him with the George V copy! Nothing loth Penzer returned to Albemarle Street with his new acquaintance to be presented indeed with the latter volume, which he received with due expressions of gratitude whereupon the donor asked him if he would like to see the firm's ledgers in the basement which had not been included in the sale and which he said would be sent for pulping as no-one presumably wanted them. Penzer accepted the invitation and found himself in the vaults staring at great piles of leatherbound volumes. These he at once recognized to be of the greatest possible importance. Sulmann told him he could have them if he wanted them. Could I save them? I jumped into action, first ringing Fred Eyles, head of the antique silver department at Garrard's and brother of my own colleague at Christie's, Reginald Eyles, and through him obtained permission to take over Penzer's offer. Realizing that this might be a considerable task I then rang John Hayward at the Victoria and Albert Museum and found he was able to come and join me. By about 4 p.m. we were in the vaults in Albemarle Street. Though half choked by the dust we disturbed humping the heavy volumes over, we found what seemed a virtually unbroken chain of ledgers from 1735 to modern times. Time pressed and we felt we could only expect to sort out and save a limited amount and worked on till about the year 1830 segregating all the volumes till then for collection next day. I then arranged for our carriers from Christie's to pick them up and take them to Goldsmiths' Hall as seeming the best haven for them, having informed my old friend the Clerk and obtained his agreement.

However there were to be two alterations to my plans. The first was that John Hayward on returning to the Museum not unnaturally told Charles Oman, Keeper of Metalwork and doyen of the study of English silver, of the find, whereupon the latter insisted that, since a member of the Museum had become involved in the saving of these documents they should be taken to the Museum. To this I could scarcely object since my only real concern was to save them from destruction. The second alteration was the news from Fred Eyles the next morning that soon after our labours in the vaults members of the purchasing firm had penetrated there, and seeing the ledgers, had informed Sulmann that since they had purchased the equity and goodwill of the company, they considered they were entitled to such records as they might wish to retain and therefore proposed to keep the first two volumes (covering 1735 to 47), the volume after Waterloo (on the assumption it might contain interesting details of presentation pieces to the heroes of the day) and that, also, they must retain the later volumes dating from the Royal Appointment, as being of a confidential nature from the royal accounts likely to be found therein. These in any case, John Hayward and I had not arranged to collect, since firstly we had felt ourselves sufficiently rewarded with the salvation of the early volumes and secondly, at that time, strange though it may now sound, scarcely regarded the Victorian period as of serious interest. So the division was made and our selection duly reached the Museum the next day. It was in this way, therefore, that the Wickes-Wakelin-Garrard ledgers were saved for posterity.

After some years I found time to make a cursory examination of the volumes and began slowly to realize the wealth of material and insight into the goldsmith's business, both particular and general, that lay waiting to be mined from them. I prepared and gave to the Society of Silver Collectors a talk on some of the interesting and, indeed, fascinating facts that had emerged from my preliminary inspection and hinted that full and detailed research into their pages would undoubtedly contribute, to an unimagined degree, to our knowledge of the craft and its organization at that time. In the fullness of time my hopes have been realized, since Elaine Barr, whose enthusiasm for silver was already of long standing, saw, in 1968, after a first sight of the ledgers, that they presented a challenge that could not be ignored and so was stimulated into further external research into George Wickes' personal history and his relationship with the Parker family, all of which, with the illustrative material of the firm's productions derived from our records at Christie's, has, I take leave to think, resulted in a major contribution to the study of English 18th century silver and the organization of the trade in its production and marketing. I am delighted to have been privileged to share with the authoress so many of her discoveries and to know that Wickes will now go down to posterity both as a Royal goldsmith of leading rank and indeed also as a name worthy to challenge that of Paul de Lamerie in the first rank of London's 'Maîtres-orfèvres'.

Arthur Grimwade

Preface

My introduction to the ledgers of George Wickes was unexpected and dramatic. It came at a time when, having leisure to study, I was quietly pursuing two passions, silver and history. Once I had opened the great leather covered volumes with their stiff metal clasps I was committed. Now, many years later, familiarity has in no way diminished their fascination.

Far from being dry records of a bygone age, these day-to-day account books of Wickes and his successors—the only goldsmiths' ledgers known to have survived the eighteenth century—have an extraordinary immediacy. Book keeping has changed little over the centuries. A glance at figures 62 and 113 a & b, all typical pages from his ledgers, will serve to shew the method used by Wickes. Each account occupies two facing pages, the debtor side on the left and the contra, or creditor, side on the right. Whilst the credit page often yields far more than routine payments, the debtor page is of greater interest to those who study and collect eighteenth century gold and silver.

Every column holds its own particular magic. Dates (in the old style of the Julian Calendar until 1752 when it was superseded by the Gregorian Calendar) are written in the first column of the left-hand debtor page: they translate easily into Assay date letters. A brief description of the object follows, sufficient to conjure up a mental picture. The next column is devoted to troy weight in ounces and pennyweights which immediately conveys size and dimensions. The fourth column is at first sight confusing: it gives the price per troy ounce which Wickes charged for the fashioning and is in itself a key to the simplicity or splendour of each piece. The basic cost of sterling silver in Wickes's day was in the region of 5s 6d per troy ounce. The fashioning charge for a standard utilitarian object would amount to very little over 6s per ounce whilst intricate casting and chasing could raise the sum to as much as 15s. Wickes occasionally charges a flat rate per ounce and then adds a further sum for the cost of making: this usually signifies an object of some importance. Engraving is invariably shewn separately and, considering the distinction of the engravers employed by Wickes, the sums are derisory. The last column of all is reserved for the cost to the client—this in itself is a social statement.

The period covered by the Ledgers was unsurpassed for the magnificence of its wrought plate and the objects themselves were, at the outset, my prime concern: the men who fashioned them were shadowy figures known only by their makers' marks. The vast amount of data needed analysing and that, initially, was my main task. Paradoxically, this brought to light occasional references of a personal nature totally unrelated to precious metals which added a new dimension to the work. Although tantalisingly cryptic these homely entries were to lead eventually to Wickes and his circle, throwing some light on the lives led by goldsmiths in eighteenth century London.

The research could at this point have changed direction and become merely a genealogical exercise. Convinced, however, that the Ledgers still had secrets to disclose (and loth to leave the silver), I resolved that the searches of wills and parish registers would have to go hand in hand with further study of the Ledgers. A picture began slowly to emerge, but there were gaps which stubbornly refused to close. I was sure that Wickes must have wed a rich woman long before I was able to prove it: their marriage eluded me for three years.

On the other hand, I had two unprecedented strokes of good fortune. The Earl of Scarbrough most generously placed at my disposal records kept by his ancestor, the third Earl, Treasurer and Receiver General to Wickes's royal patron Frederick, Prince of Wales: these hitherto unpublished documents were a veritable *embarras de richesse*. The finding of the personal papers of John Parker was another milestone. They confirmed a structure of relationships hitherto only suspected and I am indebted to the Parker family for permission to peruse and quote from them.

Whilst working on the Ledgers I was privileged to enjoy the hospitality, camaraderie and tolerance of the Department of Metalwork at the Victoria and Albert Museum. If I am partisan about the qualities of the Department it is with good reason.

Wickes has long been appreciated by discerning collectors and dealers. His work, inevitably, invites comparison with that of de Lamerie, but in spite of the charisma of the great Huguenot, Wickes has gained many converts. This book, it is hoped, will add to their number.

Chronology

7 July 1698   Wickes baptised in Bury St Edmunds
2 December 1712   Wickes apprenticed to Samuel Wastell
16 June 1720   Wickes granted freedom
9 January 1721/22   Wickes married Alder Phelpes
3 February 1721/22   Wickes registered first marks

1730   Wickes entered into partnership with John Craig in Norris St
3 June 1730   Edward Wakelin apprenticed to John Le Sage
June 1735   Wickes dissolved partnership with John Craig and moved to Panton St
30 June 1735   Wickes registered second mark

1735   Wickes appointed goldsmith to Frederick, Prince of Wales
7 March 1737/8   Samuel Netherton apprenticed to Wickes
13 March 1739/40   Wickes made liveryman of Goldsmiths' Company
6 July 1739   Wickes registered third mark

November 1747   Edward Wakelin joined Wickes
17 November 1747   Edward Wakelin registered first mark

7 September 1748   Edward Wakelin granted freedom
November 1750   Wickes/Netherton partnership
5 July 1751   John Parker apprenticed to Wickes
11 October 1760   Retirement of Wickes & Netherton—succeeded by Parker & Wakelin
31 August 1761   Death of George Wickes
4 June 1774   Death of Alder Wickes
February 1803   Death of Samuel Netherton

WICKES/BUTTS FAMILY TREE

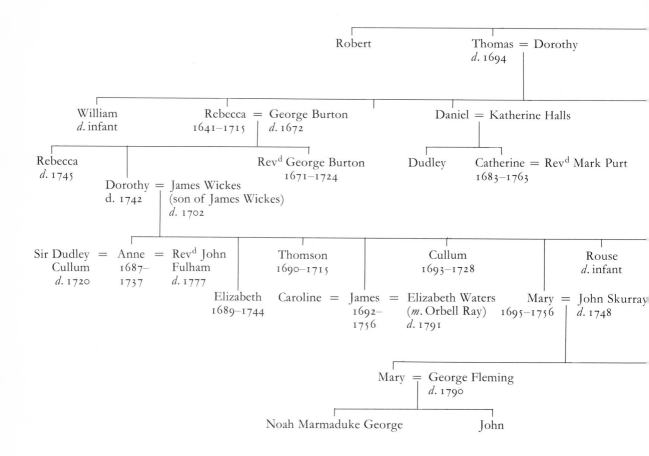

Robert   Thomas = Dorothy
d. 1694

William
d. infant

Rebecca = George Burton
1641–1715   *d.* 1672

Daniel = Katherine Halls

Rebecca
d. 1745

Dorothy = James Wickes
d. 1742   (son of James Wickes)
d. 1702

Revᵈ George Burton
1671–1724

Dudley   Catherine = Revᵈ Mark Purt
1683–1763

Sir Dudley = Anne = Revᵈ John
Cullum   1687–   Fulham
d. 1720   1737   *d.* 1777

Thomson
1690–1715

Cullum
1693–1728

Rouse
d. infant

Elizabeth
1689–1744

Caroline = James = Elizabeth Waters
  1692–   (*m.* Orbell Ray)
  1756   *d.* 1791

Mary = John Skurray
1695–1756   *d.* 1748

Mary = George Fleming
d. 1790

Noah Marmaduke George   John

PHELPES/ALDWORTH FAMILY TREE

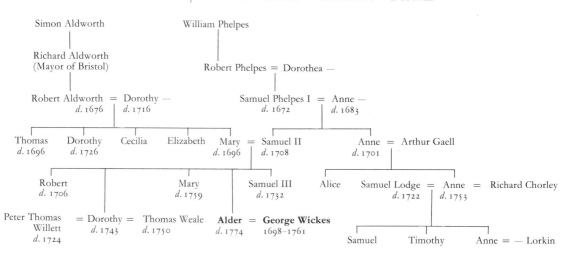

Simon Aldworth

William Phelpes

Richard Aldworth
(Mayor of Bristol)

Robert Phelpes = Dorothea —

Robert Aldworth = Dorothy —
d. 1676   *d.* 1716

Samuel Phelpes I = Anne —
d. 1672   *d.* 1683

Thomas   Dorothy   Cecilia   Elizabeth   Mary = Samuel II
d. 1696   *d.* 1726   *d.* 1696   *d.* 1708

Anne = Arthur Gaell
d. 1701

Robert
d. 1706

Mary
d. 1759

Samuel III
d. 1732

Alice   Samuel Lodge = Anne = Richard Chorley
    d. 1722   *d.* 1753

Peter Thomas
Willett
d. 1724

= Dorothy = Thomas Weale
  d. 1743   *d.* 1750

Alder = **George Wickes**
d. 1774   1698–1761

Samuel   Timothy   Anne = — Lorkin

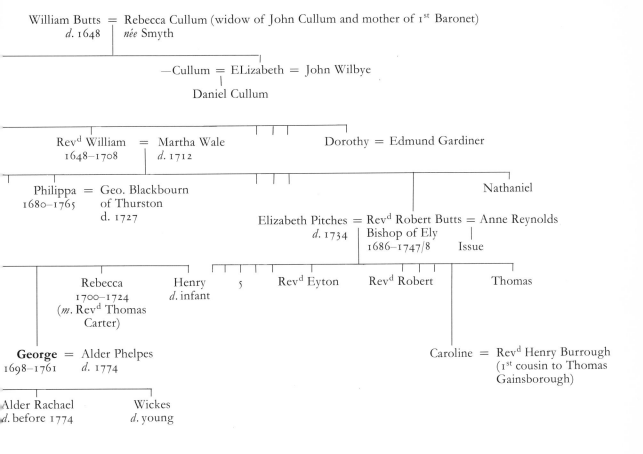

William Butts = Rebecca Cullum (widow of John Cullum and mother of 1ˢᵗ Baronet)
d. 1648 | *née* Smyth

—Cullum = ELizabeth = John Wilbye
Daniel Cullum

Revᵈ William = Martha Wale   Dorothy = Edmund Gardiner
1648–1708   d. 1712

Philippa = Geo. Blackbourn   Nathaniel
1680–1765   of Thurston
d. 1727

Elizabeth Pitches = Revᵈ Robert Butts = Anne Reynolds
d. 1734 | Bishop of Ely |
1686–1747/8   Issue

Rebecca   Henry   5   Revᵈ Eyton   Revᵈ Robert   Thomas
1700–1724   d. infant
(*m.* Revᵈ Thomas
Carter)

George = Alder Phelpes   Caroline = Revᵈ Henry Burrough
1698–1761   d. 1774   (1ˢᵗ cousin to Thomas
Gainsborough)

Alder Rachael   Wickes
d. before 1774   d. young

PARKER/NETHERTON FAMILY TREE

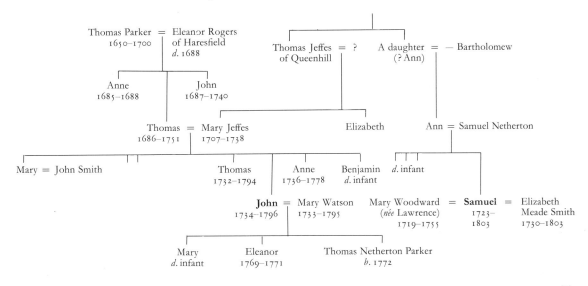

Thomas Parker = Eleanor Rogers
1650–1700 | of Haresfield
d. 1688

Thomas Jeffes = ?   A daughter = — Bartholomew
of Queenhill   (? Ann)

Anne   John
1685–1688   1687–1740

Thomas = Mary Jeffes   Elizabeth   Ann = Samuel Netherton
1686–1751   1707–1738

Mary = John Smith   Thomas   Anne   Benjamin   d. infant
1732–1794   1736–1778   d. infant

John = Mary Watson   Mary Woodward = Samuel = Elizabeth
1734–1796   1733–1795   (*née* Lawrence)   1723–   Meade Smith
1719–1755   1803   1730–1803

Mary   Eleanor   Thomas Netherton Parker
d. infant   1769–1771   b. 1772

I

George Wickes

The documentation of George Wickes begins appropriately with his baptismal entry in the register of St Mary's Church, Bury St Edmunds on the 7 July 1698. He was the eighth of ten children born to James and Dorothy Wickes between 1686 and 1701. James Wickes was an upholder or upholsterer and two of his sons, Thomson and Cullum, followed their father in this trade. That the family lived in Bury St Edmunds in reasonable comfort can be gauged by the description of the property in Cook Row (now Abbeygate Street) left to James Wickes by his brother Joseph on his death in 1693 and already occupied by James when the will was made in 1692: 'all and singular houses, outhouses edifices, buildings, yards, garden, watercourse and appurtenances in Cook Row'. It is probable that George Wickes was born in this house though it was by no means the only property in the possession of the family. The 1674 Hearth Tax Returns for Suffolk contain two separate entries for householders named James Wix [sic] in Bury St Edmunds.[1] One was taxed on six hearths, the other three. Since George's grandfather and father were both called James it is impossible to discover which man occupied the larger house. On the death of James Wickes the younger in 1702 his worldly goods were left to his wife Dorothy: they included not only the 'freehold messuage or tenement ... in Cook Row', Bury St Edmunds, left to him by his brother Joseph, but also a 'copy-hold messuage or tenement in Bury St Edmunds aforesaid in or neare a place there called the Traverse'.[2]

The family of James Wickes, upholsterer, would appear to have consisted of craftsmen living in modest circumstances, their connections with the gentry of Suffolk restricted to matters of trade. The reverse was in fact the case. There is abundant evidence that they were linked by blood and marriage to the Cullum, Pitches and Butts families, all three major Suffolk families.

Little is known of the family background of James Wickes, the father of George, save that he was probably the son of the James and Elizabeth Wickes whose children were baptized in St James's Church, Bury St Edmunds between 1665 and 1670. This is supported by the will of his bachelor brother Joseph[3] who obligingly mentions

Candelabrum, one of a pair made for Lord North, George Wickes, 1731. The branches, although unmarked, are, like the candlesticks, engraved with the crest of the Prince of Wales and his motto 'Ich Dien', presumably to commemorate Lord North's appointment in the Prince's household. (See Chapter XII, Note 2 and figure 90).
Private Collection

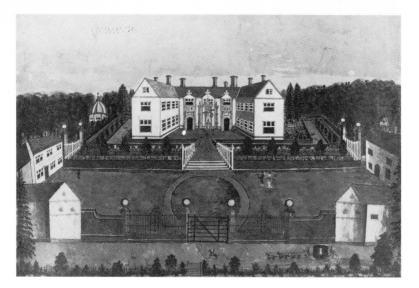

1. *Hawstead Place*, south view, watercolour by an unknown artist. In a sketch once owned by Sir Thomas Cullum the windows are mullioned. The Cullums also possessed another mansion nearby called Hardwick House. *Courtesy of St Edmundsbury Borough Council (Jarman Photographic Collection)*

in this testament his parents and names his living brothers and sisters and their children. The ancestry of George's mother Dorothy can, however, be traced more accurately. She was the second child of George Burton by his marriage to Rebecca Butts; her elder sister, also named Rebecca, figures constantly in the Wickes story; her brother George was in Holy Orders and a Cambridge don. The connection with the Butts family is of some significance. In the first half of the seventeenth century William Butts, gentleman, of White Place, Brockford, married Rebecca Cullum, née Smyth, the widow of John Cullum to whom she had borne five children, one of them the first baronet. Her daughter by her second marriage to William Butts also married a Cullum. Thomas Butts, her son, and his wife Dorothy had a large family which included Rebecca, the mother of the future Dorothy Wickes, and William, the father of Robert Butts (the future Bishop of Norwich and Ely). William himself was the Rector of Hartest, the Church being a profession much favoured by the Butts family. Dorothy Burton Wickes was therefore first cousin to the Bishop of Ely and her goldsmith son, George, his first cousin once removed.

The marriage of William Butts to John Cullum's widow was to link the families of Wickes and Butts with that of the Cullums, one of the foremost in Suffolk, but the name Wickes appears in the annals of the Cullum family in the sixteenth century. It is mentioned yet again in a will,[4] proved in 1680, of a member of a family connected with the Cullums: Symon Myddleton, the son of the eminent goldsmith Sir Hugh Myddleton of New River fame, refers to his 'sister-in-law Mrs Mary Wickes widow of Nathaniel Wickes, mercer, of London'. The

2

name appears in the records of the Worshipful Company of Goldsmiths when Thomas, the son of Nathaniel Wickes, cloth-worker, was apprenticed in 1658.

The kinship with the Cullums may have been slight from a strictly genealogical point of view, but it is obvious that the intimacy between the families was of long standing. In 1693 James and Dorothy Wickes christened their second son Cullum: he was specially favoured in the will of the third baronet, Sir Dudley Cullum, which suggests that he may have stood godfather to the boy. At the time of Cullum Wickes's birth his sister Anne was but 6½ years of age. When she was 23 she was married to Sir Dudley Cullum in Hawstead Church, Suffolk, on the 12 June 1710, by licence. Sir Dudley's first wife, the sister of Lord Berkeley of Stratton, had died in June 1709 leaving no issue. That Sir Dudley considered Anne Wickes as his kinswoman as well as his wife can be seen from the special provision in his will[5] for her burial beside him 'with such an inscription as I shall leave in writing': on her death in 1737 the significant words *Quæ Sanguine Illum attingens* were carved over her tomb.

In 1710, however, funeral thoughts must have been far from the minds of Sir Dudley and his young wife. The Cullums had several homes—they were taxed on a total of fifty-eight hearths in 1674. The Hearth Tax Returns for 1685 reveal that one of their manor houses, Hawstead Place (Fig. 1), had thirty-four hearths. This would have been the house most familiar to Wickes and it was to be the home of his sister Anne, by the terms of Sir Dudley Cullum's will, until such time as she should remarry. The massive stone figure of a woodwose or wildman brandishing a club was in fact a fountain: the date 1578 is carved on the pedestal. Hawstead Place had been bought in 1610 by Sir Robert Drury, the friend of the poet John Donne. The Drury's young daughter immortalized by Donne lies buried in Hawstead Church where Anne and her brother Thomson Wickes were later interred. The house was sold in 1656, reputedly for the sum of £17,697, to Thomas Cullum, a wealthy London draper.

Sir Dudley's second marriage, like his first, was not blessed by children; childless still in 1715, he made provision for Anne being with child at the time of his death. It is probable that Anne's younger brothers and sisters—fatherless since 1702—made frequent visits to the Cullum houses and it is plain from his will that the kindly third baronet held them all in some affection. George Wickes was twelve at the time of his sister's marriage. Her new home, Hawstead Place, set in beautiful parkland, must have left an indelible impression on his young mind. No doubt he would have been familiar with the charming legend dating from Elizabeth I's Suffolk progress in 1578. She dined at nearby Lawshall Hall on the 5 August and in the

3

evening she went to Hawstead. Tradition reports that during her visit she dropped her silver-handled fan in the moat and when it was restored to her by her host he was promptly knighted for his gallantry.

From his childhood George Wickes would have been familiar with the plate in use and on display in his sister's houses. The decision to apprentice him to a goldsmith when he reached the age of fourteen in 1712 may have been his own or one recommended to him by Sir Dudley Cullum who would have had powerful influence with the London goldsmiths through his connections with the Myddletons.[6] Six years earlier George Pitches, a kinsman of both the Wickes and Cullum families, had left Hawstead, where his father was Rector, to serve an apprenticeship to Thomas Folkingham, the London goldsmith. Elizabeth Pitches, his younger sister, had married in 1712 Robert Butts, later to become the Bishop of Ely; thus Bishop Butts had a goldsmith brother-in-law and a goldsmith first cousin once removed. This was not George Wickes's only link with the Pitches family: his aunt Elizabeth Wickes had married a Pitches, probably the Robert Pitches whose marriage to an Elizabeth Wicks [sic], single woman, is recorded in the register of St James's Church, Bury St Edmunds, on the 17 October 1683. George Pitches became free of the Goldsmiths' Company in 1715 and entered a joint mark with John Edwards in 1723. He and George Wickes were later to become neighbours, but there is no evidence in Wickes's ledgers that they ever worked together.

On the 2 December 1712 George Wickes was duly apprenticed through the Worshipful Company of Goldsmiths in Foster Lane London to Samuel Wastell for the term of seven years. The premium paid to his master was £30. He signed the Apprentice Book as 'George Wicks', although he incorporated the letter 'e' in all subsequent signatures.

Once he had served his apprenticeship through the Goldsmiths' Company and obtained his freedom—in his case by service—Wickes was entitled to call himself 'goldsmith and citizen of London'. A goldsmith, however, spent the best part of his working life fashioning silver: due to the high cost of gold, commissions for works in the more precious metal were rare. A convention seems to have existed in the eighteenth century which conferred the title of 'silversmith' on those on the fringe of the craft, though such niceties were not observed in the royal account books of the period where they are all described simply as silversmiths. Today the words are completely interchangeable and the term silversmith is in no sense derogatory. Throughout this book 'goldsmith' has been chosen for the sake of consistency and to avoid confusion.

4

In 1712 Wickes's master Samuel Wastell, like every other London goldsmith, was working solely in Britannia standard silver in compliance with the Act of Parliament (8 Wm. III c. 8 (1696–7)) which came into force on the 25 March 1697. This act raised the standard of wrought silver from the sterling standard of 925 parts pure silver per thousand in each troy pound to 958, the remaining parts being in both cases copper. The Act was introduced in order to prevent the debasement of the coin of the realm which, conveniently for the goldsmiths, was of the sterling standard previously laid down for wrought plate. Clipping the coins in circulation had become a popular method of obtaining silver which could be taken to a goldsmith and melted down for fashioning into plate. The new measures remained in force until the 1 June 1720 when the Wrought Plate Act, 1719, became effective and gave the goldsmiths the right to work in either standard. Throughout his apprenticeship Britannia silver—or New Sterling as it was known—was to be the metal on which George Wickes learnt his craft.

Samuel Wastell set up on his own shortly after gaining his freedom by service and registered his mark at Goldsmiths' Hall: the 1696 Act required goldsmiths to re-register their marks using the first two letters of their surnames and Wastell's mark in 1701 consisted of the letters W A surmounted by a bishop's mitre. The 1719 Act revived the old form of maker's mark—the initials of his christian and surname—for all work in the old standard and until 1739 goldsmiths used two makers' marks. Wastell had never registered a mark for sterling silver at the Hall but the initials S W surmounted by a mitre have been noted by Mr Arthur Grimwade on a sterling standard mug of 1722 and a teapot of 1729: it is reasonable to assume that this mark was indeed that of Samuel Wastell who had calmly flouted the Hall's regulations by using a mark that had not been registered. He added to his sins of omission by failing to notify the Hall of his change of address when he moved from Finch Lane to Cheapside, neglecting at the same time to re-register his mark. George Wickes was to be equally negligent in this respect and one can only conclude that Wastell was not in some ways the best of masters. The Minutes of the Court of Wardens record more serious offences. On the 24 February 1691 'Mr. Wastell appeared and submitted himself to this Court for selling silver worse than sterling'. He was fined the sum of one shilling, but on subsequent occasions in 1692, 1693, 1695 and 1707 he was found guilty of the same offence. The Court of Wardens, in an effort to uphold the high standard of British silver was forced to impose such fines on recalcitrant goldsmiths with monotonous regularity. On the evidence of the plate which bears his mark, Wastell was a good craftsman (in an age of fine craftsmen) most of the time

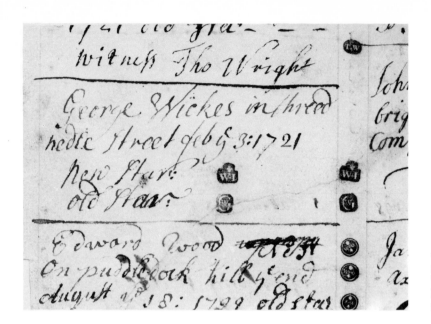

2. George Wickes's first maker's marks (entry in the Large Plate Workers' Register at Goldsmiths' Hall). *Courtesy of the Worshipful Company of Goldsmiths*

and a superb one on occasions. Wickes was at least able to learn by example if not by precept. With the exception of Wickes, none of Wastell's apprentices sought his freedom or registered a mark, but there could be normal explanations for this apparent anomaly. Although he never joined the ranks of the wealthy or prominent goldsmiths, Samuel Wastell cannot have worked without profit since his name is to be found in the ledgers of the East India Company in 1669 with an investment of £250. His will, proved in 1730, reveals little: he mentions no fellow goldsmiths and leaves no bequests to any of his former apprentices.

Wickes remained under the ægis of Wastell for some nine years. He was made free by service on the 16 June 1720. Under the provisions of the 1563 Statute of Artificers (which was not repealed until the nineteenth century) an apprentice had to be twenty four years old at least before he was granted his freedom. Wickes was only twenty two. It was not until the 3 February 1721/2 that he registered his marks[7]— unexceptional in design—for sterling and Britannia silver at Goldsmiths' Hall (Fig. 2). This entry reveals a significant fact: Wickes gives as his address Threadneedle Street. A search of the Land Tax Assessments made on the inhabitants of the Ward of Broad Street, in the City of London shews George Wickes in Threadneedle Street, in the Lower Division headed St Benet Finck, in 1722. Houses at that time were not numbered and Wickes lived between Widow Brakley and Joseph Mason. The shop sign may have been the fleur-de-lys which he incorporated into his Britannia mark, surmounting the first two letters of his surname. His neighbours included a William

Pitches (later John Pitches and son) and Thomas Folkingham, the master of his Suffolk kinsman George Pitches of Hawstead. It is obvious that Wickes had left Wastell and set up on his own.

Wickes was at this time only 23½ years of age and it is a measure of his confidence in his skill that he took such a momentous step so early in his career. He had little money of his own, possibly only the annuity of £10 left him in 1720 by his brother-in-law Sir Dudley Cullum: an identical bequest to his eldest brother James Wickes was cancelled and instead he was given outright the £100 already 'lent him towards setting upp his trade'. The other members of the Wickes family fared rather better and handsome provision was made for Anne, Lady Cullum. It is improbable that George's brothers James, a sadler, and Cullum, an upholsterer, then aged 30 and 29 respectively and both living in London, would have been in a position to give the young goldsmith much financial help. His mother may have had money set aside for her youngest surviving son, perhaps the 'overplus for benefit of my children' mentioned in her husband's will, but it is far more likely that his marriage in 1722 to Alder Phelpes, heiress, paved the way.

Notes for chapter I

1. This tax of two shillings per year levied on every hearth was imposed by Charles II in 1662 and was not repealed until 1689.
2. Arch. Sudbury Steward 402
3. Arch. Sudbury Steward 237
4. P.R.O.: PCC Prob 11/364–151
5. P.R.O.: PCC Prob 11/578–23
6. These connections were not confined to the Myddleton family. In a Cullum will of 1636 the testator, William Culham [sic] refers to his brother 'John Culham of Little Britten, London, goldsmith'.
7. All the dates quoted in this book up to 1752 follow the Julian Calendar in common use in Britain at the time. The New Year by this reckoning began on the 25 March. Wickes's ledger entries for the whole of January, February and up to the 25 March are covered by two years separated by a stroke of his pen and he does not bring the current year into his dating until after the 25 March. The Julian Calendar was superseded by the Gregorian Calendar. Introduced in Italy in 1582, this was not adopted by Britain until the middle of the eighteenth century when the Statute George II c. 23 of 1751 decreed that the 1 January 1752 should be the first day of 1752

II   The Goldsmith's Wife

Alder Phelpes, the wife of George Wickes, was the youngest of the three daughters of Samuel Phelpes by his wife Mary, née Aldworth.

The marriage allegation of Samuel Phelpes in the Registry of the Vicar-General of the Archbishopric of Canterbury records: '18 Feb 1679–80. Samuell Phelps of St Michael Bassishaw, London, Mercht., Bachr., abt. 30, & Mrs Mary Aldworth, of Blowbather Street, London, Spr., abt. 21, with consent of her mother Mrs Dorothy Aldworth, widow; at Stepney Middlesex'. Blowbather Street is a clerk's error for Blowbladder Street, a small street which at that time connected Newgate Street with Cheapside and abutted on Jackanapes Row near St Paul's Churchyard. Mary Aldworth is given the courtesy title of Mrs or Mistress, indicating a certain gentility and social position as befitted a member of a great merchant family of Bristol. It will be noted that although it was customary in allegations to name the church where the marriage was to be solemnized, in this case the information is omitted. The obvious choice in Stepney—then a country retreat—would have been St Dunstan & All Saints, but there is no record in the church register.[1] It is not unknown to find the choice of church radically changed in the time elapsing between marriage allegation and wedding, but in this case there is a possibility that the parties were non-conformist and chose to be married in the meeting house in Bull Lane, Stepney, which was built in 1674. The only marriage records available for this chapel (founded in 1644) begin in 1646 and end three years before Mary Aldworth wed Samuel Phelpes in 1680.

Samuel Phelpes must have congratulated himself on making an excellent match. The Aldworths had been interested in the exploration and commercial exploitation of the New World since Elizabethan times when a Thomas Aldworth helped to finance the first voyage of Martin Frobisher. This same Thomas Aldworth also sailed in the tenth voyage of the East India Company and is credited with the setting up of an important English trading station at Surat.

In the seventeenth century one of Bristol's greatest sons, Robert Aldworth, established the first sugar refinery. He was Master of the Society of Merchant Adventurers of the City of Bristol in 1609, 1612

3. Detail from a tapestry map of Worcestershire, English, Sheldon, woven in wool and silk. From the original set woven by Richard and Francis Hyckes in 1588. (Chacely is situated towards the bottom of the map to the right of centre.) *Bodleian Loan 1. Courtesy of the Victoria and Albert Museum (Crown Copyright Reserved)*

9

and 1625. In 1632, with his relative Giles Elbridge, he obtained a grant from the Council of New England of a considerable tract of land in America with the promise of one hundred additional acres for every immigrant, provided they founded and maintained a colony.

Mary Aldworth's father Robert was a kinsman of the eminent sugar merchant and also his godson and namesake. In his godfather's will, proved on the 12 January 1634/5,[2] he is described as the son of Richard Aldworth, mercer. It is known from an entry dated the 25 May 1605 in the Bristol Apprentices' Book that Richard was the son of Simon Aldworth, a merchant of Reading in the county of Berkshire. It is apparent from the will of the great sugar merchant Robert Aldworth that he too had strong links with Berkshire: he left £20 to his kinsman Thomas Aldworth of Wantwich and the same sum 'to beautify the church at Wantwich'. He was, however, buried in St Peter's Church Bristol (in 'mine owne ile') where his late wife Martha was interred: three sugar loaves are incorporated in the design of his handsome monument. The bulk of his fortune was left to Giles Elbridge, a member of his wife's family, who had married Aldworth's niece.

Richard Aldworth, Mary's grandfather, was also a member of the Society of Merchant Adventurers of Bristol and served as Warden in 1641 (Fig. 4). In 1643 he was appointed Mayor of Bristol and it is apparent from a pamphlet published in May 1643 by order of the

4. Basin and ewer, diameter of basin 21½ in (54.6 cm), height of ewer 14¼ in (36.2 cm), George Wickes, 1735. Made for Leonell Lyde, Mayor of Bristol. The entry in the ledger reads:

To a fine bason & ewer
275 ozs 10/10 £148 19s 2d
To graving   16s 0d

Commons 'assembled in Parliament' that Richard Aldworth was a zealous parliamentarian.[3]

Mayor Richard Aldworth's son Robert, the father of Mary, was admitted as a burgess of Bristol on the 24 January 1645/6. He died in 1676 leaving a wife, Dorothy, and five children—Thomas, Dorothy, Elizabeth, Mary and Cecilia. His widow, Mrs Dorothy Aldworth, later moved to London and enters the Wickes story in 1680 when her daughter Mary married Samuel Phelpes and eventually gave birth to Alder, the future wife of the goldsmith George Wickes. Alder's unusual christian name may have derived from her mother's maiden name, but more probably she was given the name of a godparent, perhaps a descendant of the Thomas Alder who was Warden of the Society of Merchant Adventurers of Bristol in 1566 when Elizabeth I confirmed the charter granted to the Society by Edward VI.

Mary Aldworth's husband Samuel Phelpes was the son of a wealthy London merchant residing in Basinghall Street in the parish of St Michael Bassisshaw. His family roots were, however, in Worcestershire in the manor of Chaceley. This manor, which had formerly belonged to the Priory of Little Malvern, was granted in fee to a certain George Throckmorton of Deerhurst in 1543 and was alienated by him in the following year to Robert Phelpes, his tenant. The passing of the manor from father to son can be traced through numerous chancery documents and generations of the Phelpes family can be found in the registers of the little church of St John the Baptist at Chaceley, beginning with the baptism of William, son of Robert Phelpes, in 1541. In 1612 the manor was in the possession of yet another Robert Phelpes who held it until 1626 when he and his wife Dorothea conveyed it to Christopher Helme. It returned to the Phelpes family in 1653 when it was bought by Samuel Phelpes, the grandfather of Alder Wickes (hereafter for convenience styled Samuel Phelpes I).

On the 14 October 1672 Samuel Phelpes I made his will which was proved on the 2 January the following year.[4] It is sufficiently detailed to give an interesting glimpse not only of the personal lives of the members of the family, but also of the estate real and personal which was later to appear in the ledgers of George Wickes in the accounts of his wife's sisters Dorothy and Mary, the grand-daughters of Samuel Phelpes I.

Anne, the relict, was to have one of his two houses in Basinghall Street 'for her life onely'. It is described in the will as standing 'on a parcell of ground bought of Christopher Feake'. He later grants to her and their daughter Anne 'the use of soe much of this house wherein I am now living in Basingshaw-Street London which is convenient for them whilst they are both living and unmarryed'. The exact location can be determined from a contemporary document *The Survey of Building Sites in the City of London after the Great Fire of 1666* drawn up by two seventeenth century surveyors, Peter Mills and John Oliver, and described as 'a posting book for receipts of money for staking out foundations in the ruins of the City of London.[5] Two foundations are shewn against the name of Samuel Phelpes I and a sketch reveals the location as being next to Girdlers' Hall with 'on the north side a passage of 4 foot to be left for Mr. Phelpes' on the Company's site. Some idea of the narrowness of seventeenth century City houses can be gained from the frontage—a mere fourteen feet. The depth of the site was originally ninety-three feet, but a plot thirteen feet long by eleven feet wide adjoining the garden of the Girdlers' Company is marked as 'sould to the Girdlers Company' and this is confirmed by the Company's Court Minutes which record 'the purchase of ground in the front from a Mr. Samuel Philip (sic) and his wife'. Since this is the only sketch for Samuel Phelpes it must be assumed that it covers two foundations: two houses therefore must have been built on a plot measuring seventy-eight feet by fourteen feet, with, presumably, access to the second from Baker's Alley South, the four foot passage mentioned above. The insurance policy which Alder Wickes took out with the Hand-in-Hand Company in the eighteenth century mentions three stories with garrets above.

Apart from the house in Basinghall Street, Samuel Phelpes bequeathed to his wife Anne, for the term of her life, Cumberwood Farm in Tirley, Gloucestershire, and a neighbouring farm called Sandpits. In the manner of the time, her personal property—two acres in Tirley known as Lords Meadow 'which shee bought with her owne moneyes'—was formally left to her to dispose of 'to whome she pleaseth at her death'. Cumberwood and Sandpits are still farmed to this day.

While Anne Phelpes remained a widow she was to receive one half of her late husband's profits from his 'principall stock and joynt trade' with the East India Company. There is a peculiar fascination in following Samuel Phelpes through the ledgers of the East India Company. His name appears for the first time in the Stock Journals in 1666 with an investment of £500. In 1668 he lent the Company £1,000 at interest and followed it with a further loan of £1,000 in 1669. The name of Phelpes does not disappear from the East India Company's books until 1688. Mrs Anne Phelpes died in 1683 so it would appear that the decision to end the family's connection with the Company in 1688 was made by their son Samuel Phelpes II. The entrance of George Wickes into the story is strangely foreshadowed when beneath the name of Samuel Phelpes I appears that of Wickes's master Samuel Wastell with an investment of £250 in 1669.[6]

12

By the terms of the will of Samuel Phelpes I the use of all household goods was to be shared equally between his widow and his only daughter Anne whilst they remained unmarried and each received outright one bed and furniture (the latter being the bedding, curtains, canopy, valance and counterpane, often of tapestry or rich material). His daughter Anne was left £1,500 in cash, land or houses and one piece of pasture in Tirley which, like her mother, 'she herself bought with her owne moneys'. There is an intimate touch in the bequest of the 'furniture for a bedd which shee herselfe hath been at ye working thereof', a cabinet, a pair of virginals and a looking glass. In her own will, made in 1690 and proved in 1701,[7] Anne mentions 'a looking glass sett in a frame wrought with tortoise shell'—it may well have been the one left to her by her father. No jewels were mentioned in her mother's portion, but Anne received 'all the jewels and pearls and necklaces which are her proper owne': her own will itemizes a 'best necklace of pearl . . . one gold watch a small necklace of pearls with diamond locket thereto belonging and two diamond rings'. Nowhere in the will is there any mention of plate: such a family would certainly have possessed a quantity of wrought silver and it may have been included in the household goods. Unlike her father, Anne apportioned her silver scrupulously between her daughters, 'a caudle cup a little porringer, one other porringer and three spoons' to Alice and a 'tankard a plate and three spoons' to Anne.

The bulk of Samuel Phelpes I's fortune, together with the reversions on the death of his wife, was left to his son Samuel and his heirs for ever 'to be enjoyed by him and them as their proper and peculiar right in the lawe'. Samuel Phelpes II was twenty-five and unmarried at the time of his father's death. His mother must have felt that more than adequate provision had been made for him and when she died in July 1683 the main beneficiary in her will[8] was his sister Anne, by this time the wife of Arthur Gaell, a wholesale haberdasher of the parish of St Benet Gracechurch. In the event of Anne Phelpes Gaell dying without issue the estate was to pass to her brother Samuel: this apart, he was left ten shillings 'to buy him a ring to wear in remembrance'. Gaell, sometimes spelt Gael or Gale, is a name often encountered in Suffolk, the birthplace of George Wickes, and Arthur Gaell had an aunt in Sudbury and an uncle, Edward Gaell, who was a linen draper in Ipswich. Even after her husband's death in 1684 Anne kept in close touch with them and in her will she entrusted the care and tuition of her children to that same Uncle Edward.[9]

After his father's death Samuel Phelpes II continued to live and work in London. It is probable that he carried on the business built up by his father. At least five children were born to his wife Mary, but no baptisms have come to light.[10] The Samuel Phelpes who was buried in St Michael's Bassisshaw on the 15 May 1684 may have been a child lost in infancy, but no indication is given in the register. In 1706 a Mr Robert Phelpes was interred and this ties in with a reference in the will of Mrs Dorothy Aldworth, Mary's mother, to her dead grandson 'Roben', probably named after his Aldworth grandfather. In November 1696 Mary herself was buried in St Michael's Bassisshaw: her death coincides with the birth of Samuel Phelpes III and she may well have died in childbed. Shortly afterwards Samuel Phelpes II retired and settled with his three daughters and small son on the family estates on the Worcestershire/Gloucestershire borders (Fig. 3), making the transition from merchant to country gentleman. His eldest daughter Dorothy no doubt kept house for him and helped to bring up the motherless Samuel. Phelpes's enjoyment of his manor of Chaceley was short-lived. He died, at the age of 61, on the 1 March 1707/8 and was buried in the Church of St John the Baptist at Chaceley. Some six weeks before his death he made his will.[11] He was 'sick and weak in body but of sound perfect mind' and his brief testament is that of a tired man. There are no lengthy instructions for the disposal of his worldly goods and it is obvious that he had complete confidence in his eldest daughter. All 'freehold messuages house or houses lands tenements hereditaments and premises in possession not limited in joynture' were bequeathed to Dorothy and her heirs and assigns for ever. His other two daughters, Mary and Alder, apparently received nothing and are mentioned in the will merely as joint and sole executrices with their elder sister Dorothy. The clue to the provision made for them would appear to lie in the words 'not limited in joynture'; land and monies may also have been set aside for them on the death of their mother.

By the terms of her father's will Dorothy was empowered 'to have sole management and tuition' of her small brother Samuel in all his affairs until he reached the age of twenty-one; he was to 'be kept to school and bred up in the fear of the Lord'. It is obvious that ample provision had already been made for Samuel III as his only legacy was the sum of one shilling.[12]

The death of Samuel Phelpes II is recorded in the Burial Register of the Church of St John the Baptist at Chaceley. Within the church itself a stone slab with a Latin inscription commemorates him and to it has been added, in English, the date of his son's burial in the same church on the 7 December 1732. We are indebted to this monument for the ages of both men: the elder was sixty-one when he died, the younger thirty-six.

Eight months after the death of her father Dorothy Phelpes married Peter Thomas Willett. It is apparent from the marriage allegation that she was by this time living just outside the City of

London. On the 4 November 1708 'appeared personally Peter Thomas Willett of the parish of St Mary Whitechapel in the County of Middlesex aged about 27 years & a batchelor and alledged that he intended to solemnize marriage with Dorothy Phelps of the same parish aged about 22 and a maiden haveing her freinds [sic] consent'. A licence was granted for them to be married in the Church of All Hallows upon London Wall, a short walk from Basinghall street.[13]

The young brother who had been placed in her care was then twelve years of age and would have accompanied her to London. It is probable that her sisters Mary and Alder also joined her. They seem to have regarded London as their home rather than Worcestershire though Samuel III eventually returned to Chaceley and died there, unmarried, in 1732. The Manorial Rolls record his demise with the comment that nothing was known regarding the future of his lands. He in fact died intestate and administration of his estate was granted to his eldest sister Mrs Dorothy Willett.

It is clear from the will of their grandmother, Mrs Dorothy Aldworth,[14] that she had a very real affection for the orphaned Phelpes children. On her death in 1716 Samuel Phelpes III was left a pair of silver candlesticks and a pair of silver snuffers 'which I had in a former will given his brother Roben' and a gold and coral baby's rattle, 'that is piece of corall sett in gold with three goldbells belonging to it which served all my children' and which may have served Samuel too in his infancy. He also received 'six silver-gilt tea spoons which I promised him when he was a little boy', a tea table and china belonging to it, a copper tea kettle and coffee pot and a black pot and tin lamp. In addition she bequeathed to him half of the middle part of a jewel to make him a ring and a ten shilling piece in silver 'which will serve for his children to play with if he has any'.

Samuel's sisters Dorothy, Mary and Alder were left 'all the money I have when I dye share and share alike' plus 'what other things I have which is not disposed of by Will'. Dorothy, her namesake, was also given a silver porringer and her 'largest gold colour silk quilt which will serve for her wrought bed she may line the curtains as she pleases'. A gold chain was divided between Mary and Alder and each received a silver spoon and jewels. Mary was given her grandmother's snuffbox and Alder her silver toothpick and case. Books were bequeathed to a Mr Stephen Scrope whose name appears as a witness on an Aldworth will of 1677.[15]

Alder Phelpes and her two sisters appear to have fared better than Mrs Dorothy Aldworth's own three living daughters, but here again the latter had been well endowed by their father and, moreover, her two unmarried daughters had inherited their only brother's estate in 1696. Thomas Aldworth, a wealthy merchant, having first settled his wife's personal finances, directed that his entire estate be divided into three equal parts, 'two third parts thereof unto my loving sister Dorothy Aldworth her heirs and assigns for ever' and the other third to his youngest sister Cecilia.[16] Cecilia, or Cele as their mother called her in her will, eventually inherited the entire estate on the death of her sister Dorothy which took place near Bristol in 1726. Cecilia's will has not come to light, but it is a fair guess that the Phelpes girls benefited from it. Their grandmother had left her daughter Dorothy a cabinet inlaid with mother-of-pearl for her natural life and 'a bracelet of mother of pearl to mend it if it needs—I give it to her first thinking she will value it most'. This must surely be the same piece mentioned in the will of Mary Phelpes, Cecilia's niece: 'I give to my cousin Catherine Marten [née Jackson of Bristol] of Overbury in the County of Worcester my mother of pearl cabinet after the decease of my said dear sister Wickes who is to have the use thereof for her life'. Grandmother Dorothy Aldworth had ended her testament with the words 'I desire my three daughters Elizabeth Nelson, Dorothy Aldworth, Cele Aldworth to be kind to their Sister Phelpes children', and it would seem that they honoured her wishes.

The Phelpes girls were obviously the richer by their grandmother's demise in 1716, but it is impossible to estimate their incomes at this period. Dorothy was apparently the wealthiest, but several generations of Phelpes women had owned property and it is unlikely that Alder and her sister Mary were not equally fortunate. Mary, who remained a spinster, lived in some style judging by the accounts kept for her by her brother-in-law George Wickes in his ledgers, and it is obvious that she was possessed of considerable private means. In 1716 Mary and Alder were unmarried and their sister Dorothy had by then been the wife of Peter Thomas Willett for eight years. Willett died in 1724 leaving a will written, as he was at some pains to point out, 'with my one [sic] handwriting'.[17]

He bequeathed all his moneys, goods and chattles to his wife Dorothy, naming her as 'hole excecetris'. A holograph will was not uncommon, but the testament of Peter Thomas lacked signature, seal and witnesses.[18] In order to satisfy the law it fell to George Wickes of St Benedict Finck London, goldsmith, and Benjamin Cater, broker, to identify the handwriting.[19] On the 29 November 1726, two years after Willett's death, Wickes and Cater appeared personally 'and by viertue of their oathes deposed that they severally knew and were well acquainted with Mr Peter Thomas Willett . . . several years before his death and with his handwriting character and manner of writing they having several times seen him write'.[20]

It may well have been through Peter Thomas that the goldsmith George Wickes first met his future wife Alder Phelpes. Whatever the manner of their meeting, George and Alder were married at All Hallows upon London Wall on the 9 January 1721/22, the church in which Alder's sister Dorothy had wed Peter Thomas Willett in 1708. The church register merely records the event without indicating whether it was by licence or banns: the latter is probable since no marriage allegation has been found. An allegation would have disclosed the parish in which Alder was residing at the time and, more importantly, some clue to her age though marriage allegations are notoriously unreliable on this point, 'about 21' may mean 'above 21' and therefore of legal age; Samuel Phelpes II is described as 'about 30' when we know from his funeral monument that he was in fact thirty-three years of age at the time of his marriage.

As there is no documentary evidence as to the date of Alder's baptism, her age at the time of her marriage to George Wickes must necessarily be a matter of conjecture.[21] In 1708 she was of an age to be included with her sisters as an executrix of her father's deathbed will which suggests that she was at least seventeen years old.[22] If one accepts that Alder was at least seventeen when her father's will was proved, she would have been thirty-one when she married Wickes in 1722, his senior by seven years. She may even have been as much as thirty-nine if she and her sisters were born early in their parents' marriage and within a year of each other. The latter reckoning would, however, make her ninety-one when she died in 1774, certainly a ripe old age in the eighteenth century. Twenty-one in 1708 and thirty-five in 1722 is possibly nearer the truth. In an age when marriage was frequently a calculated undertaking based on material considerations, it is strange that this young woman of independent means should still have been unwed in her thirties. It is difficult not to suspect Wickes of having married her for her money, particularly when, less than a month after his wedding, we find him registering his mark and setting up as his own master with premises in Threadneedle Street.

In the absence of any portrait of Alder Wickes, the only light on her character is shed in the wills of her relatives by blood and marriage. She was among the legatees of her husband's maiden aunt Rebecca Burton,[23] but pointedly excluded from the waspish will[24] of George's spinster sister Elizabeth who only mentioned her in order to identify a certain Mrs Joans, 'my sister Alder's acquaintance' to whom she bequeathed the sum of £5. Elizabeth Wickes left her sewing table to her sister Mary with the acid comment that she was the only person likely to use it. One might infer from this that Alder was in the opinion of her sister-in-law Elizabeth either incompetent, idle or perhaps too grand to ply a needle. The most telling reference is perhaps the wording used by an old lady in Bury St Edmunds in 1758. Mrs Catherine Purt, née Butts, widow, was first cousin to

George's mother. Her homespun will is fascinating not only for its wealth of family information, but also for its spelling.[25] She disposes of every single garment in her wardrobe in the most endearing fashion, dividing her seven best gowns plus all her 'washen gounds' amongst her female friends and relatives, but when it comes to Mrs Alder Wickes she leaves her, with a certain diffidence, 'a ring and all my cheany [china] if worth her excepting'.

Alder's accounts do not appear in George Wickes's ledgers. We know from a note in Mary Phelpes's account that a separate one was kept for Chaceley—'the Chaesley account in a smale little book in my desk'. That 'smale little book' would have been invaluable, but it has long ago disappeared. Alder's sisters' accounts are to be found mingled with those of Wickes's clients and it is not until after her husband's death, and then—due to gaps in the ledgers—only in the period 1771–1774 that Alder's own accounts may be discovered. They afford a glimpse of an elderly woman living quietly in the country supplied by her husband's successors with Hungary Water, 'cordial confection', Usquebaugh and tobacco. It is apparent from them that by this time Samuel Netherton was living with her and managing her affairs.

Notes for chapter II

1. A search of the registers of St Leonard's Bromley-by-Bow and St Mary's Stratford was equally fruitless. The records of the non-conformist Mercer's Hall Chapel at Cheapside and the meeting house in Great Yard Passage yielded no information.
2. P.R.O.: PCC Prob 11/167–3
3. The pamphlet took the form of a letter sent to the Speaker by the Mayor of Bristol and others 'Intimating the free benevolence of the City of Bristol, for the relief of the Protestants in Ireland'. Two ships, 'Meremaid' and 'Sampson', had been loaded with supplies and sent at the City's expense, the provisions being carefully listed on two invoices which accompanied the letter. Mayor Aldworth took the opportunity of thanking the House of Commons for their care of the City in sending Colonel Fines to command forces in Bristol and added that 'our fortifications are in good forwardnesse, and hath cost us very much moneys'.
4. P.R.O.: PCC Prob 11/341–10
5. Facsimile published by the London Topographical Society in 1967.
6. IOR: L/AG/1/10/1
7. P.R.O.: PCC Prob 11/460–64
8. P.R.O.: PCC Prob 11/373–87
9. It is possible that the sum of £500 left her by her mother for 'the purchase of land in the country or houses in London' was used to buy property in

Suffolk. Small copyhold estates in Aldham, Whatfield and Seamer appear in the testament of Samuel Lodge, gentleman, of Framlingham, the husband of Anne Gaell's daughter—yet another Anne—who married him in Ipswich in 1707: it is clear that the land in question had been owned by his wife before their marriage. It is perhaps worthy of note that Framlingham was also the home of the Alexanders, Quaker cousins of the goldsmith George Wickes on the distaff side, who were to become influential bankers. The firm Alexander & Gurney in Bury St Edmunds was taken over by Barclays Bank prior to the First World War and for several years after the Second World War the old brass plate of Alexander & Gurney still remained below that of its successors.

10. It is possible that they were christened privately at home, not necessarily because the parents were non-conformists. One by one, with the exception of Samuel I, II and III, the Phelpeses were buried in the parish church of St Michael Bassisshaw, a stone's throw from Basinghall Street, but in spite of an exhaustive search elsewhere there is no record of their births.

11. P.R.O.: PCC Prob 11/503–217

12. The phrase 'cut off with a shilling' has been widely misinterpreted. Blackstone, the great 18th century lawyer, makes this abundantly clear when he states 'But if the child had any legacy, though ever so small, it was proof that the testator had not lost his memory or his reason, which otherwise the law presumed; but was then supposed to have acted thus for some substantial cause . . . Hence probably has arisen that groundless vulgar error, of the necessity of leaving the heir a shilling or some other express legacy, in order to disinherit him effectually: whereas the law of England makes no wild suppositions of forgetfulness or insanity; and therefore, though the heir or next of kin be totally omitted, it admits no *querela inofficiosi*, to set aside such a testament'.

13. Little is known of Dorothy's first husband Peter Thomas Willett. His will reveals that he was a citizen of London, but although this implies that he was free of one of the City Companies the actual one is not named. It was possibly the Mercers' Company since Dorothy's account in George Wickes's ledgers shews that she had financial interests in the Company. In 1722 when the will was made he resided in the parish of St Botolph Bishopsgate. This is confirmed by his burial entry two years later in the Register of St Michael Bassisshaw—the church most favoured by the Phelpes family for burials—which specifically mentions that he was of Bishopsgate.

14. P.R.O.: PCC Prob 11/555–220

15. That surname appears more than once in the Wickes story. A Feet of Fines in the 32nd year of the reign of Charles II registered a land transaction between Samuel Phelpes II and Thomas Scrope. He was probably a member of the same family as the Thomas Scrope who was Warden of the Society of Merchant Adventurers of Bristol in 1664. An illustrious bearer of the name patronized the goldsmith George Wickes and his purchases are recorded in the Ledgers. Wickes had many Bristol clients, no doubt because of his wife's connections in that city.

16. P.R.O.: PCC Prob 11/435–243
17. P.R.O.: PCC Prob 11/612–269
18. No less an authority than Blackstone states that such wills 'need not any witness of their publication'. He points out that this does not apply to devises of land and continues 'but a testament of chattels, written in the testator's own hand, though it has neither his name nor seal to it, nor witnesses present at its publication, is good; provided sufficient proof can be had that it is his hand-writing'.
19. George Wickes was to make other such depositions in the course of his life—he performed the same service when his brother James died in 1756.
20. Before leaving Peter Thomas Willett it is perhaps worth noting that there was some connection between familes bearing the names Wickes and Willett in Suffolk. In 1655 a John Willit married an Elizabeth Wickes in St James's Church, Bury St Edmunds, and a year earlier a James Willett wed one Anne Wix in St Mary's Church, Bury St Edmunds, where George Wickes was himself baptized.
21. Alder's age does not appear on the inscription commemorating her burial in St Peter's Church in Thurston, Suffolk, nor are there any clues as to the ages of her sisters in the Burial Register of St Michael Bassisshaw.
22. An executor, according to Blackstone, could not act until he or she had attained the age of seventeen. The relevant passage reads: 'and all persons are capable of being executors, that are capable of making wills, and many others besides; as feme-coverts, and infants: nay even infants unborn or *in ventre sa mere*, may be made executors. But no infant can act as such until the age of seventeen years'.
23. P.R.O.: PCC Prob 11/743–317
24. P.R.O.: PCC Prob 11/734–161
25. Arch. Sudbury, Dalton III, 120

III The Goldsmith's Business

No records have been found which throw any light on the career of George Wickes from 1722 when he married, registered a mark and set up in business on his own in Threadneedle Street until 1735 when he opened his shop in Panton Street off the Haymarket and began the series of ledgers which form the Garrard Collection.

The real record of those years, and the most important, must be the few surviving pieces of silver that date from that period. The pair of mugs in figure 5 must have been amongst the earliest pieces to bear his mark. He registered it on the 3 February 1721/22 and the mugs were assayed at Goldsmith's Hall some time between that date and 29 May, the date of King Charles II's return to England (also his birthday), when the Assay letter was changed. Prior to the Restoration the date letter was changed on the 19 May, the feast of St Dunstan, the patron saint of metalworkers. The charm of these simple mugs is self evident: the double scroll handles relieve the plain tapered bodies with their tuck-in bases; the armorials with their wealth of detail are elegantly engraved. The mugs, which together weigh 20 troy ounces 18 pennyweights, stand $4\frac{1}{4}$ inches high and still retain traces of the original gilding.

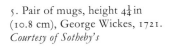

5. Pair of mugs, height $4\frac{1}{4}$ in (10.8 cm), George Wickes, 1721. *Courtesy of Sotheby's*

The workshop which produced them was presumably a fairly modest establishment in Threadneedle Street. The Land Tax Assessments for the Ward of Broad Street in the City of London shew that Wickes was still there in 1729. After that year his name disappears and little is known about him until June 1735 when he inserted an advertisement in *The London Evening Post* describing himself as 'late partner with Mr John Craig, the corner of Norris-street'. Norris Street still exists today connecting Lower Regent Street with the Haymarket. In a survey of London and Westminster published in 1754 Norris Street is described as 'a place of a pretty good trade for salesmen'.

It is probable that Wickes joined John Craig in 1730, but, like his master Samuel Wastell before him, Wickes did not inform the Goldsmiths' Company of his move nor did he re-register his mark on his change of address in compliance with the Hall's regulations. The Norris Street premises were held in John Craig's name which appears variously in the Accounts of the Overseers of the Poor of the Parish of St James's Westminster, the Preacher Assistant Rate and the Watch from 1726 onwards. Prior to that, John Craig in Norris Street is mentioned in the Court Minutes of the Goldsmiths' Company in 1722 for refusing to allow a search by the Wardens. His business would appear to have been fairly substantial judging by his advertisement in *The Daily Journal*, No. 2564, dated the 27 March 1729, announcing the loss of a 'fine roundish brilliant [diamond], weighing about 16 grains'. It continues: 'whoever brings it to Mr Craig's, a jeweller, the corner of Norris-St., St James's, Hay-Market, shall have 50 guineas reward, paid by the said Mr Craig and no questions asked.' An ambitious goldsmith like George Wickes would hardly have entered into partnership with a minor jeweller.

Although it is not possible to pin-point the exact date when Wickes moved to Norris Street, the year 1730 seems even more likely when one notes that for the 2 December 1731 the Apprentices' Book (Volume 5) at Goldsmiths' Hall records that David Craig, the son of John Craig of the parish of St James Westminster, jeweller, bound himself apprentice to George Wickes, 'citizen and goldsmith of London', for the term of seven years. The amount of the premium normally paid to the master has been omitted and it is probable that Wickes waived the fee for his partner's son. The apprenticeship record also reveals that John Craig was a jeweller, but the absence of the significant word 'citizen' shews that he was not free of any of the City Livery Companies. Wickes was certainly working with Craig in 1733 for on the 6 April of that year John Hervey, first Earl of Bristol, wrote in his diary 'Paid George Wickes & Mr Craig for a silver coffee-pott at 5s 9d [per ounce] & all demands £11 18s'.

6d

6a. One of a pair of serving dishes, width 20 in (50.8 cm), George Wickes, 1741. *Courtesy of Christie's*

6b. One of a pair of serving dishes, Edward Wakelin, 1749. *Courtesy of Christie's*

6c. One of a pair of serving dishes, width 13½ in (34.3 cm), Frederick Kandler, 1749. *Courtesy of Christie's*

6d. One of a pair of serving dishes, width 17¼ in (43.8 cm), Paul de Lamerie, 1741. *Courtesy of Christie's*

The similarity of these four dishes by different makers shews the universality of the prevailing taste of the day.

An earlier entry in the Earl's diary is of even greater potential interest. On the 20 May 1724 he recorded the payment of £4 10s to 'Ben Godfrey, for ye use of *his master John Craig*, in full for ye tea-pott I gave Mrs Sellars'. Benjamin Godfrey was not apprenticed through the Goldsmiths' Company and efforts to trace him in the records of other City livery companies have proved fruitless. This casual reference in the Bristol Diary suggests that he may have served a somewhat irregular apprenticeship to John Craig who was, by his own definition, a jeweller and not a goldsmith. The Earl may, however, have used the word 'master' in the loose sense of 'employer'.

Had Godfrey's master been named as Abraham Buteux, the Huguenot goldsmith who was Craig's neighbour in Norris Street, there would have been little cause for surprise since shortly after Buteux's death in 1731 his widow, Eliza (née Pantin) married Ben Godfrey. Although the marriage took place on the 6 February 1731/32, Godfrey did not register his first mark until the 3 October 1732, giving as his address 'The Hand, Ring & Crown' in Norris

Street, the premises (two houses) which Eliza had inherited from Buteux and which she continued to run after his death, having entered a mark in her own right on the 15 November 1731.

John Craig had clearly been dealing in silver, probably as a middleman, long before he was joined by Wickes, but the intriguing possibility exists that wrought plate was actually manufactured on the premises, by Benjamin Godfrey, before the advent of Wickes. Godfrey may indeed have remained with John Craig until 1732, in which case he would certainly have worked under Wickes for a short time. There can, however, have been little intimacy between the three men for Godfrey's will, made in 1732, was witnessed not by Craig or Wickes but by Paul de Lamerie.

No joint mark was entered by George Wickes and John Craig— the goldsmith side of the business was obviously in the hands of Wickes who continued to punch his work with the maker's marks he registered in 1722.

The partnership with John Craig is the only one for which there is any documentation in the 1730s. One cannot, however, ignore the brief but categorical statement made by E. Alfred Jones[1] which joins Wickes to Paul Crespin in a partnership lasting from 1733 to 1738. Another eminent scholar, the late Dame Joan Evans[2] publishes this as a statement of fact. Neither author quotes documentary evidence in support of this theory. No mention of Paul Crespin occurs in Wickes's ledgers, which admittedly do not start until 1735, and a search of *The London Gazette* and other newspapers of the period yielded no information on such a partnership. The brothers Crespel were later to be closely associated with Wickes's firm, but the name of the great Huguenot goldsmith Crespin does not appear. Crespin and Wickes catered for the taste of the time and there is inevitably a similarity in certain pieces produced by them (Fig. 7a). They both

7a. Soup tureen, width 14¾ in (37.5 cm), George Wickes, 1738. Made for Sir Robert Walpole to match a tureen by Paul Crespin dated 1733. *Courtesy of Sotheby's*

7b. Soup tureen, Benjamin Godfrey, circa 1735. *Courtesy of S. J. Shrubsole Ltd.*

made use of William Kent's designs for wrought plate when they were published by Vardy in 1744, but so did many of their fellow goldsmiths, among them John Swift, John Jacobs and Thomas Heming.

Crespin and Wickes shared the patronage of certain distinguished clients including that of Sir Robert Walpole. Walpole no doubt bought from other goldsmiths too, but the Ledgers, certainly from 1737 onwards, record substantial purchases from Wickes. The sale at Sotheby's in July 1964 of a pair of matching soup tureens engraved with Walpole's armorials brought to light a curious link between the two makers (Fig. 7a). One was the work of Paul Crespin, hallmarked 1733, and the other bore the mark of George Wickes and was assayed in 1738. Any suspicion of plagiarism is dispelled by two entries in Sir Robert Walpole's account in Wickes's ledgers: they are consecutive and read as follows:

1738 July 29 To a tureen   151 ozs 4 dwts   8/5   £63   2s 0d
             To graving 4 crests and garters   8s 0d
             To byling and doing up a tureen as new   £1 10s 0d

There is a strong possibility that the refurbished tureen was the work of Crespin which had been brought to Wickes so that he could repair it and make a second one to match it. The high fashioning charge of 8s 5d per troy ounce supports this argument since the tureen is a handsome one. Yet another tureen is also known, identical with those made by Crespin and Wickes, save that Sir Robert Walpole's armorials are absent (Fig. 7b). This third example, the work of Benjamin Godfrey, was a duty dodger struck three times with his maker's punch: in the absence of assay marks it is a matter of conjecture whether it preceded or followed the tureens made by Crespin and Wickes; it was certainly produced prior to 1741, the year of Godfrey's death. It is tempting to dwell on the possibilities of such a partnership—the imagination and skill of Paul Crespin allied to the skill and business acumen of George Wickes. Had it existed Wickes might have benefited immeasurably from it as Crespin was indisputably the finer artist. It is difficult to fault Wickes as a craftsman, but the soaring inspiration which fired Crespin and so many of his fellow Huguenots is missing.

It would have been interesting to have found a link between John Craig, jeweller, of Norris Street, London, and the American goldsmith James Craig who inserted this advertisement in the *Virginia Gazette* on the 25 September 1746.

'James Craig, *Jeweller, from* London, makes all sorts of jeweller's work, in the best manner, at his shop in *Francis* Street, (facing Main Street) opposite to Mr. *Holt's* new store.'

By 1752 he is styling himself in the same newspaper 'James Craig, *Jeweller*, in Williamsburg'; an advertisement of 1772 gives his address as The Golden Ball in Williamsburg—the same silversmith's shop under the same sign has been reconstructed and stands in Williamsburg today on the site occupied by James Craig in the eighteenth century.

In a letter sent from Williamsburg to John Norton, a London merchant, dated the 21 April 1768, he writes 'please purchase for me a ticket in the lottery for this present year . . . I should rather have a small n° than a large have it registered in the name of John Craig and please send me the n°.' Unfortunately he gives no address for John Craig, but goes on to mention goods ordered from a Robert Cruickshank, goldsmith, in the Old Jewry, who, Craig writes, 'is acquainted w^t my manner of describing what things I want as I have had things from him . . . Desire him to get ye jewelers work, toys, & cutlery from one Mr William Webb, the silver work Mr Cruickshank will make'.[3] There is no mention of Norris Street, but it is possible that by 1768 the Craig establishment had long been closed.

Wickes's partnership with John Craig ended in June 1735. There could have been several reasons for its termination. Wickes may have felt that it was high time that he had his own establishment again. Craig was possibly in failing health—he died eighteen months later on the 14 December 1736. He left no will and administration of his estate was granted to his widow Anne: a will might have made provision for his son David who, if he was still alive, would have been five years into his apprenticeship with Wickes; it might also have referred to a relative who had emigrated to America and set up as a jeweller in Virginia. Wickes may not have relished the prospect of an uneasy alliance with John Craig's wife Anne and feared for the future of the business. Anne Craig appears to have been an able business woman: she was joined by John Neville and they registered a joint makers' mark on the 15 October 1740. Some fine plate has survived bearing their mark. Whatever the reason, the partnership was dissolved. Wickes thereupon set up his own shop in Panton Street on the other side of the Haymarket and directly opposite Norris Street. He was probably by this time goldsmith to Frederick, Prince of Wales though this is not mentioned in the advertisement which Wickes inserted in *The London Evening Post* No. 1184 19–21 June 1735. It is worth quoting in full:

George Wickes, Goldsmith and Jeweller, late partner with Mr. John Craig, the corner of Norris-street, is removed to the King's Arms in Panton-street, the second door from St James's, Hay market, where he continues (*as the maker*) to make and sell all

8. Maker's mark registered by Wickes on moving to Panton Street in 1735 (entry in the Large Plate Workers' Register at Goldsmiths' Hall). *Courtesy of the Worshipful Company of Goldsmiths*

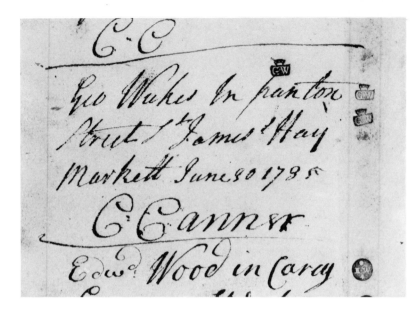

sorts of curious work in gold and silver, jewels and watches after the best and newest fashion; and buys and sells all sorts of second-hand plate, jewels and watches.

The italics, but not the parentheses, are my own. It is interesting that Wickes should have emphasized that he was continuing 'as the maker' almost as though that in itself was a guarantee of high quality craftsmanship. The network of subcontractors that the firm was later to use had not yet come into being.

The shop sign for his new premises in Panton Street is entered on the 24 June 1735 in an account in the first ledger headed proudly 'my house' not as the King's Arms of the advertisement, but as 'The King's Arms and Feathers'. The feathers consort oddly with the King's armorials, but were undoubtedly added to proclaim his Royal appointment to the Prince of Wales. The sign cost £14 3s 6d—Wickes was setting up in some style in Panton Street. The total cost of the work on the house was £364 10s 2d. Separate amounts are entered for the carpenter, painter, joiner, carver, glass grinder, sign painter, mason, bricklayer, plumber and glazier. Since there is no itemized description of the actual work carried out it is impossible to deduce the rates prevailing in London in the 1730s. By far the largest sum involved was the £100 paid to the carpenter. An interesting corollary to this list of artisans is their reappearance in their own right in the Gentlemen's [Clients'] Ledgers, identifiable in the ledger index by their trades which are written against their names.

On the occasion of this move Wickes complied with the Hall's regulations. On the 30 June 1735 he registered a new mark, crudely

designed, with his initials surmounted by a crown. His change of address was duly noted: Panton Street, St James's, Haymarket (Fig. 8). The attractive trade card shown in figure 9 must have been printed at this time.

In 1735 Panton Street, described nearly twenty years later as 'a good open street well built, and inhabited by tradesmen', would have been considered an excellent location for a fashionable goldsmith, but it had not always been so salubrious.[4] On this site, which may well have included a midden within the enclosed walls of Scavengers Close, Thomas Panton built, on the North side, at least three houses running from the Haymarket to Oxenden Street. It was in one of these houses that Wickes took up residence in 1735, 'the second door from St James's, Hay market' (Fig. 10). His neighbour on one side was an apothecary called Thomas Otway whilst, on the other side, the corner premises fronting the Haymarket were occupied by John Carpenter, a pewterer; his house, as well as that of Wickes, adjoined the Golden Head in the Haymarket, for many years in the possession of Samuel Boler, with whom Wickes shared a 'necessary' or outside lavatory.

We are given a glimpse of an eighteenth century goldsmith's shop in three trade cards of the period. In Phillips Garden's card (Fig. 11) the shop is elegantly furnished and there is no visible sign of a workshop unless it be sited behind the gothic screen on the right. In Peter de la Fontaine's trade card (Fig. 12) the forge and two silversmiths at work are clearly visible beyond the counters of the shop. A third trade card issued by one Morris, a jeweller, goldsmith and toyman of 'The King's Arms' at the corner of Norris Street, shews journeymen working at a bench beneath a window (Fig. 13).

As far as Wickes's shop is concerned, a written description has survived. The partnership indenture drawn up in September 1760 when John Parker and Edward Wakelin took over the business lists not only the fittings of the shop, but also the actual rooms. The passage concerning the house is worth quoting in full.

On the front of the house, the coving covered with lead—The Kings Arms and Feathers—the painted cloth on the said coving— all the sashes in the front of the shop, with the presses, counters, drawers, shew glasses and looking glasses, and all other things as they are now fixed in the shop. In the parlor, behind the shop, the

10. Detail from Horwood's Plan of London 1792–1799. *Courtesy of the Archives Department, Westminster City Libraries*

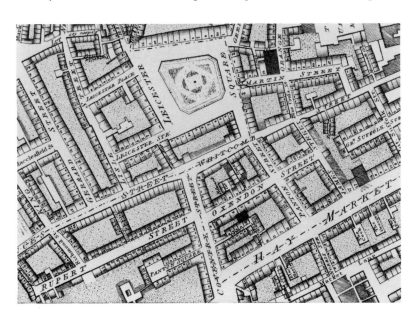

11. Trade-card of Phillips Garden, Broadley's *Annals of the Haymarket*.
Courtesy of the Archives Department, Westminster City Libraries

12. Trade-card of Peter de la Fontaine. This representation of the interior of a goldsmith's shop should perhaps be treated with a certain reserve. Research by the present writer has failed to throw any light on the mysterious Peter de la Fontaine and his trade-card, allegedly engraved by Hogarth and bearing his signature, is viewed with suspicion by Hogarth scholars and omitted from their catalogues raisonnés of the artist's work. *Ambrose Heal Collection. Courtesy of the Trustees of the British Museum*

closet with shelves; the marble chimney piece and slab, and outside shutters to the windows—in the kitchen, a double closet, and all the shelves and dressers—in the fore room even with the kitchen, all the sashes, shelves, two closets and a bottle rack—in the dining room, a marble chimney piece set with gally tiles, and slab, and marble hearth—in the back marble chimney pieces in the chimney, a marble slab, the chimney set with gally tiles—two pairs of stairs; the rooms wainscotted up to the cieling, shutters to the fore windows—in the garret, a large sash door, which is usually put up in winter. Outside shutters to the dining room windows.[5]

A later description of the property, albeit brief, exists in the archives of the Hand-in-Hand Insurance Company for 1781. The house, which was constructed of brick, had four stories, each with a square footage of 619 feet. The record gives the measurements—32 feet 6 inches by 19 feet, the latter being the street frontage. From the earliest of the documents relating to the house with which John Parker armed himself when he took over the lease we learn that the depth from North to South was 60 feet. The house was valued for insurance purposes (in 1781) at £500. A single story counting house, eight feet square, which stood behind the house was separately assessed at £25. Six years were to elapse before 'an indenture of bargain and sale' between George Pauncefort, the freeholder, and Parker was registered in John Parker's name. This deed reveals that the parcel of land backed on to a yard belonging to Samuel Boler; cellars are also mentioned. One of the witnesses to this document was Benjamin Sparkes 'of the Inner Temple London gentleman' from whom Wickes and his successors frequently sought counsel's opinion.

This then was the house to which Alder and George Wickes repaired in 1735 and where he was to spend the rest of his working life. Samuel Netherton must have accompanied George and Alder when they moved from Norris Street. He was the ward of their old friend William Lawrence whose accounts in the Ledgers suggest that the lad had been living with George and Alder Wickes for at least four years prior to his apprenticeship to Wickes in 1738 at the age of fifteen.

Panton Street must have become the family focal point for by this time nearly all George's close relatives had moved from Suffolk to London. His sister Mary, three years his senior, had married John Skurray, an upholsterer, in St Anne's Church Soho on the 24 April 1731 and was living in nearby Gerrard Street ('a very good street, well built, and inhabited by gentry'—a far cry from today's huddle of Chinese restaurants and strip clubs). The Skurrays had three children, a boy who was given the name Wickes, and two daughters, Mary and

Alder Rachael. Wickes Skurray's name disappears from family wills after 1753 and Alder Rachael is not mentioned after 1761; their sister Mary survived and was obviously a favourite with her uncle judging by the provisions he made for her in his will. George's mother, Mrs Dorothy Wickes, may have lived with the Skurrays or near them since the Burial Register of St Anne's Soho records that she resided in Gerrard Street. Her spinster daughter Elizabeth probably lived with her though she later moved to Chelsea near her cousin Mrs Elizabeth Blose, a Butts kinswoman, who, being George's client as well as his cousin, had an account in his ledgers. His mother's sister Miss Rebecca Burton moved to London from Radwinter and took up residence in the parish of St Andrew Hatton Garden near Ely Palace,

14c

14a. Tankard, height 7¼ in
(18.4cm), George Wickes, 1726.
Courtesy of Christie's

14b. Sugar bowl or slop basin
George Wickes, 1724. *Courtesy of
Christie's*

14c. Caster, height 7½ in (19cm),
George Wickes, 1727. *Courtesy of
Christie's*

the London seat of her cousin Bishop Butts. Cullum Wickes,
George's upholsterer brother, was already dead by this time: he was
buried in the south aisle of St Peter's-upon-Cornhill on the 28 July
1728. His remaining brother James was still alive, living in the
Fenchurch Street area with his wife Elizabeth. Wickes's sister Anne,
the widow of Sir Dudley Cullum, was by this time residing in Surrey
having taken another husband, the Reverend Mr Fulham. She died in
1737 and two years later the cleric remarried. He went as a matter of
course to his brother-in-law Wickes for the new wedding rings and
jewellery. The gold hoop ring is followed closely by a diamond
hoop ring: the two appear together frequently in the Ledgers
suggesting that they were worn in concert as engagement and
wedding rings are today. In this case the client supplied the diamonds
which Wickes set at a cost of one guinea. With the exception of eight
rows of pearls costing twelve guineas, no new jewellery was
purchased, the thrifty groom resorting to new settings for stones
which were probably taken from pieces of jewellery originally
bestowed on Anne Wickes by Sir Dudley Cullum. In 1739 large
buckles made of rose diamonds, diamond cluster earrings with bow
knots and necklaces of eleven rows of pearls with broad loops were
obviously in fashion. If Wickes had any qualms about breaking up the

jewellery of his dead sister and resetting it for her successor he kept them out of this transaction: conduct which might be considered insensitive today was not so regarded in the eighteenth century.

Alder Wickes had her sister Mary Phelpes close at hand: her accounts in the Ledgers suggest a modish woman of some means. She was obviously on intimate terms with Wickes's family, witnessing their wills and making them trustees and beneficiaries of her own testament. She appears to have been especially fond of George's sister Mary Skurray and her children and devoted to that apparently universal favourite Samuel Netherton.

Alder's sister Dorothy, the widow of Peter Thomas Willett, had already left London. She may have joined their brother Samuel in Chaceley where she was, by virtue of her father's will, the lady of the manor. The Bishops' Transcripts for Chaceley record that on the 8 September 1734 'Mr Thomas Weale of ye parish of Tewkesbury and Mrs Dorothy Willett of this parish were married by licence'. Thomas Weale had been a widower for six years and practised as an apothecary in Tewkesbury. This second marriage may not have been a happy one. There are several reasons for thinking that it was not, not the least being Dorothy's burial in June 1743 in the church of St Michael Bassisshaw in London beside her first husband Peter Thomas Willett instead of in the Weale family vault in the south aisle of the Abbey Church at Tewkesbury.

Apart from the comings and goings of his own family, the household in Panton Street would have been enlivened by the presence of George's apprentices. Wickes's reputation and attainments (Fig. 14) would have made him much sought after as a master. On the 13 March 1739/40 he was considered sufficiently senior and worthy to be made a livery man of the Goldsmiths' Company (Fig. 15). As such, however, he took little part in the Hall's business, contenting himself with the expansion of his own.

Notes for chapter III

1. *Catalogue of Plate belonging to the Duke of Portland, K.G., G.C.V.O. at Welbeck Abbey*, London, 1935.
2. 'Huguenot Goldsmiths in England and Ireland', *Proceedings of the Huguenot Society*, Vol. XIV, London, 1933, fn. 4, pg. 26.
3. I am indebted to Dr Edward M. Riley, Director of Research, Colonial Williamsburg, for this information on James Craig.
4. A very interesting document came to light in the papers of John Parker which have been preserved by his descendants. John Parker was Wickes's last apprentice: later, in partnership with Edward Wakelin, he took over the firm founded by George Wickes. Parker was a careful man, the brother of a Worcester attorney, and when the time came to assume responsibility for the house in Panton Street he made sure that he held all papers and titles pertaining to it. They included a ratification by Charles II of a grant of land to Thomas Panton made presumably prior to the Restoration. The document, dated 16 August 1671, begins with a flourish:

> Charles the Second. To all to whom these presents shall come greeting. Whereas our trusty and wellbeloved subject Thomas Panton Esq. by his humble peticion setting forth that he had been at great charges in purchasing a parcell of ground lyeing at Pickadilly ... In reference whereunto the said Thomas Panton has sett out the ground layed severall foundations and built part thereof before our late proclamacon hath brought us to grant him our Royal proclamcon that he may proceed in his said intended building according to the draught presented to us and delivered to our Surveyour Generall the examinacon of the which allegations we were grahously pleased to order should be referred to Christopher Wrenn Esq. our Surveyour Generall.

These letters patent describe the location of the land:

part of it being the two bowling greens fronting the Hay markett the other part lyeing on the north of Tennis Court upon which severall old houses were standing which he had demolished to improve the same and make the place more uniform.

Christopher Wren was required to 'consider whether in case the petitioners request should be granted the building will cure the noysomnesse of the place and how the ditches and sewers will be changed and kept sweet'. Wren reported that 'he had viewed the said places and duly fnd the peticoners allegacons to be true and that the designe of building shewn to him might bee very useful to the publick especially by opening a new street from the Hay market into Leicester fields which would ease in some measure the great passe of the Strand and would cure the noisomness of that part'.

Permission to proceed was granted to Panton with the proviso that the front walls and the out walls of the houses he intended to erect should 'be built of and with brick and stone or one of them with party walls sufficient scantings goode substantiall paveing in the streets and such sewers gutters . . . as shall be sufficient for the drayning and carrying of the Water through and from the said streets houses and buildings'.

We are indebted to the caution of John Parker for further details on the land developed by Thomas Panton. It had been acquired by Panton on the 15/16 June 1669 from James Baker of Evercreech of Somerset, gentleman, and Grace his wife for a consideration of £1,500. A week later a further copy lease and release were drawn up 'reconciling difference between Sir Henry Oxindon and Thomas Panton' and dividing 'the capital messuage etc. as to one moiety to use of Oxindon his heirs and assigns, as to the other moiety, to use of Panton his heirs and assigns'. The site consisted originally of 'a capital messuage or great house situate in Pickadilly in St Martin in the Fields with appurtenances and the tennis court and other buildings and the upper ground or bowling green and the lower ground (now the Duke of Monmouth his agents or servants), all formerly known by the name of Scavengers Close or the Conduite Close, sometime since inclosed with a brick wall; the tenements and ground on the outside of the upper and lower grounds in Hedge Lane with the messuages etc. which abut on lands late of the Earl of Suffolk (S) and the Earl of Leicester's land and Hedge Lane (E) and the King's highway (N and W)'.

5. The word 'gally' which is used to describe the tiles surrounding the fireplaces in the two principal rooms is of interest. Its precise derivation is not known, but it is thought to date from the sixteenth century when galley fleets were used to transport Hispano-Moresque ceramic ware from the Mediterranean. In 1760 when the schedule quoted above was written the word 'gally' would have struck an old fashioned note as by that time these tin glazed lustre ware tiles were usually loosely termed 'Delft' even when they were manufactured in the English factory at Lambeth. They were often plain white with small blue decorations, but the gally tiles in situ in the Panton Street house may have been there when Wickes took over the premises in 1735 and could have been quite different in style.

IV The Apprentices

A good master was the first essential for an aspiring goldsmith. Apprentices served a term of at least seven years and a premium was normally paid to the master. When, as was usually the case, the master was a freeman of the Worshipful Company of Goldsmiths, the apprenticeship was recorded in the current Apprentices' Book at Goldsmiths' Hall and the applicant presented himself and signed the entry.

The apprenticeship was also required to be registered with the State and a stamp duty paid. The Statute of Apprentices in 1565 forbade anyone to enter a trade who had not served an apprenticeship. Although the full rigour of this rule was modified by subsequent Acts of Parliament and by legal judgements, it remained on the Statute Book until 1814. In 1710 the Statute 8 Anne c. 5 imposed a stamp duty on indentures of apprenticeship and from 1710 to 1811 the Commissioners of Stamps kept registers of the money they received. Duty was payable by the master on premiums up to fifty pounds at sixpence in the pound and thereafter at the rate of one shilling. The last date for payment was one year after the expiry of the indenture (later extended), but the records shew that the stamp duty was usually paid within a few months of a master taking on an apprentice.

In the case of two of his apprentices—David Craig and Samuel Netherton—Wickes appears to have waived the premiums since no figures are given in the archives of Goldsmiths' Hall nor is there a record of either indenture in the stamp duty registers at the Public Record Office. In view of the relationships existing in both instances—Craig was the son of Wickes's partner and Netherton the ward of a close friend—it could well have been an act of generosity on the part of the goldsmith. There is, however, the possibility that he was in fact defrauding the Revenue—premiums may have been paid to him for both boys, father and guardian conniving at the age-old sport of bilking the tax man.

Some of the master's obligations to his apprentices were set out in 1760 in the partnership indenture of Wickes's successors Edward Wakelin and John Parker and make interesting reading.

It shall and may be lawfull to and for each and either of the said parties to have and take by turns one or more apprentice or apprentices or turnover to be employed in and about the business of the said joint trade as they the said parties shall think convenient the first apprentice or turnover to be taken by the said John Parker which apprentice or apprentices turnover or turnovers or other servant or servants shall be maintained and provided for out of the said joint stock after the rate of ffifteen pounds for each by the year and the money or other consideration to be had and received with such apprentice or turnover shall be brought into the said joint stock for the equal benefit of the parties to these presents and not for the particular use and benefit of the master taking such apprentice or turnover and if any imbezlement or other loss or damage shall during the said term arrive or happen unto the said parties or either of them or unto their joint stock or the gains thereof by the breach of trust or infidelity of any such apprentice or turnover the same shall be born and sustained by the said joint stock and therefore for the better preventing any such loss or dammage. It is hereby agreed that no apprentice or turnover shall be received into the service of either of the said partners during the said term but such as before he or they shall be bound or turned over shall give security for his or their honesty and fidelity.[1]

A clause dealing with board and wages follows.

The charge of the dyet or wages of such journeymen and apprentices or other servant or servants as they shall hereafter agree to take and employ in their said joint trade and business allowing also for the board of every such servant or servants after the rate of ffifteen pounds by the year to such of the said copartners or other person or persons who shall find or supply such servant with board.

Inflation must also have been the scourge of eighteenth century London for we find the £15 increased to £20 in 1770 when the co-partnership was extended for a further ten years.

Wickes was to take seven apprentices between 1722 and 1751. The first, William Woodward, was turned over to him in Threadneedle Street on the 8 October 1722, his first master William Pearson having died before the completion of the term of apprenticeship. Woodward was made free by service in 1726, but he may have remained with Wickes, working as a journeyman, until 1731 when he registered his first mark. The entry in the Large Plate Workers' Register at Goldsmiths' Hall reveals that he had by then changed his address to

Fenchurch Street. In 1723 Wescombe Drake was turned over to Wickes after serving two years of his apprenticeship with John Saunders. Drake obtained his freedom in 1728 and subsequently moved to The Golden Ball in Norton Folgate.

The first of Wickes's apprentices, as opposed to turnovers, arrived in 1727 in the person of Charles Woodward, a premium of £20 being paid to Wickes. Like his namesake William Woodward, Charles was of the parish of St Olave, Southwark, the son of Robert Woodward, butcher. William's father Henry Woodard (sic) had also been a butcher and in all probability the boys were close relatives. Charles Woodward did not seek his freedom until 1740. His only mark was registered in April 1741: at that date he had left Wickes and was working in Tooley Street, Southwark.

Charles Woodward was followed by David Craig on the 2 December 1731. Wickes was by this time in partnership with the boy's father, John Craig, jeweller, in Norris Street, Haymarket. As we know, no premium changed hands, but in all fairness it should be pointed out that the boy was living under his father's roof and eating with his family; Wickes would have trained him but was probably spared the cost of boarding him. It is doubtful whether David Craig remained with Wickes after his apprenticeship or whether he even completed it. There is no record of his freedom in the Court Minutes of the Worshipful Company. Goldsmiths working within the City's limits came under the Hall's jurisdiction and were bound by the rules of the Company to make a formal application for their freedom, with the payment of a fee of 10s by service, 44s by redemption. The Company was unable to exercise the same control over goldsmiths working outside the City boundaries and many journeymen with no prospect of setting up on their own account were reluctant to pay for a privilege which brought them no financial return. Ten shillings, or fifty pence, seems little enough today but in the eighteenth century it could have represented the wages of a week or so for a struggling journeyman with a family to support. David Craig in the parish of St James's Westminster may well have taken this view. The fact that he was not made free would not have debarred him from his right, established in law at the beginning of the eighteenth century, to enter a mark. No mark of David Craig has come to light, but it is possible that he entered one as a small plate worker in the volume covering the period 24 May 1739–13 July 1758 which is missing from the Hall's archives.

In August 1736 Wickes took a Suffolk boy as his apprentice. Robert Hayward came from Hawstead (spelt Halstead in the Hall's Apprentices' Book), a village near Bury St Edmunds. His father Thomas Hayward was a schoolmaster, possibly of the Cullum Charity

16. Account for Wickes's
apprentice Robert Hayward.
Courtesy of Garrard & Co. Ltd.

School at Hawstead. Sir Dudley Cullum and his wife Anne, the sister
of George Wickes, were married and buried in Hawstead Church.
Thomson, the eldest brother of Anne and George, was also interred
there in 1715 at the age of twenty-five. The Cullum crest, a pelican in
piety, can still be seen on buildings in Hawstead today.

The Haywards would have been well known to the Cullum and
Wickes families. An account relating to Robert Hayward appears in
the first ledger in the Garrard Collection. It is in a Gentlemen's
(Clients') Ledger entered under the name of a relative, Mr Edmund
Howard (Fig. 16). The names Hayward and Howard were interchangeable in Suffolk and Wickes's spelling was infinitely variable.
This same Edmund Hayward was appointed co-trustee and executor,
with George Wickes's maternal uncle the Reverend George Burton,
of Sir Dudley Cullum's will. These family considerations did not,
however, prompt Wickes to forgo Robert Hayward's premium and
£25 was duly paid.

As will be seen, Robert Hayward is referred to familiarly as 'Bob'
and the account covers the charges of a barber for 2¾ years (£1 7s 6d)
and sundry articles of clothing. It also records the expenses of an
illness he suffered in 1740: payments were made to a nurse and a
surgeon (for twice bleeding—5s 0d). By far the largest fee involved
was that paid to Mr Nevell the apothecary whose role in the

eighteenth century approximated to that of the physician today. Mr Nevell's name also appears in the Gentlemen's Ledgers as a client of Wickes.

It would appear from the Hayward account that a master was not expected to provide clothes or the services of a barber for his apprentices, nor be responsible for costs incurred by illness. Chicken and wine were obviously not part of the daily diet of an apprentice: the £15 allowed to each one annually for board would not have permitted such luxuries and the meals of the apprentices would have been far more spartan. Alder Wickes does not seem to have taken any part in nursing him judging by the payments over four weeks to a nurse and the cost of three weeks 'board for Bob' to a Mrs Shaw, but the boy may have had an infectious illness necessitating his removal from the house in Panton Street. It will be noticed that the mending of Bob's clothes is also charged to this account.

The account was transferred to Wickes's small ledger which unfortunately has not survived and Robert Hayward disappears from the story. He never sought his freedom nor registered a mark at Goldsmiths' Hall. It is possible that he worked as a journeyman for Wickes, but there is no way of proving this since the first Workmen's Ledger—which must have contained a wealth of valuable information—is also missing.

On the 7 March 1737/38 a significant entry was made in the Apprentices' Book at Goldsmiths' Hall. The wording, in the form that has changed very little over the centuries, reads as follows:

Be it rembred that I Samuel Netherton son of Samuel Netherton late of Fleet Street of London undertaker dsed do put myself apprentise to George Wickes citizen & goldsmith of London for the term of seven years from this day there being paid to my s^d ma^r the sum of.

The last ten words were crossed through. The signature, written 'Saml Netherton', appears under the entry (Fig. 17).

17. Entry for Samuel Netherton from the Goldsmiths' Company Apprentice Register, Vol. 6, p. 247, 1737. *Courtesy of the Worshipful Company of Goldsmiths*

Samuel Netherton first appears in the Wickes story in 1735 in the account of his guardian William Lawrence (Wickes invariably spells it 'Lawrance'), a London merchant living in Rolls Buildings, off Chancery Lane, Fleet Street. Samuel was obviously boarding with Wickes three years before his apprenticeship began and was possibly a member of the household prior to that date. There can be no doubt that the Sam who appears in William Lawrence's account is indeed Netherton since he was later to be named as son-in-law and co-heir in Lawrence's will.[2] The boy—and his mother Ann—was certainly known to Wickes in 1734 when the goldsmith and Lawrence were summoned before the Court of the Arches—the ecclesiastical Court of Appeal for the Province of Canterbury—for non-payment of a legacy which they, as executors of the will of John Waldron, were bound to honour.

The testament of John Waldron bears examination in some detail since, with the exception of the wronged legatee, all those who benefited from the will were members of the Wickes circle with, in some cases, accounts in the goldsmith's ledgers. John Waldron, 'of Hornsey Middx. gent. blind but in sound health' made his will on the 8 July 1733[3]: one of the witnesses was John Skurray, upholsterer, the husband of Wickes's sister Mary.

Amongst the legatees were Ann Netherton and her son Samuel with bequests of £60 and £30 respectively. In addition they received—as did George Wickes and his wife Alder—ten pounds each for mourning apparel and a remembrance ring to the value of twenty shillings. After payment of the testator's just debts and legacies the rest and residue of his real and personal estate was left equally to Wickes and Lawrence their heirs and assigns for ever. The will was duly proved by Wickes and Lawrence, but by the following May the dilatory executors had failed to pay a legacy of £100 to Hannah Gray, a spinster and a minor. Her guardians thereupon commenced suit against them in the Court of the Arches stating 'that the sd. legacy of one hundred pounds is yet unpaid and the aforesd. George Wickes and William Lawrence the executors of the sd. will have been often at least once requested by the sd. curators to pay or cause to be paid to the sd. minor or her guardians . . . but do still absolutely deny or refuse at least delay to pay the same'. It was furthermore stated 'that the goods chattels and credits of the sd. John Waldron . . . which have come to the hands and possession of George Wickes and William Lawrence are more than sufficient to pay the just debts of the sd. deced. and the legacies given and bequeathed by the sd. will'. Wickes and Lawrence had ineluctably to find the sum of £100 and the goldsmith deposited it with the Court of the Arches on the 30 May 1734. The findings of the Court include, however, a stipulation that should the estate of John Waldron prove insufficient to pay the legacy Wickes and Lawrence were to be reimbursed. There is a touch of sardonic humour in the Court transcript: the clerk records the guardians' deposition that Wickes and Lawrence were 'often at least once requested . . . to pay' and 'do still absolutely deny or refuse at least delay to pay the same'. With the passing of over two hundred years it is impossible to say whether Wickes and Lawrence were acting in bad faith or the minor's guardians merely importunate.[4]

Samuel Netherton was himself a minor aged ten years when he was left £30 by John Waldron. He was born to Samuel and Ann Netherton on the 28 November 1723 and baptized at St Bride's Church, Fleet Street, on the 2 December 1723. The church's Burial Register chronicles a sad little procession of Netherton children: Elizabeth in February 1721, Hanna in June 1722 and John in January 1724. Samuel's father was certainly dead at the time of his son's apprenticeship, but the exact date of his demise is unknown and no will or administration has come to light. The family originated in Worcestershire, but Samuel's father lived in London where he worked as an undertaker in Fleet Street. He was married to Ann Bartholomew at the Church of St Edmund Lombard Street in 1716.[5]

Long before her marriage to Wickes, Alder would have known the Nethertons and the Bartholomews if only through their connection with the Parkers of Longdon who lived a mere four miles as the crow flies from Chaceley, the home of the Phelpes family. At this point an interesting relationship emerges: Samuel Netherton, Wickes's apprentice, was second cousin to John Parker who was also to become Wickes's apprentice and later succeed him and Netherton in the business. Parker's mother Mary was the daughter of a Thomas Jeffes of Queenhill near Longdon whose sister wed a Bartholomew. A daughter of that marriage, Ann, married Samuel Netherton, the Fleet Street undertaker, and became the mother of Wickes's protégé Sam.

The relationship between Samuel Netherton and John Parker is plain to see in certain pedigrees drawn up by John's brother Thomas based on a long series of entries in the Longdon parish register and other sources. After the death of Thomas these documents must have passed to John since they contain additional information in his handwriting. Further annotations were made by John's son Thomas Netherton Parker when, through the good offices of John Wakelin, the son of his father's old friend and partner, Edward Wakelin, he entered into correspondence in 1797 with Lancaster Herald with a view to registering at the College of Heralds his entitlement to bear the arms used by the Parker family for three centuries.

A closer examination of these documents reveals the apparently unimportant birth of a daughter Mary to 'Thomas Parker gentellman by Ann his wife' on the 17 November 1660. This was John Parker's great-aunt Mary: a margin note states that she 'married Anthony Lawrence whom she survived and died a widow'. The Longdon parish register records the burial on the 23 February 1724 of Mrs Mary Lawrence, widow. Lawrence is not an uncommon name and whilst there is no evidence to link Anthony Lawrence with William Lawrence, the guardian of Samuel Netherton, it may well be that the Lawrences were kinsmen or close friends of the Parkers and Nethertons. Included among the Parker family papers are several abstracts of titles to land, one a mortgage in November 1708 to a John Lawrence the younger and his heirs, followed by a conveyance in fee in January 1712/13 to the same John Lawrence regarding the tithe to two acres of land called The Twitchells. In William Lawrence's will, proved in 1751, a brother John Lawrence was left a silver cup.

We can follow William Lawrence's ward, the boy apprentice Samuel Netherton, for a few brief years in the Ledgers through the account of his guardian and then that, too, was carried into Wickes's small ledger and is now, alas, lost to us. The account tells us that 'a cap for Samuel' was bought for six shillings on the 16 September 1735; the following year in November 'a pr. leather britches Sam' is entered, also costing six shillings, together with a wig at £1 1s. The next entry, dated the 9 April 1737, records the purchase of 'twelve coat and two breast buttons, carved', weighing 4 troy ounces 2 pennyweights, but it is not clear whether these were intended for William Lawrence or Samuel. 'A mettle attwe [étui] gilt for a lady in Woerstersheire—returned' in July 1738 was surely a matter for Lawrence: it would have been interesting to have known the identity of the lady in Worcestershire and the reason why the étui was returned.

The purchase of a peruke £1 1s is entered on the 17 May 1741 as well as 12/- for the cost of alterations to a coat and banyan, the latter being a loose gown, jacket or shirt of flannel; Sam was obviously growing fast and his clothes needed letting out. In the winter of 1742 he was the recipient of a velvet cap (5/-), two pairs of shoes (12/-) and a great coat (£1 5s). Two months before the expiry of his apprenticeship in January 1745 Sam acquired another coat: on this occasion it cost £3 6s and was obviously a more splendid garment befitting a young blood of twenty-two.

By far the most interesting items in William Lawrence's account are the payments to 'ye drawing master' (£1 5s 3d) and 'Mr. Goosetree the writing master' (£2 2s). The latter's tuition was not wasted on the boy: Samuel's handwriting, which begins to appear in the Ledgers from 1739 onwards, is both elegant and legible, unlike that of Wickes who appears to have been constantly at odds with a scratchy quill. The employment of a drawing master suggests that Sam may have been an artistic boy: the ability to design wrought plate or to make a swift sketch to interpret a client's requirements would have been of some value in a goldsmith's establishment.

Netherton did not seek his freedom by service at the end of his apprenticeship nor did he register a mark singly or jointly with Wickes at Goldsmiths' Hall. He appears instead to have become Wickes's right-hand man in the day to day running of the business, leaving the master to fashion the silver and oversee the journeymen. It has been suggested that he may have taken over the jewellery side of the firm but most items of jewellery recorded in the ledgers in the period 1735–1747 were run of the mill articles, almost certainly bought in from sub-contractors and stocked as a side line. They were purchased for the most part by the bourgeoisie—very little appears in the accounts of the aristocratic clients who obviously patronized the specialist jewellers.

After Netherton Wickes took no more apprentices for thirteen years and his acceptance of John Parker in 1751 may have owed much to Netherton's powers of persuasion. Parker's mother was, as we have seen, first cousin to Netherton's mother and the ties with Worcestershire seem to have endured. Since Netherton was not himself free of the Goldsmiths' Company he was not eligible to take apprentices and George Wickes became John Parker's master on the 5 July 1751. Wickes, a hard-headed business man, exacted a premium of £50 ignoring the ties between Netherton and Parker and the fact that the boy's family lands abutted those of Alder Wickes in Chaceley.

John Parker came from a long line of Worcestershire landed gentry. The White House, Longdon, his family home, still stands. The earliest authenticated owner of the house according to family sources was the Thomas Parker who appears in the parish register as the father of a daughter, Alice, baptized in December 1563.

In 1686 Thomas, the father of John Parker, was born. He died on the 13 March 1751, a widower, leaving a young family of two sons, Thomas and John, and four daughters, Mary, Eleanor, Elizabeth and Ann. His will, dated the 28 December 1744, was proved on the 4 June 1751[6] and a month later his younger son, then aged 16½, was apprenticed to Wickes. By the terms of the will the Longdon estate passed to the elder son Thomas whilst John's inheritance, consisting of lands in Gloucestershire which had once belonged to his grandmother, Eleanor Rogers Parker, the daughter and co-heiress of John Rogers, gentleman, of Haresfield (a fine memorial to the Rogers family can still be seen in Haresfield Church), was to come to him when he reached the age of twenty-one.

The Bishop's Transcripts and the Longdon church register record the baptism of John Parker on the 12 November 1734. Three and a half years—and two child births—later, on the 8 March 1738, his mother Mary died at the early age of thirty-one, five months after the death of her last child Benjamin who lived only three weeks. Her memory was preserved for her children in a charming portrait by Joseph Highmore: there is both sweetness and delicacy in the slender woman holding a garland of flowers (Fig. 18).

In 1751 John Parker left behind him in Longdon a family of four spinster sisters, three of them in their early twenties, and a brother aged eighteen. Judging by the 'tribute of filial regard' which John was later to erect in Longdon Church, Thomas Parker must have been a loving father. The monument tells us that 'he was a religious observer of the duties incumbent on a good Christian, among which a liberal and unaffected charity to the distressed was the most eminent'. He made generous provision in his will for his servants and the poor of the two parishes in which his lands lay. His portrait by Highmore—the companion to that of his wife—shews us a kindly, warm man (Fig. 19).

The transition from the serenity of Longdon to a fashionable goldsmith's establishment in the heart of London must have been a strange and exciting one for the young John Parker. His cousin Samuel Netherton, his senior by some eight years, would have been there to welcome him. They were obviously close and Netherton became on the 1 January 1770 godfather to Parker's second daughter Eleanor who, in her father's own poignant words, lived '1 year, 11 months & 4 days'. Two years later Netherton was again chosen to be godfather, this time to a son born 'Thurs^y 13 Feb. 1772 at half after 11 at night'. He was christened Thomas Netherton Parker at St Martins-in-the-Fields on Sunday, the 23 February, 1772.

Before leaving the apprentices it might be of some interest to mention a small treatise published in London in 1747. Entitled *The London Tradesman*, it is described as 'a compendious view of all the trades, professions, arts, both liberal and mechanic, now practised in the Cities of London and Westminster calculated for the information of parents, and instruction of youth in their choice of business'.

In the section on goldsmiths, the author R. Campbell Esq., tells how

'the goldsmith makes all his own moulds, and for that reason ought to be a good designer, and have a good taste in sculpture. He must be conversant in alchemy; that is, in all the properties of metals: he must know the proper menstruums for their solution, the various methods of extracting and refining them from their dross and impurity; the secret of mixing them with their proper alloy: he must know the various ways of essaying metals, and distinguishing the real from the fictitious. From hence it must be conjectured that he ought to be possessed of a solid judgment as well as a mechanical hand and head. His education, with respect to his business, does not require to be very liberal: a plain *English* education will suffice; designing is the chief part of his early study, previous to his Apprenticeship: but as his employment is the most genteel of any in the mechanic way, and that it requires a large stock to set him up, I should advise a youth for this business to have such an education as I have described in Chapter XIV.

The reader may be spared Chapter XIV, but to the above might be added with profit the niceties required of a would-be gold and silver lace-man.

He ought to speak fluently, though not elegantly, to entertain the ladies; and to be master of a handsome bow . . . but, above all, he must have confidence to refuse his goods in a handsome manner to the extravagant beau who never pays, and patience as well as stock to bear the delays of the sharping peer, who pays but seldom.

The author includes a homily on the behaviour of apprentices under a chapter headed 'Advice to the young apprentice, how to behave during his apprenticeship, in order to acquire his business, obtain the good-will of his master, and avoid the many temptations to which youth are liable in this great city'. He is expected to be diligent and honest and able to live in peace with his master and family, interfering as little as possible in the concerns of the house and avoiding tattling between servants or carrying stories between husband and wife. He must expect to take his master's correction with the same submission as though he were his father and 'consider him in the place of a parent'. A lad grown to some years 'must carefully avoid idle company and ale-houses' and resist the advances of wanton women, 'another strong temptation to apprentices to go astray. The blood runs warm in their young veins, and they are naturally prone to gratify the new-grown appetite'. His spare time, the author suggests, ought to be spent 'in learning to write, read, cast accompts, drawing, or any other qualification suitable to his station.' Gaming and early marriage were also to be frowned upon, whilst reverence for religion was much advocated, it being 'too much the fashion now-a-days to laugh at religion, and even to be ashamed of acts of devotion'.

The book provides useful tables on apprenticeship premiums, the amount of capital needed to set up as a master and the hours of work. The premium shewn for goldsmiths is £20–£50, the capital £500–£3,000.

Notes for chapter IV

1. The insistence on the honesty of apprentices was no doubt prompted by the memory of the unfortunate law suit in which de Lamerie was involved in 1721. It makes fascinating reading in P. S. S. Phillip's definitive biography of Paul de Lamerie and it will be sufficient to recall that the case revolved around an attempt by a dishonest apprentice to defraud a small chimney sweep of a jewel he had found and taken for evaluation to de Lamerie's shop. The great Huguenot goldsmith, an innocent and unsuspecting party to the fraud, was held by the Court to be responsible for the misdeeds of his servants. The case, listed as Armoury v Delamirie [sic], has become part of legal history and remains to this day a classic reference for the vicarious liability of an employer. (1721 I Stra. 505).

2. P.R.O.: PCC Prob 11/788–182

3. P.R.O.: PCC Prob 11/661–275

4. Cases in the Court of Arches 1660–1913 (E. 30/156)

5. Curiously enough a Samuel Netherton made a brief appearance in the Court of the Arches in 1668 in a dispute connected with a nuncupative will made by his kinswoman Barbara Netherton of Netherton in the parish of Cropthorne, Worcestershire. She left her bees and 'six sheeps' to her stepbrother and to Samuel Netherton a mere five pounds. Had this been young Samuel's father he would have been in his seventies when the boy was born and it is more likely that he was his grandfather.

6. P.R.O.: PCC Prob 11/788–185

V The Workshop

20. Wire-drawing. Detail from an illustration commissioned by the Goldsmiths' Company in 1707 (see endpapers).
In this picture the journeyman is turning the wheel with his hands, but larger machines required the use of the right hand and right foot to manipulate the wheel.
Courtesy of the Worshipful Company of Goldsmiths

21. Goldsmiths at work. Detail of engraving (see Fig. 20). *Courtesy of the Worshipful Company of Goldsmiths*

It is clear from the Ledgers that Wickes prospered and it must soon have been obvious to him that he needed extra space. Accordingly on Lady Day (25 March) 1744 he took over a second house in Panton Street. It is probable that at this point he moved the actual workshop to the new premises, retaining the original dwelling as his home whilst continuing to display and sell his wares in the shop on the ground floor. The schedule relating to the house which was appended to the partnership indenture of John Parker and Edward Wakelin applied unquestionably to the original house and makes no mention of a workshop. The intricacies of the goldsmith's craft in the eighteenth century—as indeed today—would have called for furnaces and benches, bulky equipment for drawing silver wire (Fig. 20) and an astonishingly large number of stakes and tools of all shapes and sizes. Such an atelier, apart from generating heat and sweat, is of its very nature noisy and too close a proximity to it would not have pleased a goldsmith's clients (Fig. 21).

The volume of Wickes's business would no doubt have borne the expense of removing the workshop to another house, but it is worth noting the death of his wife's eldest sister, Mrs. Dorothy Wale, in June 1743. The event is in fact recorded in the Ledgers in the account of the middle sister, Mary Phelpes, which is debited as follows:

1743 June 24 To cash p[d] for the fees of
the church [St Michael's Bassisshaw] for
sister Wale's buriing[1)] . . .   £8 0s 0d

As Dorothy's co-heiresses in entail, Alder and Mary became possessed of the two houses in Basinghall Street which their grandfather Samuel Phelpes had had built after the Great Fire of London and the family estates in Worcestershire, of which the Manor of Chaceley formed part. Alder's share of the rents would have provided a welcome addition to Wickes's working capital.

The new workshop was next door but one to Wickes's home-cum-shop at the Haymarket end of Panton Street. It was to be used as such by the firm until 1779 when the workshop was transferred to more palatial premises on the corner of Oxendon Street and the north side

49

of Panton Street. This latter, the corner house, is shewn in the Rate Returns for 1760 as being in the possession of Wickes, thereafter Edward Wakelin's name appears until his retirement in 1777. In 1779 John Wakelin, Edward's son, and William Tayler, the partners who succeeded John Parker and Edward Wakelin, took it over and it is described in the Ledgers of that year as 'our new workshop'. The collector of the Poor Rate noted in the margin of his account book that 'much money has been lay'd out in alterations and diging vaults'. An entry in John Parker's account for 1779 reveals that he owned the lease and that 'the new workshop was insured [with the Westminster Fire Office] for £500 more than before on acc^t of the improvements'.

No lease or agreement has come to light for the original workshop, but it is clearly to be seen in successive Rate Returns under Wickes from 1744 until 1760 when it changes for one year to Wickes and Netherton. In 1761 Edward Wakelin's name appears and remains until 1769 when it is deleted and 'Parker & Wakelin' substituted; John Wakelin and William Tayler take over in 1777 for two years then it passes into the hands of one John Nickells and out of the annals of the firm.

Without the evidence of a written indenture such as those which exist for other houses which John Parker acquired, it is impossible to do more than make a guess at the size and layout by comparing it with one of the houses for which there is not only an excellent schedule set out in an indenture of 1806, but also a ground plan sketched in the margin of a later indenture for the same house dated 1836 (Fig. 22). This house which is most likely to have resembled the workshop of 1744 is identified in the indenture as number 24 Panton Street and would have been reached by crossing Oxendon Street and walking a few paces up Panton Street towards Whitcomb Street keeping to the north side.

The house which Wickes leased for a workshop in 1744 may have differed slightly from number 24 Panton Street but the dimensions of the latter will at least serve to give a general idea of the size and layout of Wickes's new atelier. The frontage on Panton Street measured 18 ft 10 ins and the house was 33 ft 4 ins in depth with the yard beyond a further 27 ft 3 ins. 'Iron pallisadoes' (railings) at the front of the house enclosed a basement area with two coal vaults, complete with doors, and a 'dust binn'. A door from the area opened into the house and two windows, each with twelve panes of glass, protected by 'bowed ironwork', provided light for the basement kitchen. The floor of this room was boarded, but the back kitchen, probably a scullery, had brick tiles and was lit by a single casement window with three lights or panes. The whole of the basement is for the purpose of this exercise critical since in Wickes's second house it would almost

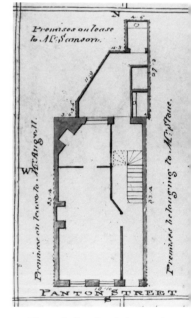

22. Ground-plan sketch in margin of Indenture of 1836 for No. 24 Panton Street. The adjoining premises were leased to Joseph Angell I. *Private Collection*

23. A chaser at work. The tricorne hat suggests a skilled goldsmith rather than a journeyman. Detail (see endpaper).

certainly have been converted into a working area. A passage floored with brick tiles ran through the house to the back yard which was paved with flag stones. In the yard an earth closet or 'necessary' with three seats occupied a space 4 ft 6 ins wide by 6 ft 9 ins long: it had a tiled roof with a lead gutter and a door with an iron handle. Rain water drained into the yard via a lead pipe fitted to a wooden water trap on the roof of the house. The shutters for the outside of the shop when not in use were stored in the yard behind a screen. The ground floor comprised a further 627 square feet lit by two 'bow window fronts with forty lights' at the street end and a single twelve-paned sash window overlooking the yard.

The basement may not have provided sufficient space to house the bulky equipment as well as all the journeymen and apprentices and, as was the case with the later workshop on the corner, the ground floor would probably have been incorporated. Chasers and engravers need maximum light and their benches would have been placed near the windows (Fig. 23). On dark winter days they would have worked by candlelight—a year's supply in 1767, according to the Ledgers, cost five pounds.

The installation of a workshop on the two lower floors would have left the house without cooking facilities. A room on the first floor may have been used as a kitchen/dining room, but it is more likely that the apprentices and boarded journeymen took their meals at the main house or that food was brought to them in their workshop by Alder Wickes's servants.

The living rooms would have been situated on the first and second floors: it is interesting to note in the schedule of 1806 'a closet to receive a bed' in a room on the second floor. One can only surmise that from 1747 onwards these floors housed Edward Wakelin and, later, his family. He married Ann Allen—'aged upwards of twenty nine years and a spinster', according to the marriage allegation—at Ely Chapel, on the 7 May 1748, the Reverend Charles Allen officiating. Their first child, a son baptised Francis, was born on the 28 July 1750 and lived only a few days. John, the future partner in the firm, was born on the 29 July 1751. A daughter, Elizabeth, came into the world on the 25 March 1753 and left it on the 4 June 1754. A second girl, also christened Elizabeth, arrived on the 6 July 1755 followed by a son, Edward, on the 23 January 1757. He, like his siblings, was baptised at St Martins-in-the-Fields. The demands of a growing family may explain why Wakelin's name appears in the Rate Returns of 1761 as occupier not only of the workshop but also of the house on the corner of Panton Street and Oxendon Street, Ann and the children living in the latter whilst his other family, the apprentices and journeymen, continued to inhabit the floors over the workshop.

Edward Wakelin took his first apprentice, James Ansill, on the 7 September 1748. He was the son of James Ansill, husbandman, of Stowe. The Apprentices' Book at Goldsmiths' Hall records Ansill's apprenticeship and that of a second Staffordshire boy, Stephen Gilbert; his village, Hickston, lay close to Ansill's home, Stowe. Wakelin was himself born in Uttoxeter and it may perhaps be permitted to wonder how their regional accent mixed with the long drawn out vowels of Suffolk which, judging by his phonetic spelling, Wickes must have retained to his dying day.

Prior to their apprenticeships both lads had been employed by the firm. Ansill would have been a mere twelve years of age when he started in 1746 with an annual wage of eight pounds. He was probably required to sweep the floors and run errands until, two years later, Wakelin took him formally into apprenticeship. Gilbert was even younger, a child of eleven. His wages for the first year, 1749–50, amounted to five pounds, rising to six pounds the following year. The payments to Stephen Gilbert stop with a settlement of £3 15s, his wages for seven months and fourteen days, on the 8 May 1752, the very day he was apprenticed to Wakelin.

The boys and servants would normally have slept in the garret rooms, one lit by a 'three leaded iron casement' and the other two relying for light and air on one lead light apiece. Two fireplaces served the three rooms. Access to the roof of Wickes's workshop was gained through a bolted trap door in the garret. A skylight with twelve panes lit the attic staircase. It is possible that not all the servants and apprentices could be accommodated in the garret rooms—in overcrowded premises they were often reduced to sleeping on pallets in the workshop.

Notes for chapter V

1. It is followed by an entry relating to the purchase of black earrings and a necklace at eight shillings which were presumably items of mourning jewellery. The two sisters shared the funeral charges and Mary's credit balance shews that she duly received from Alder £29 9s, being 'one moety of the funerall exspences of sister £58 18s'. The very next entry credits her with cash paid to 'br[other] Weale (sic) for a inkstand at 14 ozs 14 dwts ... 5s 8d ... £4 3s'.

VI The Journeymen and Sub-Contractors

One of the most important volumes in the Garrard Collection is that labelled 'Workmen's Ledger No. 2' which contains a complete record of the sub-contractors employed by the firm over a period of years. Unfortunately, it does not start until 1766 by which time Wickes's immediate successors John Parker and Edward Wakelin were six years into their partnership. The preceding volume—Workmen's Ledger No. 1—is missing: whilst it may have been started in Wickes's time, it is more likely that it dated from October 1760 when Parker and Wakelin took over the business. Many of the accounts in the extant second ledger are headed 'carried forward from W.L.1.' and in that missing first ledger there may well have been similar information linking it with past records kept by Wickes. As it is, the number of imponderables precludes even an educated guess at the exact state of the workshop in Wickes's time.

Although Wickes took pains to stress his continuing role 'as the maker' in 1735, the sheer volume of objects entered in the Gentlemen's (Clients') Ledgers could not possibly have emanated from one workshop, let alone one pair of hands. He presumably restricted his personal effort to the more elaborate and prestigious pieces: even then part of the work would have been done by his journeymen,

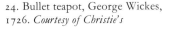

24. Bullet teapot, George Wickes, 1726. *Courtesy of Christie's*

assisted by the apprentices, under his supervision. Wickes is unlikely to have entrusted a difficult piece to a journeyman in its early stages and it would be interesting to know when he handed it over and at what point he resumed work on it himself.

So much of his early work was hollow ware that he must have been an expert at raising silver. Hollow vessels of any shape may be hammered from one piece of sheet metal without a join and objects such as teapots, bowls, jugs and beakers have their beginnings in flat pieces of silver cut to the requisite shape (Fig. 24). A circle is used for a round bowl and the mark made by the point of the compass remains for all time and is easily recognized on the base. After being roughly shaped with a wooden mallet in a series of depressions gouged out of a tree stump, it is ready to be raised (Fig. 25), that is to say hammered concentrically, starting at the compass point, until the whole surface is covered with rings of small circular dents. This intensive hammering causes distortion of the crystal structure of the silver alloy, inducing stresses which result in an ever increasing resistance to further work. A goldsmith develops an instinct which enables him to feel through his fingers this reluctance and his ear becomes attuned to the sullen metallic sounds emitted by silver that has reached a point when it must be annealed (Fig. 26). This is the moment when it is put to the flame to release the stresses and create a new undistorted crystal structure. The degree of heat and the time needed to soften the metal back to a state of malleability is gauged by the colour which first turns a smokey black then gradually changes until it glows a dull ruby red. If the heat is too great and exposure to it too long, the silver will crack when it is reworked and the piece will be ruined. The bane of all goldsmiths—and collectors—is firestain, a surface discolouration caused by the oxidation of the copper in the alloy which forms copper oxide. This is the result of an inherent defect in the particular piece of silver which is aggravated by intense heat; the resulting blemish becomes more pronounced each time a piece is annealed; it can only be eradicated by hard polishing or, in extreme cases, by the removal of a skin of silver. Modern techniques have to a great extent overcome this danger, but such niceties were unknown in the eighteenth century though no doubt Wickes had his own remedies.[1]

The raising ends when the metal has been gradually stretched by the hammer to the required height and diameter. A skilled worker can judge this by eye though calipers and gauges would have been available in Wickes's workshop to check the measurements.

At this point the object is again annealed and is then ready for planishing. As early as 1607 the Goldsmiths' Company abhorred the custom of employing specialist workers for each branch of the craft, castigating those 'of the idler sort' who 'betake themselves to the sole

25. Raising plate. Detail (see endpaper).

26. Annealing in a furnace. Detail (see endpaper).

27. Cheese stand, width 14 in (35.5 cm), height 5⅞ in (14.9 cm), Edward Wakelin, 1760. *Courtesy of Christie's*

practice and exercise of one slighte and easy part . . . some to be only hammermen', but it was common practice in Wickes's day and no doubt it helped to streamline the work and cut down on production time in a big workshop.

The planisher starts, as the raiser did, at the compass point, working concentrically as before but this time with a special smooth faced hammer which gently flattens the marks caused by the raising. As and when the metal becomes mulish it is annealed. A delicate touch is essential in planishing and the work was frequently carried out by women in the eighteenth century.

The final stage is the removal with pumice of the faint marks left by the planishing. This task would have been given to Wickes's apprentices. Stoning and polishing is hard and monotonous work which leaves the fingers stiff and raw, but the sense of achievement when the silver becomes satin smooth is recompense enough. The inside of a vessel and the area under a raised foot were often left unstoned and in such pieces the original hammer marks are readily discernible. Occasionally with a piece made from Britannia silver slight crescents can be observed amongst the regular pittings: the purer standard, being softer than sterling, is easier to work, but a hammer struck at the wrong angle can leave a deep indentation and the difficulty of eradicating it is the penance paid by every inexperienced goldsmith.

Wickes, and later Wakelin, would have kept a wary eye on the beginners, it being the master's duty to give them proper training. The chasing and piercing (Fig. 27)—the latter involving the use of very small saws—needed not only a steady hand, but skill and artistry. Only experienced men would have been employed on such work and, with the engravers, they would have been seated in the best positions with good lighting and elbow room, whilst the others would have worked in conditions which would not be tolerated today.

The master would have been able to leave his own work and move from bench to bench, keeping every employee under close scrutiny. Then, as now, a worker encountering difficulties would have paused in his task and waited for the master to come to his assistance. In this way practical advice given on the spot would avert the ruin of a piece which would otherwise have had to be consigned to the melting pot with the consequent loss of valuable time.

Run of the mill objects would have been left entirely to the senior journeymen who would not normally have registered a mark at the Hall: in such cases the master's punch would have been used (Fig. 28). This was common practice and when a coveted maker's mark is found on a very modest everyday object it is salutary to remember that it is highly unlikely that it was fashioned by the great man himself. Later, in the early nineteenth century, an extra mark is found—particularly in the case of flatware—a minute symbol or solitary initial, the 'signature' of the journeyman who actually made the piece.

Outworkers with marks registered at Goldsmiths' Hall would have punched their work as a matter of course. Occasionally pieces are found with the maker's mark overstamped with that of the retailer. This seems to have occurred more frequently in the latter part of the eighteenth century. Hester Bateman's work, if indeed she ever wielded a hammer, was frequently subjected to this malpractice—the number of her spoons overstamped by George Gray must run into hundreds. Wickes does not appear to have indulged in overstamping, but the joint mark of Parker and Wakelin has been found on candlesticks, superimposed on that of John Winter of Sheffield, in 1774. Wickes's acceptance of the marks of his journeymen and out-workers may well account for the disparity between the vast quantity of wrought silver recorded in his ledgers and the paucity of pieces bearing his mark.

As far as the workshop was concerned there were, obviously, physical limits to the number of employees who could be adequately supervised by one master and when the volume of business exceeded the resources of his own premises Wickes, in common with other successful goldsmiths, engaged out-workers and specialists. Wickes would have had no qualms in sub-contracting work to skilled men with a lengthy and thorough training behind them, knowing that many of them were only prevented by lack of capital from attaining his own enviable position. He himself had had the good fortune to marry a rich woman, but outstanding goldsmiths like Edward

28. The Master striking his maker's mark on a bowl. Detail (see endpapers).

Wakelin had no option but to serve established men—in his case Le Sage and Wickes—for many years, biding their time until they had accumulated sufficient funds to set up on their own. The waiting time was not wasted when a man could work at his craft in a reputable atelier, steadily acquiring knowledge and experience.

It is difficult to understand the reason for the years which frequently elapsed in the eighteenth century between the end of an apprenticeship and the registration of a mark. The seeking of freedom by service or patrimony involved the payment of a fee, but a goldsmith's right to register a mark was his by law and in no way dependent on his having taken up his freedom. Moreover the cost, if indeed any existed, was negligible. Paul de Lamerie registered his first mark the day after he received his freedom, but this was not common practice. It can only be assumed that it was not a matter of great importance to the majority or that they were discouraged by employers who preferred to see the house mark stamped on all silver made on their premises.

The only records available on the journeymen employed by Wickes are tucked away in the back pages of the Associates' Ledger. The earliest date from the beginning of 1748, a few months after Wakelin joined the firm. Only four out of a total of twenty listed in these pages have been positively identified in Mr A. G. Grimwade's *London Goldsmiths 1697–1837: their Marks & Lives* as having registered marks at Goldsmiths' Hall.[2] Those four men were entrusted with tasks requiring the most skill and this may be significant. The ledger yields some information on their work, but it is of a general nature, unlike Workmen's Ledger No. 2 which affords a mass of detail.

The Associates' Ledger identifies William Solomon, who registered his mark as a large plate worker on the 19 October 1747. Cast work, melting and flatting are mentioned together with a passing reference to 'waste in piercing'. He remained with Wickes and Wakelin until the 22 December 1759. The account of James Peltro, whose mark, also as a large plate worker, was entered in June 1739, was started, at least in this ledger, early in 1748 and ends in March 1751. Peltro, like Charles Bichel who followed him in 1752 and remained with the firm until 1760, can only be associated, from the meagre information available, with 'silver took off'. Andrew Killick, another large plate worker (mark registered on the 7 September 1749), was employed from February 1753 until October 1755 and appears to have spent those years filing and polishing.

A fourth worker, John Christopher Römer, was almost certainly a relative of the well-known goldsmith Emick Römer, an emigrant from Norway, whose work for Parker and Wakelin is recorded in their second Workmen's Ledger. John Christopher's name is written in full on the first page of his account which was begun prior to May 1752; it was later abbreviated to John Romer, but his signature is clearly J. Chr^{tr} Römer. A mark—the initials IR enclosed in four lobes—has been found on silver of the period, notably on a tureen dated 1764, and it is probable that it was recorded in the missing Large Plate Workers' Register. He appears in the 1773 Parliamentary List of Goldsmiths as 'plate worker' in Compton Street, Soho. Casting would seem to have been his forte and he was still with the firm in 1760. By that time he was sufficiently senior and capable to be promoted by John Parker and Edward Wakelin to some kind of managerial position. He must have been serving in this capacity when the lease of 'the house'—presumably the workshop since John Parker was living in 'The King's Arms & Feathers'—was transferred to him on the 11 October 1760, the day the business was acquired by Parker and Wakelin. This transfer of lease was obviously an internal arrangement since his name is absent from the Parish Rate Returns of that period, but the facts as stated in the ledger are clear:

1760

Octr 11   To cash allow'd for patterns
fixtures & the lease of the
house to be tranfer^d to him   £400 0s   0d

To 2 beds 2 bolsters
4 blankets 2 coverlids
a grate fire shovell & tongs
6 chairs a large candle box
& a safe   £7 7s   0d

Had the new partners' first workmen's ledger survived it would have been possible to follow John Christopher Römer's progress: the pages allotted to him would also have revealed a wealth of detail related to the running of the workshop and he himself would have emerged from the shadows as the man chosen to assist, even to replace, Edward Wakelin as works manager.

Cornelius Woldring was another journeyman of long standing. He joined the establishment on the 25 May 1748 and his account at the back of the Associates' Ledger ends on the 25 June 1761. His work appears to have been confined to casting and burnishing. There is a foreign ring to his name—he may, like Römer, have been Scandinavian.

Woldring, as a caster, was working in a specialized field. Heavy ornament and solid parts such as finials and feet cannot be raised and are fashioned by pouring molten silver into moulds designed for the purpose. Small objects would have been cast whole, but for larger pieces the goldsmith would have resorted to halved moulds, the resulting twin castings being joined together with silver solder, powdered borax being used as a fusing agent. Whatever the size, the casting would have emerged in a rough state and the edges would have needed to be filed off and the piece burnished and polished before it could be soldered to the main body of the object (Fig. 29). It is interesting that Wickes (and, incidently, de Lamerie) invariably wrote 'soder' when referring to 'solder', presumably because it was so pronounced in their day.

Cornelius Woldring appears to have been joined for a short time by a relative: a John Woldring was employed from the 13 August 1754 until October of the following year. John Fisher, on the other hand, served Wickes from 1748 until 1757 working principally as a chaser.

Melting and flatting, the latter being the hammering of ingots into sheets, were the province of John Jehner and John Holst who started working for Wickes in January 1747/8 and continued until 1752. Jehner was credited with the making of 'silver wyre' as well as 'flatted silver'. To produce this wire, which was mainly used for rims, edging and decoration, strips of annealed and malleable silver are drawn through a series of holes, diminishing in diameter, until the requisite size is achieved. The machine used for this purpose in the eighteenth century was big and cumbersome, the worker holding the wire with his left hand whilst his right hand and often his right foot were employed in manipulating the four handles of a large wheel (see Fig. 20).

The word 'skillet' occurs frequently in the Ledgers in connection with the workshop and was used to describe a thick flat piece of silver or other precious metal.[3] Wickes would have bought a large proportion of his silver in ingot form, but some of the articles which were traded in by clients would have been melted down into skillets in his workshop by such men as Jehner and Holst. The wealth of early masterpieces of the goldsmith's art, at the time out of fashion, which has been lost by this practice is beyond calculation.

The name of Pierce Stirrup occurs in these pages from 1753 to 1762, but the nature of his work is not disclosed. This also applies to Samuel Paddison whose account ends abruptly on the 29 January 1757 to be followed closely on the 16 February 1757 by one headed Elizabeth Paddision—probably his widow—in which she is described as a polisher. 'Bills of turning' are entered under the name of George Elger (January 1747–September 1759), but nothing else is known of him. In common with the workers mentioned above he was paid for 'jobs of work' and the irregular dating of their payments suggests that they were out-workers who did not live on the premises.

The employees who were paid regular wages, on the other hand,

29. A solderer at work. Detail (see endpaper).

would probably have worked and slept in Panton Street. Seven are listed, but, with two notable exceptions, they stayed for relatively short periods, ranging from four months to two years and five months. Judging by their low wages, averaging just under £5 10s per annum, the tasks carried out by them were of a menial nature.

The two exceptions were James Ansill and Stephen Gilbert who, it will be remembered, started as very young boys and shewed sufficient promise to be taken on as apprentices by Edward Wakelin in 1748 and 1752 respectively.

Throughout the seven year term of his service an apprentice did not normally receive any financial remuneration, but Ansill, who was first employed by Wickes in 1746, continued to be paid an annual wage throughout his apprenticeship which was increased by one pound a year until by 1755 he was receiving ten pounds. In December 1748, five days before Christmas, a 'suit of cloathes' was bought for him, the cost—£3 5s—being deducted from his wages.[4]

Once out of his apprenticeship, Ansill almost certainly remained with Wickes, working as a journeyman under the ægis of Wakelin. He was four years ahead of Gilbert who did not finish his term until 1759. Sometime after 1759 and before 1766 they became partners and judging from the large number of pages devoted to 'Messrs Ansill & Gilbert' (far more than any other sub-contractors) in Workmen's Ledger No. 2 (carried forward from Workmen's Ledger No. 1), they were the main outside suppliers of wrought silver to the firm. So close were their links with Panton Street, which must have been their home for many years, that they can hardly be classed as sub-contractors. It is obvious from their output that they had received a thorough all-round training. Unlike the specialist goldsmiths, their accounts cover a wide range of objects large and small including raised hollow-ware and dishes. They seem to have been content to work as an adjunct of the firm; they apparently never registered a joint mark and the objects they fashioned would have been punched initially with the maker's mark of Edward Wakelin, superseded in 1760 with the mark he entered with John Parker. The only mark known for Stephen Gilbert is that registered with Andrew Fogelberg in 1780, presumably after the death or retirement of his life-long friend James Ansill.

Specialization was already beginning to spread in the 1730s. Goldsmiths who at one time would have turned their hands to all aspects of their craft found better markets for their wares when they concentrated on one or more articles in popular demand. Spoon making had long been a specialist craft handed down from father to son and master to apprentice so that certain names are invariably linked with spoons and flatware.

Without the kind of documentary evidence that is found in

Workmen's Ledger No. 2 it is useless to speculate too closely on Wickes's choice of sub-contractors. Had their names, or even their initials, been written in the clients' ledgers against the items supplied, it would have been possible to identify some of them. Parker and Wakelin followed faithfully the book-keeping methods adopted by Wickes and there is no information on outside sources in their clients' ledgers either, but, conversely, the clients' names are noted against the objects recorded in the sub-contractors' accounts in Workmen's Ledger No. 2. Wickes must have kept a separate ledger for the specialist goldsmiths he employed—he was too good a business man to have relied on a haphazard system of verbal orders and initialled receipt slips—but no such volume was found in the Garrard Collection.

It is possible that the established specialists whose names appear in Workmen's Ledger No. 2 were retained by Parker and Wakelin because they had long ago been selected by Wickes and had proved their worth during the years when he was in charge. Any surmise must, however, be of necessity restricted to a handful of men. Isaac Callard may have been one such, a maker on whom Wickes could have relied for spoons. He first registered a mark in 1726 and in 1766 he was still supplying the firm. James Tookey, free of the Goldsmiths' Company in 1741, was another spoon maker favoured by Parker and Wakelin: Wickes could well have patronized Tookey back in the early 1740s when orders from a royal goldsmith would have been eagerly accepted by the spoon maker.

Wickes probably relied for salt cellars on David Hennell, the founder of the well-known firm of goldsmiths whose descendants continued the family business which flourishes to this day. David Hennell registered his first mark in 1736: he was certainly retained by the firm prior to 1766 since his account is headed 'carried over from W.L.1.': he was joined later by his illustrious son Robert Hennell I whose name appears with that of his father in Workmen's Ledger No. 2.

Thomas Pitts, *épergne* maker *par excellence*, was free by 1744 and his name figures largely in the later extant ledger. Wickes, who had himself made many superb *épergnes* in his time, would have been quick to appreciate the skill of Thomas Pitts and was probably responsible for bringing him into the network.

The services of Ebenezer Coker would also have been available to Wickes. A specialist maker of waiters, salvers and candlesticks, he worked in Clerkenwell, registering his first mark in 1738. He certainly made large quantities of plate for Parker and Wakelin and pieces bearing his mark can still be traced, through their engraved armorials, in the firm's clients' ledgers. Walter Brind is another goldsmith who

can be considered here. Free in 1743 and with a mark registered from Foster Lane in 1749, he made sturdy papboats, panakins and cream jugs. The list of sub-contractors working for Parker and Wakelin before 1766, from which the above names have been taken, contains many omitted from this perusal. Some were still in their apprenticeships in Wickes's day and only those whose working lives coincided with his own bear serious consideration. Information which might have been of some use in an attempt to reconstruct the network has vanished with the missing Register of Small Plate Workers' Marks which covered twenty years of Wickes's career.

There is also no documentation in the Garrard Ledgers of the everyday tasks which, whilst essential, were not directly connected with the fashioning of wrought silver. The pieces produced in Panton Street, after being punched with Wickes's maker's mark (at least up to 1747), had to be conveyed to Goldsmiths' Hall in Foster Lane on the days appointed for assaying.

The Assay Office was adjacent to the Hall—as it still is today—and there must have been an established procedure whereby slips were made out in advance, simpler versions of the current Hall Notes, listing the objects for assay, one for retention by the Assayer, the other a form of receipt signed by the receiving officer and returned to the goldsmith. This counterfoil would then be presented when the hall-marked objects were collected.

Wickes's work did not end with the return of the pieces sent for hall-marking, it being accepted that they should be submitted for assay at a point just short of completion and the finishing touches added after they had been collected and brought back to the workshop. On hollow-ware, plates and salvers the marks would

160

The Earl of Radnor Dr

1812 Bro.t from 7/300 . . . . . . 2 5 6

remain pristine, but those stamped on bottom-marked flatware were often distorted as a result of the final hammering-over which was necessary to give a smooth edge to the stems. As spoon collectors know to their chagrin, marks are often indecipherable as a result.

Once an object was finished to Wickes's satisfaction one small touch remained: the engraving of the weight on the base. It is invariably the figure entered in the clients' ledgers. This engraved weight is the third and final piece of information required when searching the Ledgers for pieces of Wickes's silver as and when they come to light today, the other two being the armorials (to identify the client) and the assay date letter. When they are weighed they are usually found to be a few pennyweights lighter, due not so much to any inaccuracy in Wickes's scales, but to the wear and tear of the centuries. When an object weighs more than the figure engraved on the base it is a useful pointer to later repairs or embellishments which were often carried out by the firm and duly recorded in the later accounts of the clients or their descendants (Figs. 30a & b).

The Ledgers give no indication of the system employed by Wickes for delivering his plate to clients. It is probable that it was taken from the workshop to 'The King's Arms & Feathers', entered into the appropriate accounts and then taken round to the client's house or, in the case of a visitor to London, to the place where he was staying: it is not unusual to find in the index the name of an inn or the address of furnished chambers noted alongside the entry for a client. For those living outside the United Kingdom arrangements were made by Wickes to convey the plate to a port: charges were made for the cost of carriage as well as the fee paid for the debenture which was issued when the objects were shipped and enabled the owner to recover the six pence per ounce duty already paid on them.

Since pieces appear to have been entered in the Ledgers on the date they were delivered to the client, rather than at the time the order was placed, some note of the requirements must have been made initially and a copy passed to the workshop. Unfortunately no such instructions have survived to prove the point.

Notes for chapter VI

1. Nowadays these firestains on antique silver can easily be concealed by silver-plating, but no serious collector would resort to this dubious solution: the silver thus deposited is eventually dissipated by normal domestic cleaning and the original firestain glaringly exposed.

2. It must be emphasized that research on eighteenth century makers' marks has been bedevilled by a gap in the Archives of the Worshipful Company of Goldsmiths: two registers, one for Small Plate Workers covering the period 24 May 1739–13 July 1758 and another for Large Plate Workers 30 September 1759–7 March 1773, were not returned to the Company after the Parliamentary Scrutiny of 1773 and it is feared that they perished when part of the Houses of Parliament was destroyed by fire in 1834.

3. Once formed, the skillets, like the ingots, had to be hammered into sheets; machinery was introduced later in the century and today they are rolled evenly and effortlessly by the same means whilst the modern goldsmith can not only choose from many gauges when buying raw silver, but also stipulate the exact shape he requires.

4. Another small item in his account is of some interest: the debiting of one ounce of silver at the end of March 1755 during the seventh and last year of his apprenticeship. Were it not for the fact that Ansill was not made free of the Worshipful Company until 1764, it would be tempting to connect this with the rule promulgated by the Company as early as 1607 in the Order for the Masterpiece. Disturbed by the fact that 'very few workmen are able to furnish and perfect a piece of plate singularly . . . without the help of many and several hands', the Hall laid down that before being granted his freedom a craftsman had to produce a piece wrought by his own hands without help from his master or fellow workers. In order to ensure that this order was stringently observed the Company went to the lengths of installing a workshop on its own premises and insisting that the masterpieces should be made there. This provision was minuted in the seventeenth century, but not raised by the Court again so there is no firm evidence to prove that it still obtained in the eighteenth century.

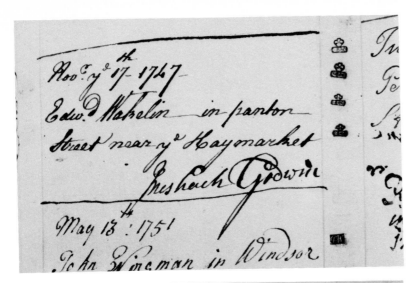

31. Edward Wakelin's first maker's mark (entry in the Large Plate Workers' Register at Goldsmiths' Hall)

32. 1739 maker's mark of George Wickes. By the Statute of 1738/9 (12 Geo.11c.26) goldsmiths were ordered to destroy their marks and register new ones at the Hall consisting of initials only, of a different style of lettering from that used before. It was hoped that this measure would help in the detection of counterfeit marks

33. Wickes's maker's mark and hall-marks for 1742 at the base of a candlestick. *Courtesy of Spink & Son Ltd.*

VII The Associates

Wickes's reputation as a goldsmith was firmly established and orders flowed into the new workshop set up in 1744. Although Netherton would certainly have been a great help to him, only Wickes would have been capable of running the manufacturing side and the hard work must have started to take its toll. There can be no doubt that he had competent journeymen working for him, but obviously none of his own calibre. He needed a goldsmith of some experience with exceptional talent and an impeccable working pedigree. He had probably been looking around for some time making a survey of likely candidates: his short list would make interesting reading today. It must have been soon apparent to him that Edward Wakelin, the ideal man for the job, was working in nearby Suffolk Street in the atelier of John Hugh Le Sage at the sign of the Golden Cup. Wickes would have been well aware that Le Sage was frequently entrusted with work for the Royal Family farmed out to him by the King's goldsmith Thomas Minors. He would also have known that Wakelin's chances of a partnership with Le Sage were slender since the master's son was himself a goldsmith, apprenticed to his father.

Unlike de Lamerie and Le Sage, Wickes himself had not enjoyed the benefits of Huguenot training and whereas he would probably have been as quick as the other native goldsmiths to hold out against the Huguenots earlier in the century, by 1747 they were established and accepted in England and Wickes was too good a craftsman not to recognize and appreciate their peculiar gifts.

Edward Wakelin moved to Panton Street in November 1747. The son of Edward Wakelin, a baker, of Uttoxeter, Staffordshire, his father was already dead at the time of his apprenticeship to Le Sage on the 3 June 1730. Although by 1747 Wakelin had been out of his apprenticeship for some ten years, he had made no attempt to seek his freedom by service of the Goldsmiths' Company nor did he do so on joining Wickes. Instead he waited a year until the 7 September 1748, presumably sparing himself the fee—ten shillings—until such time as he was sure that he could work harmoniously with Wickes. He did, however, register his first maker's mark at Goldsmiths' Hall on the 17 November 1747, giving as his address Panton Street (Fig. 31). He did

34a

34b

34c

34d

not, as might have been expected, enter a joint mark with Wickes, but instead he adopted the latter's format and the initials EW beneath the feathers of the Prince of Wales are so similar to Wickes's last maker's mark (Fig. 32) that even experts have been known to confuse them (Fig. 33).

Wakelin was clearly no ordinary employee. Wickes needed a goldsmith of proved excellence to take over the fashioning side of the business and, judging by the magnificent pieces which bear his mark, Wakelin was a superb artist and craftsman (Fig. 34). Wickes's mark is rarely, if ever, found on plate assayed after 1747 and it is apparent that Wakelin had replaced him 'as the maker'. Wickes was forty-nine in 1747; he had worked hard since the age of fourteen and he may have felt it was time to leave the strenuous physical work to a younger man. His health had possibly deteriorated—a working goldsmith needs considerable stamina—or he may have found greater satisfaction in running the administrative side of a thriving business and dealing personally with clients who became with each year more illustrious.

34a. Cream jug, height 4¾ (12 cm), Edward Wakelin, c. 1750. Few of Edward Wakelin's pieces are as grotesque as this rococo cream jug. Whilst the design on the body of the jug is of considerable interest, the handle is out of character. *Courtesy of Sotheby's*

34b. *Epergne*, Edward Wakelin, 1751. *Courtesy of Christie's*

The ledgers were kept principally by Netherton, though occasionally one recognizes the handwriting of Wickes.

It has been suggested that Wakelin became Wickes's partner in 1747, but this is belied by the handsome trade card which appeared in 1750 in the joint names of Wickes and his protégé Samuel Netherton (Fig. 35). Netherton was at this time barely twenty-seven years of age: though Wakelin was seven years his senior he had only just joined the firm and probably did not have the capital to purchase an interest.

Netherton may have anticipated the partnership when he took to wife Mary Woodward, widow, on the 17 February 1749/50. They were married by licence in the Bishop of Ely's London Palace chapel by the Reverend Henry Burrough, son-in-law of Wickes's kinsman the late Bishop of Ely, Robert Butts, and first cousin to the artist Thomas Gainsborough. Three Butts children were baptised at Ely Palace and Henry Burrough had wed Caroline Butts there in 1750.

Mary Woodward was the daughter of Netherton's guardian William Lawrence. She was born in 1719 and was therefore four years older than Samuel. Her late husband may have been a relative of Wickes's first two apprentices of that name, which in all three cases was frequently written as 'Woodard'.[1]

The only appearance of a Mrs Woodward in Wickes's ledgers occurs in the account of a Mrs Short ('In new Broad Street'). The entry is dated 20 December 1735 and reads: 'To new setting 3 stay one girdle buckle Mrs Woodward ... £3 3s'. In 1735 Mary would have been a mere sixteen: either she was a very young and modish bride or the buckles were reset for her mother-in-law. Mrs Short herself was certainly well-known to Wickes—in company with the goldsmith and his wife Alder, William Lawrence and Samuel Netherton, she was a legatee of John Waldron, whose will landed Wickes and Lawrence in the Court of the Arches.

Samuel would have known Mary from the age of ten at least. She may have been very kind to her father's ward and with only a few years between them they were probably close friends. There is, of course, the possibility that it was a marriage of convenience engineered by Lawrence and Wickes. If so, Lawrence must have had a great deal of confidence in Netherton for when he made his will on the 30 May 1751[2] after sundry bequests (some of silver to relatives), he left the rest of his estate equally between his brother and his 'son-in-law Saml. Netherton of Panton Street, Silversmith', who were named joint executors. The will was proved on the 14 June 1751, four days before the funeral. William Lawrence was buried in the Church of St Dunstan-in-the-West, a few hundred yards from his home in Rolls Buildings. Strangely enough, there was no mention of Wickes in his

34c. Soup tureen, width 15¾ in (40 cm), Edward Wakelin, 1753. Finials in the shape of fruit, vegetables, flowers and crustacea were popular rococo decorations. The split pomegranate fashioned by Edward Wakelin had its origins in the legend of Persephone; it is found frequently in Renaissance ornament; its introduction into English design is believed to date from the arrival of Catherine of Aragon, the pomegranate being a symbol of the House of Aragon. *Courtesy of Sotheby's*

34d. One of a set of four entrée dishes, width 10 in (25.4 cm), Edward Wakelin, 1755. *Courtesy of Christie's*

will. Mary was also excluded, but it is more than likely that, between her father and her late husband, she was already comfortably endowed. When she herself died in 1755 Samuel Netherton applied for administration of the 'goods, chattels and credits of Mary Netherton, formerly Woodward' which suggests that she had enjoyed certain assets in her own right.[3]

Samuel and Mary Netherton set up home in Panton Street living in the first house acquired by Wickes since it is probable that Wakelin and his family and, almost certainly, the apprentices, would have lived over the workshop next door but one. Samuel was to all intents and purposes the son of the house and Mary was already well acquainted with Wickes and his wife Alder. Netherton's marriage—as barren as that of Wickes—was short-lived. Mary died in October 1755, possibly in childbed though this is not stated, and was buried in the parish church of St Martin-in-the-Fields. This brief description of her interment is to be seen in the Church's Burial Book:

[aged]36 w[oman]	Mary Netherton from Panton Street
Oct 1755	Church Vt. Gt. Bl.
	6 m prs candles
	Tuesday at 11.30

The church fees amounted to £16 14s 8d.

34e. One of a pair of candelabra, height 17½ in (44.5 cm), Edward Wakelin, 1751. *Courtesy of Simon Kaye Ltd.*

35. Trade-card of George Wickes and Samuel Netherton, 1750. *Courtesy of the Trustees of the British Museum*

Judging by the constant mention of Samuel Netherton in their wills, he was greatly loved by all the members of George and Alder Wickes's families on both sides. It is strange in an age where it was universally accepted that remarriage often followed swiftly on the heels of a bereavement that Netherton, now aged thirty-two and in the prime of life, chose to remain a widower for the next seventeen years. No portrait of him has as yet emerged and we have no knowledge of his physical appearance, but he seems to have been a man of singularly attractive character and—an important factor in an unsentimental and materialistic age—his enviable financial position would have ensured him a wide choice of marriageable young women.

For the next five years his cursive script fills the ledgers as before but Samuel makes his appearance as junior partner in only one volume—a strange form of stocktaking ledger involving the firm of Wickes & Netherton and its associate Edward Wakelin.

Notes for chapter VII

1. A search of Woodward/Woodard wills and administrations produced only one likely candidate, Richard Woodward, late of the parish of St Margaret Westminster. Unfortunately he died intestate in 1742; administration of his estate was granted to Mary, his widow. The case is weak, resting solely on the fact that in no other Woodward will or administration found was the widow named as Mary. If this Richard Woodward was indeed Mary Lawrence's dead husband, he may have been a kinsman of Richard and Thomas Woodward, the unfortunate goldsmiths and bankers who were declared bankrupt in 1731. *The Gentlemen's Magazine* for March of that year reported 'that the cause of their failure is charged of the Jews, who borrowed large sums of them . . . but took no care to reimburse'. The Archives of the Worshipful Company of Goldsmiths record the apprenticeships of two Richard Woodwards, one in 1692, the other in 1719. The older apprentice would have been about sixty-four in 1742 and may well have been the bankrupt. The younger man would have been thirty-seven in that year and Mary Lawrence Woodward twenty-three years of age. The question is purely academic: administrations—the bane of all researchers—do not give the trade of the deceased and, unlike wills, contain no personal details and we are none the wiser about the identity of Mary's dead husband, who may not have been, after all, a goldsmith.
2. P.R.O.: PCC Prob 11/788–182
3. P.R.O.: Admon. Prob 6/131

1753 Messrs Wickes & Netherton Debtors | Contra Creditors

Nov 5 To 8 Wax Candlesticks	4.7		
To a Tureen & Cover	120.8	1/4 r 10.11	By O S 200
To a plain Trowell	5.16	r	By Do 500
14 To a foot & cover to a Gilt box	2.12	r	By Do 500
To 2 pr Neckd Candlesticks & Nozles	101.19	1/6 r 7.13	By Cash 10.10
a Branch	23.9	2/6 r 2.11	By Cash ....
To 2 Chaisd Soup Ladles	20.10	r 2.1	By Do 400
To a Neckd fluted Cream boat	6.13	r .1	By Cash 40
To a Bread Basket	59.3	r 7.1	By Do 10.10
To 2 Dishes	142.9	11r 6.11	By O S 568.16
To a Saucepan	12.17	r 1.1	By Do 400
To 2 pr of Neckd Candlesticks & nozils	117.20	r 8.1	By N S 37 4.7
To 12 Plates perls	218.14	12.14	By Cash 10.10
To 2 hand Waiters	23.1	r 1.1	
To a hearing trumpet	15.18	r 2.	2695.16 71.14.7
To 12 knife handles	32.3	1.1	
To 2 Dishes	38.2	r 1.11	By a Bread Basket 66.8 at 8/5 ... 27.19
To a fish plate	21.5	r 1.1	By 12 Table knife handles 12 frh at 26.2 ... 20.0
To 2 Bread Baskets	129.10	r 15	By 12 D Spoons ... 30.1 ... 2.7.6
To a Neckd Do	64.10	23r 7.1	By a Night Soup Ladle ... 5.2 ...
To a Chaisd Cream boat	11.5	r 1.1	By 8 Buckles & 2 Wires & pepper castor & spoons 4.10.2
To a Neckd Inkstand & 3 Boxes	59.7	r 5.1	54.16.8
To Do & 4 Boxes	37.17	r 4.1	By 1 Years House Rent ... 40.0.10
To a Bill of Jobbs to Decr 2d 1753	8.12	8.12	15.1
Broet from ye 1st folio	1282.13	122	Broe from ye 1st folio ... 7767 ... 263.2.11
From ye 2d folio	2114.13	1174	From ye 2d folio ... 2452 ... 83.5.10
From ye 3 folio	2155.16	280	From ye 3 folio ... 3578.16 ... 339.8.6
From ye 4th folio	2377.11	172	From ye 4th folio ... 1863.13 ... 263.16.4
From ye 4th folio	2374.19	228	From ye 5th folio ... 1428.1 ... 324.17.7
From ye 5th folio	1897.12	256	From ye 6th folio ... 1299.6 ... 231
From ye 6th folio	2485.2	376	
Difference of Weight	14687.13	2617	Difference of Weight ... 21045.18 1674
	14688.2		By Cash due to Ballance ... 21046.5 1302.10.8
To Duty for 14688		359	£ 2976.13.11
To Sterling due to Ballance	6358.3 £2976		
	21046.5		

Decr 3 1753 Settled the above accounts this day
& remains due to Messrs Wickes & Netherton a
ballance of Six thousand three hundred & fifty
eight ounces threepennyweight of old Sterling & to
Mr Watkin a ballance in Cash of Thirteen hundred
& two pounds ten shilling & threepence
Saml Netherton

VIII The Associates' Ledger

The Associates' Ledger appears at first glance to be a crude attempt at arriving at some kind of balance, expressed in terms of money and sterling silver, between Wickes, Netherton and Wakelin. It no doubt made sense to them at the time and formed the basis of their business relationship, but it is something of a conundrum today. It merits close examination since it is the only volume in the Garrard Collection which throws any light on Wakelin's role in the firm in the period 1747 to 1760.

This ledger does not shew sales or profits, but it is laid out in the conventional way with two pages headed 'Debtor' and 'Contra Creditor'; each is divided into five sections (Fig. 36). The left-hand page—the debtor side—is headed with the names of Wickes and Netherton and consists of a list of wrought articles apparently made or acquired during the accounting period and unsold at the date when the balance was struck. The right-hand creditor side is concerned with a miscellany of entries which appear to relate to the workshop. Wakelin's name does not appear except in the summing-up of assets at the end of each stock-taking.

On the debtor side the first of the five columns is reserved for the date whilst the second and largest column is devoted to a brief description of the objects. The third gives the troy weight in ounces and pennyweights and is followed closely by a fourth so similar to that reserved for the fashioning charge in the Clients' Ledgers as to bear serious comparison. This latter is shewn in shillings and pence, but the space is often left blank, possibly because the piece was bought from a client or subcontractor and not made by the firm's workshop. An assessment of the value of the article is written in the fifth and last column. A typical entry reads as follows:

Nov.ᵣ 18 To a cruet stand   22 oz   4/3   £4 13s 6d (Fig. 37).

It will be seen that the last figure (£4 13s 6d) is arrived at by multiplying the fashioning charge (4s 3d per troy ounce) by the weight (22 ozs), the same method in fact as that used consistently in the Clients' Ledgers.

Interspersed amongst the silver are entries for duty: in one

36. Settlement in the Associates' Ledger for the year 1753. The names of Wickes and Netherton appear at the top of the debtor side on the left-hand page. The right-hand page is headed Contra Creditor and Wakelin's name is omitted although it is clear from Netherton's note at the bottom left-hand corner of the illustration that Wakelin was responsible for the workshop.
It was not possible to photograph the whole of the cost column, the last on the debtor side, or the date column, the first on the creditor side, without risking damage to the ledger. *Courtesy of the Victoria and Albert Museum*

73

37. Oil and vinegar cruet, George Wickes, 1742. The design of this cruet and stand is conservative for its date. A very similar one on identical feet was made by Paul de Lamerie in 1727 and is now in the Ashmolean Museum. Wickes's version is far more delicate: the piercing is exceptionally fine. *Courtesy of Brand Inglis Ltd.*

instance, in 1752, the sum of £359 7s 6d is recorded as being due to the Excise on 14,375 ozs of silver, the duty payable being at that time 6d per troy ounce.

The opposite page—the right-hand side headed 'Contra'—is also divided into five columns, the first one giving the date. Quantities of unfashioned silver appear in the second column, the standards described as OS (old sterling—925 parts fine per thousand) and NS (new sterling or Britannia standard—958 parts fine per thousand); occasionally pure silver makes an appearance. The troy weight follows, the fashioning charge column is left completely blank and the overall value is entered in the fifth column. Fashioned silver is sometimes found on this page, but it was probably intended for melting down.

Apart from raw silver, the second column also carries such diverse items as sea coal, charcoal, emery paper and patterns, all of which would have been in daily use in the workshop. House plates also make an appearance and pit tickets. The latter may have been silver tokens for melting down; they appear frequently on the credit side of an account of an actress client, Mrs. Horton, suggesting at first glance that the members of the Wickes household were avid theatre goers. Two important items figure on this side—the annual rent and taxes of the house-cum-workshop (£40 0s 10d) and the amount of cash in hand.

At each balance two columns were totalled on both sides: the weight of silver in the third and the sums of money in the fifth. The final figures were then examined and when the weight of silver on the contra side exceeded that on the debtor side the amount required to equalize the two was quite simply added to the left-hand page. The same procedure was adopted for the cash on the contra side. Thus we find 16 December 1752 the following totals:

	Debtors	Wickes & Netherton					Creditors				
	ozs	dwts	£	s	d			ozs	dwts	£	s	d
	17,806	14	2,432	16	0			23,833	4	1,442	7	8
To silver due to balance	6,026	10					By cash due to ballance			990	8	4
	23,833	4								2,432	16	0

By this very simple adjustment an agreement seems to have been arrived at which was acceptable to all three associates. It was followed by a note couched in the following terms and, in this instance, signed by Netherton.

Decr: 16. 1752 settled the above accounts this day & remains due to Messrs Wickes & Netherton a balance of six thousand & twenty-six ounces eleven pennyweights [it was in fact ten] of old sterling & to Mr Wakelin a ballance of nine hundred & ninety pounds eight shillings & four pence in cash.

The table that follows gives the amounts involved in the period 8 April 1748–27 December 1759.

Date	Due to Wickes— Sterling Silver	Due to Wakelin— Cash
8 April 1748	2,700 ozs	—
14 July 1749	4,499 ozs	£423 16s 2d
16 November 1749 [?1750]	4,717 ozs 18 dwts	£647 0s 11d
	Due to Wickes & Netherton	
1 December 1751	2,943 ozs 13 dwts	£547 15s 0d
16 December 1752	6,026 ozs 10 dwts	£990 8s 4d
3 December [1753]	6,358 ozs 3 dwts	£1,302 10s 8d
14 December 1754	7,884 ozs 8 dwts	£1,033 2s 4d
9 August 1755	15,328 ozs 10 dwts	£1,182 0s 7d
11 August 1756	6,735 ozs 13 dwts	£1,647 18s 2d
1 October 1757	6,486 ozs 4 dwts	£1,660 10s 4d
7 September 1758	6,503 ozs 8 dwts	£1,595 0s 5d
27 December 1759	5,099 ozs 3 dwts	£166 0s 8d

It must be stressed that the figures given above are those used by the Associates in an extremely arbitrary way to balance their books and appear to be merely paper figures.

What, then, was the real purpose of this ledger? A clue to the answer would seem to lie in the third column on the left-hand page—the debtor side—which contains what appear to be fashioning charges: they are significantly below those paid by clients for comparable objects in the Clients' Ledgers. One possibility is that these sums were the monies actually owed to Wakelin as head of the workshop, he being responsible for paying the journeymen who had fashioned the articles. It must, however, be borne in mind that the number of objects listed in each accounting period is puny compared with the output recorded in sales in the Clients' Ledgers. It would seem, therefore, that the pieces listed in the Associates' Ledger were those made for stock and unsold at the time when the balance was made. There is only one other ledger in which fashioning charges at such low levels are to be found—the second Workmen's Ledger. This unfortunately does not start until 1766 and the volumes which preceded it are missing from the Garrard Collection.

Wakelin's position in the firm has always been something of a mystery. His competence and skill as a goldsmith were obviously beyond dispute and his exclusion from the partnership may well have been due solely to his lack of ready money. When Netherton became a partner in November 1750 Wakelin had only been in Panton Street for three years. He would hardly have been able to save sufficient money in that time or prior to it since his wages even as a senior journeyman with Le Sage would not have been princely. By the time Wickes and Netherton retired in 1760 he was in a position to raise the £2,700 needed to buy him a half share in the capital joint stock when, in partnership with John Parker, he took over the firm. It should be pointed out, however, that both men were assisted by a loan from Wickes. He must have had confidence in their ability to have invested in them, receiving 5% interest per annum on the loan. It was covered by a bond dated the 11 October 1760 and was not finally discharged until the 16 June 1772, long after Wickes's death. On that date the sum of £1,800 was paid out of the joint stock to Alder Wickes.

The indenture of partnership between Parker and Wakelin stipulates that entries should be made in 'proper books' of 'all buyings sales receipts and payments & of all cash goods notes debts & other stock belonging to the joint trade'. It also lays down that 'the partys shall every year . . . within twenty days after or before the 1st Novr join in making up a gen^l account & reckoning & an estimate acc^t & calculation of all jewels plate ready money debts . . . & set down in

38. Brandy saucepan, diameter
4¼ in (10.8 cm), George Wickes,
1728. *Courtesy of Sotheby's*

two books to be prepared for that purpose the true particulars of such
accts clearly as the same shall be computed by both partys by their
mutual consent which books or transcripts are to be mutually signed
by each party & each to have one for his own use, the first of which sd
accts to be made stated signed & sealed on or before 1st November
1761'. These two books are lost to us, each partner, presumably,
taking his personal copy with him when he retired.

A similar exercise can be seen in the second Workmen's Ledger
when settlements were made with Ansill and Gilbert and, later, with
the Crespels, all principal subcontractors of the firm. In the case of
these workmen the system is far more straightforward. On the
debtor side one finds entries for the silver they received in bulk from
the firm interspersed with cash advances and it is only the latter that
appear in the money column; the silver is not valued but shewn in
ounces and pennyweights. On the credit or contra side are listed the
wrought articles in their finished state, the amount of silver used for
each item and the workman's charge for fashioning it. Some idea of
the system employed by the firm can be gained from a piece made by
Ansill and Gilbert for Wickes's widow in 1772. The Workmen's
Ledger records

'June 15 To a small saucepan Wickes 6 ozs 19 dwts . . . 6s od.'

In the Clients' Ledger it appears as follows in the account of Alder
Wickes:

'June 16 To a small saucepan 6 ozs 19 dwts 5/9 £2 os od'
(Fig. 38).

Ansill and Gilbert received just over 10d per troy ounce for their
labour. After deducting their 6s from the £2 charged to Alder Wickes,
Parker and Wakelin were left with £1 14s which would not have

covered the cost of the silver and their overheads. It is obvious that in this instance they were prepared to make a gesture to the widow of their late master.

Close study of the Associates' Ledger leads to a conjecture that may bear examination. Was Wakelin paid an agreed sum when an article was made, the partners taking the chance that it would eventually be sold? It goes without saying that under such an arrangement he would also have received a percentage of the profits from the goods manufactured in his workshop for specific orders. The journeymen in the firm's workshop were paid wages, but sub-contracted articles would have been treated as piece work. It would have been Wakelin's responsibility to farm out such pieces and oversee the work at all stages. In such cases he must have received a proportion of the profit accruing to the firm once the out-worker had been paid. The lion's share would certainly have gone to Wickes and Netherton as owners of the firm and, moreover, the overheads of the shop, as opposed to the workshop, would have had to be deducted. The debts incurred by the workshop, including the rent, appear to have been Wakelin's province, but these outgoings are shewn on the contra side of the Associates' Ledger implying that Wickes and Netherton were the creditors and received these sums, at least on paper, from Wakelin. This was the method used in their dealings in the Clients' Ledgers, but this is no ordinary ledger and we have to draw from it what information we can.

One entry stands out. Dated 2 April 1748 it reads:

By cash as by agreem^t for
ye assignm^t of the house
& ctra . . . £400

This could only have applied to the workshop since Wickes did not relinquish the lease of the first house, the shop-cum-dwelling place, until 1760 when the remainder of the lease was bought by John Parker. The word 'assignment' may have been used loosely in this case since the workshop remained under Wickes's name in the Rate Returns until 1761 when Wakelin's name appeared for the first time. If, however, Wakelin did pay £400 for some kind of assignment as well as £40 per annum rent, then one can only assume that the workshop was a very profitable concern and his business arrangement with the partners as regards his salary or percentage a highly satisfactory one. The Associates' Ledger confounds confusion, but one impression emerges: Wakelin was the works manager albeit under the overall control of his masters Wickes and Netherton who ran the business from 'The King's Arms & Feathers' and kept firmly in their hands all matters pertaining to sales and administration.

IX The Designers and Modellers

John Parker must have worked for some time alongside the partners to have acquired the business knowledge which enabled him to take over the firm in 1760 at the age of twenty-six. Nine years had elapsed since the commencement of his apprenticeship to Wickes and it would be interesting to know how many of those years, if any, were spent at the bench and the furnace. Wakelin, on the other hand, had spent thirty years in the workshop. Despite the eighteen years which separated them, Wakelin was content to enter into partnership with the youthful Parker: their indenture places great emphasis on the 'joint and equal' basis of their business relationship. It does not, unfortunately, delineate the duties of each man. Wakelin at forty-four was clearly in charge of the fashioning side which was to remain his sphere of influence whilst Parker took over the duties formerly shared by Wickes and Netherton. He may also have possessed talents which served him well on the design side.

The author of *The London Tradesman* made it clear that whilst a goldsmith 'ought to be a good designer' he should also 'have a good taste in sculpture'. He might have added that a working knowledge of modelling was even more essential. Although very few have survived, pattern books are known to have been in general circulation, many of them emanating from the Continent. In the early decades of the century clean simple lines were in vogue and the goldsmith could rely heavily on engravings and drawings or on his own eye and hand. Some of the working sketches for fine furniture which have survived are amazingly rough and ready, but the eighteenth century was an age of superlative craftsmen who were so skilled that they could work from the merest outline. This must have been equally true for the goldsmith. By the 1730s, however, when the rococo style had reached England, no goldsmith's establishment could have functioned without the services of a modeller. *Rocaille* extravagances had first to be drawn then expressed in wax or base metal before being made into moulds and translated into cast gold and silver.

Apart from those made in base metal (and this would have applied particularly to ornament in constant use), the models themselves were of their very nature ephemeral, but the sculptural talent was captured for all time in the fashioned silver. William Kent's baroque designs were available, perpetuated by their publication by Vardy in 1744, and were used by Wickes, Crespin and Wakelin. Had Robert Adam never sketched a candlestick or vase there would still have been sufficient examples of attic shapes in the collection of Sir William Hamilton and the much-acclaimed volumes of d'Hancarville[1] and Wood & Dawkins[2] to enable goldsmiths to satisfy the neo-classical tastes of the latter half of the eighteenth century. Flaxman and his fellow artists receive their just dues, but—Moser apart—the modellers of rococo silver are unknown and unsung and when one of their swirling fantasies compels the imagination today a thought might be spared for the goldsmith's modest collaborator who first gave it life.

Wickes would almost certainly have employed outside modellers, but their identity has perished with the early Workmen's Ledgers. He would not have had far to go to find them. A short walk from Panton Street would have taken him to Old Slaughter's Coffee House, the haunt of the denizens of the St Martin's Lane Academy which William Hogarth founded in 1735 to teach artists and craftsmen the rococo style. Sir Joshua Reynolds, writing Moser's obituary, related how the Swiss chaser and enameller, long domiciled in England, 'presided over the little societies which met first in Salisbury Court, and afterwards in St Martin's Lane, where they drew from living models.' Mark Girouard, writing in *Country Life*,[3] has suggested that the 'little societies' were the true nursery of English rococo design. This elitist group included Hogarth, Gravelot, Moser and Hayman— the first three known to have been associated with the goldsmith's and jeweller's trades. The young Gainsborough and his fellow pupils in Gravelot's studio were at hand and no doubt impecunious: Wickes might well have had his pick of promising students from the St Martin's Lane Academy who would have happily accepted modelling commissions from one of the most reputable goldsmiths of the day.

As Mr Gerald Taylor has pointed out, the figures on the magnificent cistern by Charles Kandler, which was acquired by Catherine II of Russia, were modelled in wax by Michael Rysbrack, who was frequently employed by Frederick Prince of Wales on works of sculpture. The cistern, which weighed 8,000 ounces, was based on a sketch by George Vertue, the antiquary, and designs by Henry Jerningham, a goldsmith. Unable to dispose of such a costly piece, Jerningham petitioned to have it included in a state lottery. £100,000 was needed towards the cost of a new Westminster Bridge and in the Spring of 1735 a bill to authorize a lottery to raise funds was before the House.[4] References to lottery tickets occur in clients' accounts in

Wickes's ledgers, but there is no proof that he himself participated. John Parker's involvement is, however, documented. He wrote down the numbers of his tickets in his account with an optimistic flourish and then erased them with fine ruler lines after the results of the lottery had been published.

There are, unfortunately, few references to modellers in the extant ledgers. Only one appears to be named—merely by chance—in the account of John Fisher, the firm's chaser from 1748–1757. The entry, dated the 8 November 1748, states:

'Cash p^d Hole for the pattern of a candlestick . . . £1 6s'.

This may conceivably refer to the 'fine chaised candlestick' costing £90 which was made for the first Lord Mountford in August 1748: the 'expence of the pattern' (presumably the finished mould)—£70—was extremely high. The fact that it is included in the chaser's account suggests that John Fisher was deputed to settle with Hole. If indeed this was Lord Montford's exceptional piece, the three months interval could well have been the result of some haggling by the capricious nobleman who in fact returned the candlestick within weeks of its delivery. The discrepancy between the comparatively small amount paid for the pattern and the large sum charged the client was possibly due to the difficulties of the intricate casting and chasing.

A client was expected to meet an additional charge incurred when Wickes was put to the expense of employing a modeller for an unusual piece. In 1759 the Earl of March's account contains the entry: 'To a drawing of a sauceboat and a pattern of a plate in lead . . . 5s'.

When the client was dissatisfied with the final design he found himself obliged to meet Wickes half way: the Earl of Ashburnham was debited on the 23 August 1755 with four guineas, the 'moiety of the expence of a dye for the spoons not executed'. The spoon must have been out of the ordinary and may even have been made to the Earl's own design which turned out to be a disappointment to him when realized in metal. Had it been a complete artistic failure Wickes would probably have extracted from him the full cost of his whim: it was possibly perfectly acceptable to the goldsmith and the die quietly added to the firm's stock.

In 1758 a client was required to pay £48 13s incurred in the 'moddling & chaising two terrines & covers'. There is an inference here—as with Fisher and Hole—that some inter-relationship existed between modellers and chasers in the eighteenth century. The modeller in this instance may also have carried out the chasing. It is significant that the next line reads: 'To the prime cost of making the terrines & finish^g them *in part* . . . £25'.

Wickes's client John Trever was obviously a man who was not content to choose a stock object. Amongst a long list of pieces in his account in 1740 is an exceptionally heavy sugar dish: it weighed 20 ozs 17 dwts at a time when the average was 11 ozs 13 dwts. A making charge of £2 12s 6d was added to the basic cost of £6 7s and was accompanied by an entry which reads: 'To cheasing the pattern in copper for the suger box ... £4 4s'. The lines which follow are something of an anticlimax:

To altering 2 bottle into canisters w^t joynts	£3	0s	0d
To lyining the canisters with lead		4s	0d
To a shagreen case	£5	5s	0d

The shagreen case must have been extremely large or very ornate. The pieces were not engraved with armorials so that if they were to come on to the market the only means of recognition would be the unusual sugar bowl; the canisters would have been so expertly altered that no one would suspect that they had once been bottles.

John Trever's account is also interesting for 'a flower pot ring with brill^{ts}' bought at a cost of £4 4s on the 28 March 1740. This is the first of only two references to flower pot rings in Wickes's ledgers.[5]

A modeller is mentioned but not named in the account of the Earl of Coventry in 1758. The entry is curiously worded:

To cash p^d the modeller & cabinet for making patterns of epargnes	£23 12s

The role of the modeller is clear, but the word 'cabinet' does not make immediate sense on its own and it was perhaps meant to have been 'cabinet maker'.

The supporting role of the cabinet maker is underlined by a reference dated the 27 October 1747 when a client was charged an extra £10 on account of 'the cabinet makers bill for the backs & ironwork of the sconces'. The sconces, nine in all, weighed 2,326 ozs 17 dwts and cost £639 17s 8d.

The close relationship between silver and furniture design in the eighteenth century has long been recognized. It did not require the promptings of such as Kent and Adam to bring about the collaboration that existed between goldsmith and cabinet maker who instinctively appreciated that the two crafts were inter-dependent. Their known ability to work from rough sketches argues a general level of visual perception which is very rarely found today. It was no happy accident that the pie-crust moulding which appeared on small tripod tea tables in the 1730s was echoed in the borders of silver waiters

39. One of a pair of piecrust waiters, diameter 11½ in (29.2 cm), George Wickes, 1744. *Courtesy of Sotheby's*

40. Title page from a book of rococo designs by Augustin Heckel. Augustin Heckel, the son of Michael Heckel (a goldsmith and chaser of Augsburg), was a chaser, draughtsman and engraver. He was mentioned by Vertue in 1732 as being one of the four best chasers of gold watch cases and snuff boxes and again in 1749 as a chaser, together with G. M. Moser. *Courtesy of the Victoria and Albert Museum*

(Fig. 39). The waiters, moreover, rested on feet which were themselves often small replicas of those used on the furniture of the day. When the rococo style came into fashion, the goldsmiths and cabinet makers bent with the wind and the parallels proliferate. The carved figures of Chinamen on Chippendale mirrors appear on silver tea canisters and candlesticks, the mirrors themselves taking the same outlines as the asymmetrical cartouches chased and engraved on wrought plate (Fig. 41). As far as decorative motifs were concerned, the same design sources were readily available to both crafts and they adapted them to their own materials, keeping pace with fashion and each other (Fig. 40). The die-stamped shells and scrolls which decorate 'fancy back' spoons for some thirty years from 1735 were second cousins to those carved and inlaid in the furniture of the period.

The services of specialist modellers would have been reserved for Wickes's more exacting clients. His other customers would have been content to make their selection from the wares arranged on the shelves of his shop in Panton Street. Pieces would have been placed on the counter for their inspection and appraisal. If the items required were not in stock the customer would have been able to leaf through the firm's design book, a form of illustrated catalogue, and an order for the objects chosen would be passed to the workshop next door but one.

A totally different procedure would have been needed for the noblemen and cognoscenti. Their requirements would have necessi-

tated the presence of a man of some authority, conversant with the most up-to-date modes, familiar with foreign phrases and able to interpret airy descriptions with a quick sketch. Such dealings would have required tact and skill, and Wickes would scarcely have entrusted them to a humble assistant. Netherton may well have been groomed for this role, leaving Wickes free to fashion the silver and supervise the journeymen and sub-contractors.

It may then have been Netherton who was confronted with the design for two 'fine chais'd candlesticks & branches & false nozils' ordered by the Earl of Kildare and delivered to him on the 27 May 1745 (Fig. 42). They eventually weighed 308 ozs 13 dwts and to the prime cost of £95 3s 6d was added a making charge of ten shillings per ounce (totalling £154). More interesting even than the splendid objects conjured up by these figures is the entry:

'To cash p^d for a book of drawing & binding . . . 18s 6d'.

At first glance this suggests a client with an interest in designs and it may reasonably be assumed that the book contained drawings or engravings of silver objects. Interest deepens when it emerges that the Kildare candelabra were copies of the famous piece by the great

41a. Rococo coffee pot, height 9⅜ in (24.8 cm), George Wickes, 1742. *Private Collection*

41b. Detail of the rococo coffee pot in figure 41a shewing a typical cartouche. *Private Collection*

84

42. Pair of candelabra made for the Earl of Kildare, George Wickes, 1744. The candelabra were copies of the piece to which the French goldsmith Thomas Germain is pointing in his portrait painted by Nicolas de Largillière in 1736 (see Fig. 43). *Courtesy of Thomas Lumley Ltd.*

43. *Portrait of Thomas Germain and his Wife* by Nicolas de Largillière, 1736. See figure 42. *Courtesy of the Gulbenkian Foundation, Lisbon*

44. *The artist and his family at tea*, unsigned, *c.* 1730. Three versions of this painting are known. Objects from left to right: sugar bowl with cover, tea canister, jug, slop basin, teapot on lamp stand. In the centre sugar tongs and a spoon boat holding spoons. The silver is typical of the Queen Anne/George I period. *Courtesy of the Worshipful Company of Goldsmiths*

French goldsmith Thomas Germain[6] to which he is pointing in the portrait painted by Nicolas de Largillière in 1736 (Fig. 43).

Kandler appears to have been the first goldsmith to have used the design in England. Hall-marked with the date letter for 1738, his pair weighed 405 ozs. The next known copy was made by John Le Sage in 1744 and was engaged with the royal arms of George II.

Had Wakelin joined Wickes two years earlier, he would have instantly recognized the design chosen by the Earl of Kildare—as senior journeyman in Le Sage's atelier he could even have been responsible for making the royal candelabra. Wickes and Netherton may have been equally well acquainted with it and were no doubt able to employ Le Sage's modeller or even borrow the moulds. The same ones were perhaps used by Parker and Wakelin in 1770 for the pair now in the Fairhaven Collection at Anglesey Abbey. The last known copies were made by Paul Storr in 1816.

Whilst Netherton may have been very useful once he had acquired sufficient experience, in 1735 Wickes was on his own and every aspect of the business had, of necessity, to be kept within his grasp. He had built his reputation on the plain unadorned styles popular during the reigns of Queen Anne (Fig. 44) and the first two Georges (Fig. 45) and he had somehow to make the transition to the rococo without the benefit of Huguenot training. From 1747 onwards Wakelin was no doubt invaluable, but from 1735 to 1747 Wickes worked alone. So well did he assimilate rococo techniques that the best of the pieces he produced in that period are worthy of comparison with any wrought by de Lamerie and his fellow Huguenots who were more conversant with the casting techniques so essential to the rococo style than were their British counterparts (Fig. 46).

One suspects, however, that Wickes was more at home in the workshop than the design studio and it could well be that Netherton, who had studied as a boy under a drawing master, made this his sphere of influence, to be joined later by John Parker.[7] There is ample evidence in the many bequests made to them in wills—one notable one to Netherton by a client of the firm—that they were men of unusual charm and gifts. These qualities they would need to deal with their clients and to translate their requirements into wrought plate. It

45. Pair of sauceboats, width 8¾ in (22.2 cm), George Wickes, 1731. *Courtesy of Sotheby's*

46. One of a pair of rococo soup tureens, length 13 in (32 cm), George Wickes, *c.* 1745. Maker's mark only, struck four times (duty dodger). *Courtesy of Christie's*

is perhaps possible to see the young Parker of the Cotes portrait in such a role (Fig. 47).

It is known from the all too few extant design books compiled by goldsmiths that it was their practice to fill them with small line drawings in the manner of scrapbooks. The silver and armorial engravers of the eighteenth century adopted the same method. These volumes contain a wealth of additional information pertaining to techniques, clients and designs. No such design book has survived from Wickes's day though one used by Robert Garrard's son has fortunately been preserved for posterity. Some of the sketches appear to have been removed from an earlier volume and pasted into this book. Robert Garrard II is known to have had a particular interest in the reproduction of past styles, including pieces in the Queen Anne manner (Figs. 48, 49, 50, 51). His firm was making objects in the fashion of the early eighteenth century at least by 1840.[8]

Without direct proof it is impossible to assess the part played by the Associates in the field of design. Netherton's failures to seek his freedom and register a maker's mark strongly supports the belief that he never became a working goldsmith. John Parker did obtain his freedom, but belatedly in 1762 and probably only, initially, in order to be eligible to take apprentices. He certainly registered a joint mark with Edward Wakelin, but that was in a sense a necessary endorsement of their partnership. In the event, it was written into their indenture that Parker's initials be placed above those of Wakelin, Parker having purchased on his own account the remainder of Wickes's lease on 'The King's Arms & Feathers'.

Bolstered by the knowledge that by the terms of his father's will he would inherit at the age of twenty-one a considerable family estate in Gloucestershire, it may well be that from the very outset John Parker intended to eschew the manual work and concentrate instead on the management and, possibly, the design side of the business. Wickes may have insisted on both Netherton and Parker spending sufficient time in the workshop to become familiar with the problems that had to be overcome to enable a sketch to materialize into fashioned silver. They would have had to learn the rudiments of the techniques involved in raising, casting and chasing gold and silver and the limitations imposed by the metals themselves.

The initiative which took John Parker to London, when he could so easily have remained in Worcestershire managing the Longdon estates for his attorney brother until such time as he could enter into his own inheritance and live on his estate on the Gloucestershire borders, presupposes an intellectual curiosity and a realistic nature. By becoming a tradesman and succeeding in his trade he could count on a reasonably early retirement (such as Netherton achieved) secure in

47. *Portrait of John Parker* by Francis Cotes, 1766, 35 × 27 in (89 × 68.5 cm). An entry dated the 15 July 1766 in John Parker's personal account in the Ledgers reads 'To cash pd. Cotes the painter . . . £31 10s'. The sum covered this painting and a companion portrait of Parker's wife.
John Parker is wearing a dark green coat and white waistcoat. The ring on the little finger of his left hand is an intaglio set in diamonds. Plain buttons decorate his waistcoat, but those on his coat are more ornate: the firm was to supply many such buttons to its clients judging by their frequent appearance in the Ledgers. *Private Collection*

48a. Melon teapot, height 4¼ in
(11 cm), George Wickes, 1731.
*Courtesy of the Visitors of the
Ashmolean Museum*

48b. Page headed 'R.G.
(Melonized)' from the Design
Book of Robert Garrard II.
Courtesy of Garrard & Co. Ltd

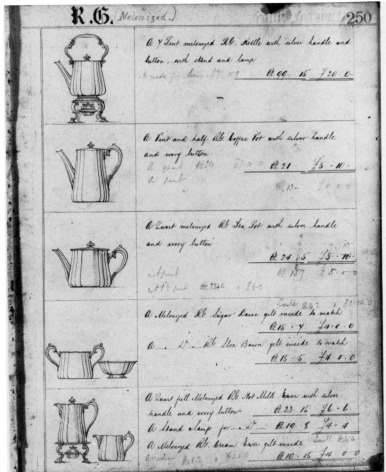

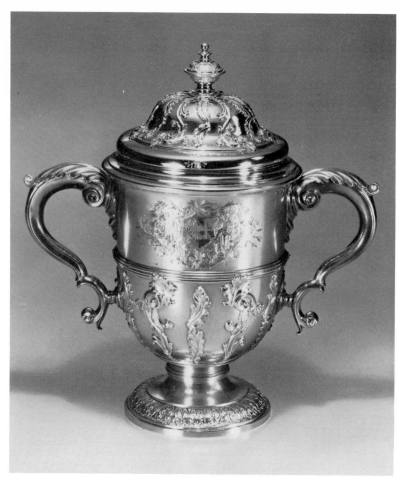

49a. Cup and cover, George Wickes (transposed marks). This piece bears the hall-marks for 1737 on a disc cut from an object already hall-marked and let in between body and foot ring. This was a favourite method of duty dodging. The marks would normally have been struck on the body of the cup. *Courtesy of James Walker Goldsmith and Silversmith Ltd.*

49b. Detail from Design Book of Robert Garrard II. Such was the popularity of silver of an earlier period that the firm founded by Wickes continued to make and stock this cup and cover (similar to that shewn in figure 49a) as late as 1884. *Courtesy of Garrard & Co. Ltd.*

the knowledge that he could at will revert to his old standing as a country gentleman.

The outline of a structure begins to emerge. From 1735 until 1747 Wickes was in sole control of workshop and saleroom. The high quality of the silver struck with his mark during this period bears witness to his remarkable skill as a goldsmith. It was not sufficient to be a fine craftsman—commercial acumen and capital were also needed, as goldsmiths like Phillips Garden found to their cost. Wickes was an able businessman and the firm prospered. Gradually more and more of the administration was entrusted to Netherton who

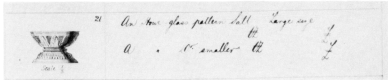

50a. Two salt cellars from a set of six, silver-gilt, Edward Wakelin, 1754. This design had long been popular. A similar pair made by Anne Tanqueray in 1726 is in the Victoria and Albert Museum. *Courtesy of Thomas Lumley Ltd.*

50b. Detail from Design Book of Robert Garrard II. The salt fashioned by Edward Wakelin in 1754 (Fig. 50a) was not considered sufficiently ornate in the latter part of the nineteenth century and extra decoration was added to meet the prevailing taste. *Courtesy of Garrard & Co. Ltd.*

may also have been responsible for the design side. After 1747 Wakelin took over as goldsmith maintaining the high standards set by Wickes and controlling the growing network of sub-contractors. In November 1750 Netherton moved into the limelight becoming junior partner to Wickes. The following July his cousin John Parker joined the establishment working diligently for nine years possibly under the wing of Netherton. During that time a good working relationship developed between Parker and Edward Wakelin so that in October 1760 'for and in respect of the mutual confidence and good opinion they have of each other', they entered into partnership and took over the firm when the heir apparent, Netherton, decided to accompany George and Alder Wickes into retirement.

The Associates' Ledger ends appropriately with this entry in John Parker's hand which in his excitement he failed to sign:

Debtor		Contra	
To ballance due this day ye 11ᵗʰ Oct. 1760	£1,500	By a mojety of the stock in trade of Messrs. Wickes	
To my bond dated this day Oct. ye 11 1760	£1,100	& Netherton transferrᵈ to me this 11ᵗʰ of	
	£2,600	October 1760	£2,600

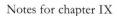

Notes for chapter IX

1. d'Hancarville, *Collection of Etruscan and Roman Antiquities from the Cabinet of the Hon^{able} Wm Hamilton His Britannick Majesty's Envoy Extraordinary at the Court of Naples*, 1766–7.

2. Wood and Dawkins, *The Ruins of Palmyra*, 1753; *The Ruins of Balbec*, 1757.

3. Mark Girouard, 'Coffee at Slaughters' and 'The Two Worlds of St Martin's Lane' ('English Art and the Rococo', I & III), *Country Life*, 13 January and 3 February 1966.

4. Gerald Taylor, *Silver*, page 194.

5. See Charles Oman, *British Rings 800–1914*, page 25 and colour plate IV.

6. The design was to be used by the great *orfèvre's* son, François-Thomas Germain, twenty-two years later when in 1757 he fashioned a pair of almost identical candelabra which is now in the Espirito Santo Collection in Portugal.

7. John Parker's son was a more than competent artist and the goldsmith's granddaughter Mary, later Lady Leighton, had talent of a high order judging by her published sketches not only of the famous gothicized cottage of the Ladies of Llangollen, but of the Ladies themselves who counted amongst their intimates Mary's parents, Thomas Netherton Parker and his wife Sarah. Such artistic gifts could well have been their heritage from John Parker.

8. I am grateful to Mrs Shirley Bury for this information on Robert Garrard II.

51a. Set of three condiment vases and ladles, John Parker and Edward Wakelin. Two dated 1759 and one 1762. These rococo vases with their realistically fashioned strawberry finials were a natural progression from the urn condiments Wickes made for the Leinster Service in 1746/7 (see Fig. 115). By 1760, however, severe neoclassical forms were preferred and it is unusual to find such flamboyantly rococo pieces at this date. *V. & A. No. M.1675–1944. Courtesy of the Victoria and Albert Museum (Crown Copyright Reserved)*

51b. Detail from the Design Book of Robert Garrard II. These casters which were in the firm's stock as late as 1906 bear a striking resemblance to the vase-shaped condiment set made by Parker and Wakelin in 1759. (See Fig. 51a). *Courtesy of Garrard & Co. Ltd.*

52a. The Pelham Gold Cup with
the original case. Wickes frequently
supplied cases for important pieces.
Designed specially for the objects,
they were of sturdy construction
and lined with silk or velvet. *Private
Collection*

The Influence of William Kent

The splendid objects made by Wickes and Wakelin for the nobility which surface from time to time (sacrificed often by the need to meet death duties) give the impression that the goldsmiths spent most of their time creating masterpieces. The Ledgers belie this attractive theory: aristocratic accounts frequently reveal an astonishing number of tedious repairs.

This was not, however, so in the case of the Hon. James Pelham who in 1736 ordered a gold cup (Fig. 52) to the tune of £301 1s. Such an object, weighing 58 ozs, is in itself of interest, but the real significance of this handsome piece only emerged with the publication in *The Connoisseur* of July 1969 of the second of Dr John Hayward's intensive researches into the architect William Kent's designs for gold and silver plate.[1] The cup bears neither hallmarks nor maker's mark and the case for Wickes as the maker rests on an entry in Colonel Pelham's account in the ledger dated 26 October 1736 which reads:

To a gold cup	58 ozs @ £3 15s 6d	£218 19s 0d
To makeing		£80 0s 0d
To a case		£2 2s 0d

The design for the cup (Fig. 53) was included in *Some Designs of Mr. Inigo Jones and Mr. Wm. Kent* published by John Vardy in 1744— Vardy describes it in his 'table of the several plates' as 'a gold cup for Colonel Pelham' and includes an alternative design, also for Colonel Pelham, which Wickes executed in silver for Sir Charles Hanbury-Williams in 1745 (Figs. 54, 55). In 1736, however, Wickes must have worked from the original drawing commissioned by his client from William Kent. Colonel Pelham was at the time Private Secretary to Frederick Louis, Prince of Wales, and his choice of designer and goldsmith understandable since both enjoyed the patronage of the Prince.

The design is of particular interest: it is basically late baroque without so much as a hint of the rococo which was just beginning to become fashionable in London: its classical restraint strangely foreshadows Robert Adam. Whilst the finial with the Prince's device

was probably chosen to commemorate the Colonel's royal appointment, it is possible that the cup was originally intended as a gift to his royal employer, Pelham speedily reversing the decision when in the autumn of 1737 he realized the imminence of yet another of the unseemly father-son quarrels which so frequently beset the House of Hanover.

The design was to be copied many times, notably by Heming, John Jacob and John Swift, but, as with other designs by Kent, Wickes appears to have been first in the field, and most of the later versions fall far short of his serene almost neo-classical simplicity.

Wickes was to return to Kent's designs: Dr Hayward has identified two other pieces, the fantastical *'surtoute'* or *épergne* made for the Prince of Wales in November 1745[2] and the magnificent soup tureens with handles formed as horses' heads which Wickes made for Lord Mountford of Horseheath.[3] From a later description these were obviously faithful interpretations of the original Kent design which appears in Vardy's table as 'a terrine & cover for Lord Mountford' (Fig. 56).

These tureens have a strange history. When Lord Mountford ordered them from Wickes he could scarcely have foreseen the straits to which his extravagance would drive him (culminating in his suicide in 1755). Some years earlier the pair of tureens appears in the Ledgers as one item in a long list of plate ordered by Mountford. The entry, dated the 18 January 1744/45, makes no reference to Kent and is worded as follows:

54. Vardy's engraving of an alternative design for Colonel Pelham's Cup by William Kent. *Courtesy of the Victoria and Albert Museum*

55. Silver mug, height 5½ in (14 cm), George Wickes, 1745. One of a pair made for Sir Charles Hanbury-Williams to William Kent's alternative design for a cup for Colonel Pelham. *Collection of the late Sir John Hanbury-Williams*

To 2 fine chais'd tareens [sic] &			
covers 452 ozs 11 dwts @ 6/2^{d} [per oz]	£139	10s	10d
To making @ 7/6 [per oz]	£169	14s	2d
To graving 4 coats [of arms]	£1	4s	0d
To an iron bound case	£2	2s	0d

It is somewhat incongruous to find that an iron-bound case to house the tureens should have cost so much more than the fine quality engraving which is such a feature of all Wickes's pieces.

The work did not end there: two months later further embellishments appear. Eight screws weighing 6 ozs 4 dwts and costing £6 2s were added as well as two 'lyenings' (116 ozs @ 9/2 per oz— £53 6s 6d). Two under-dishes (not included in the Kent design) were fashioned to complement the tureens; these weighed 201 ozs and must have been magnificent pieces in their own right judging by the charge of 10/2 per oz which brought the cost of the dishes alone to £102 3s 6d. Four coats of arms were engraved (£1 4s) and a further cost of fifteen shillings incurred for 'exchainging of a case for the turreens'. The overall weight of the tureens with their matching under-dishes and liners was 775 ozs 4 dwts and the total cost £476 2s. At first glance it would seem that the dishes with their high fashioning charge of 10/2 per troy ounce must have been even more elaborate than the tureens, but it will be noticed that Lord Mountford paid a further making charge of 7/6 per ounce for the latter to cover the extraordinary fine casting and chasing involved in Kent's design.

It is strange that Lord Mountford did not order ladles *en suite*. He had previously purchased a far more modest pair of 'fluted tareens', complete with ladles, in March 1743 which he traded in against the cost of the new ones, but he presumably kept the ladles by way of economy or simply because Kent in his wisdom had omitted to design one to accompany the tureen.

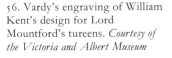

56. Vardy's engraving of William Kent's design for Lord Mountford's tureens. *Courtesy of the Victoria and Albert Museum*

Lord Mountford's bill for the period November 1742 to February 1744 amounted to £1,471 13s 8d, but he handed in for melting down or resale unwanted plate to the value of £1,067 14s, paying Wickes the balance of £404 in cash.

Contrary to general belief, the tureens did not then vanish from sight to re-emerge in 1921. After Lord Mountford's death in 1755 his massive collection of plate and his equally massive debts passed to his son and heir. Undeterred by his father's fate and his own precarious financial situation, he too placed orders for plate with the firm: had Wickes had an inkling of the difficulties that were later to plague the account, he might well have hesitated before accepting them.[4] Already in 1756 the new Lord Mountford was obviously in difficulties for he brought the Kent horse-head tureens back to Wickes and they duly appear on the credit side of his account on the 2 June 1756 as '2 terrines, lynings, covers, dishes & ladles . . . @ 5/6 [per oz] . . . £219 3s 6d'. As previously stated, no ladles were supplied *en suite* with the Kent tureens and their presence here no doubt accounts for the increase of 21 ozs 16 dwts in the overall weight.

Wickes made no allowance for the additional high making charge of 7/6 per ounce which appeared in the original price and he lowered the fashioning figures from 6/2 and 10/2 (the latter for the under-dishes) to an overall 5/6 per troy ounce which was in fact the current price for silver traded in. Mountford had no option but to accept this valuation and it is obvious from entries on the debtor side of his ledger account that he was hoping that Wickes would be able to dispose of the objects for him. Wickes was in no way guilty of sharp business practice: his estimate was a strictly realistic price based on the prevailing taste for silver of a different style. Handsome as the tureens undoubtedly were, they proved difficult to sell: Wickes's clientèle, by now attuned to the heady influence of the rococo, obviously found Kent's design far too ponderous. Wickes had them on his hands for a year and he accordingly charged the new Lord Mountford '1 years interest to be allowed for keeping the terrines till sold . . . £11.'. He piled Pelion on Ossa by debiting the nobleman's account with £6 6s, 'the prime cost of boyling & burnishing the terrines etc.' plus a further £6 7s, the latter sum being enigmatically described as 'the moiety of £12 14s being the neat profit of ye terrines'. Both these entries are dated 25 May 1757: on that very day the two tureens, complete with covers, liners, dishes and ladles appear in the account of the ninth Earl of Lincoln and thereafter they ceased to be an embarrassment to either Wickes or Mountford.

Lord Lincoln acquired them for £250. Bearing in mind the original price charged to Lord Mountford—£426—it was a shrewd purchase, the new owner having been spared the high making charge imposed

57a. Two sauce tureens (from a set of eight) made to Kent's horsehead design but on a smaller scale by Benjamin Smith in 1807 for the third Duke of Newcastle. These were obviously intended to complement the Mountford soup tureens acquired by the Duke's father from Wickes in 1757. *Courtesy of Partridge (Fine Arts) Ltd.*

57b. Lid of the sauce tureen in figure 57a. *Courtesy of Partridge (Fine Arts) Ltd.*

by the intricacies of Kent's design which had, perforce, been borne by Mountford. No mention is made of erasing the previous armorials, but this was obviously done since three pounds were added to Lincoln's bill to cover the cost of 'graving 8 coats supporters garters & cor[ts]'.

The present location of the Mountford soup tureens is not known, but some idea of their splendour can be gained from the set of sauce tureens made to Kent's horsehead design but on a smaller scale by Benjamin Smith in 1807 for the third Duke of Newcastle (Fig. 57). They were obviously intended to complement the Mountford soup tureens acquired by his father from Wickes in 1757.

The Earl of Lincoln's appreciation of Kent may have been fostered by the acquisition in 1755 by his wife Catherine, residuary legatee of all the Pelham fortunes, of the gold cup, designed by Kent, made for her distant cousin Colonel James Pelham by George Wickes in 1736. On 6 December 1755 a significant entry appears in the Earl of Lincoln's account: 'To graving 2 crests, coronets & garters on a gold cup & cover—10/-'. When the cup left Wickes's hands in 1736 no armorials had been engraved upon it.

The Pelham wealth was not the only asset enjoyed by Lord Lincoln as the husband of a great heiress: he was also granted his wife's uncle's title on reversion and became in 1768 the second Duke of Newcastle, changing his name from Fiennes Clinton to Pelham Clinton. He continued to patronize Wickes's successors Parker and Wakelin and in December 1775 he augmented his collection with two 'small fine terrines and dishes', complete with liners and four coats of arms engraved 'in the chased compart^{mts} on ye terrines'. The total weight was 275 ozs 13 dwts and the cost £146 7s 1d. As with the Mountford soup tureens, there is nothing in the Ledgers to suggest that this later pair was made to Kent's design. Dr Hayward was fortunately able to establish the identity of the Wickes Mountford tureens when he recognized them as Lot 18 in the sale of the plate from the Duke of Newcastle's seat at Clumber which was held on the 7 July 1921. The wording in Christie's sale catalogue gives a clear and detailed description of Kent's design:

> A pair of soup-tureens, covers and liners, chased with applied vine branches and grapes and the handles formed as horses' heads, on gadrooned stands with shell ends—by Edward Wakelin, 1744.

The maker is given not as Wickes but Wakelin. This erroneous attribution of objects made in 1744 to Wakelin, who did not register a maker's mark until 1747, is by no means the first of its kind. The similarity between the marks of Wickes and Wakelin can pose very real problems and many a fine piece made by Wickes prior to 1747 has been in the past mistakenly credited to Wakelin. One is tempted to believe that the latter's mark was so designed deliberately in order to emphasize the continuity of the firm. Advances in scholarship and research into makers' marks have eliminated many of these errors, but it is still a trap for the unwary and the disappearance of these tureens from archives and records may well be due to this misattribution.

Lot 19 which followed the Wickes soup tureens—which may reasonably now be said to have been made to Kent's design—is described as 'A pair of oval soup-tureens, covers and liners, similar— by Parker and Wakelin, 1775'. It would not have been surprising had these later objects been smaller versions of the Kent tureens, but in

58. One of a pair of soup tureens with horse-head handles, John Parker and Edward Wakelin, 1775. These tureens were commissioned by the second Duke of Newcastle. Whilst the horse-head handles which were such a feature of the tureens made to Kent's design by Wickes have been retained, these pieces were clearly influenced by the neoclassicism of Robert Adam and could scarcely have been intended to complement the Kent tureens. The ledger entry describes them as '2 small fine terrines and dishes . . . 245 ozs 8 dwts @ 11/- . . . £134 19s 4d.'; liners weighing 300ozs 5 dwts accompanied them and cost a further £10 11s 9d. *Courtesy of Thomas Lumley Ltd.*

the event the cataloguer used the word 'similar' advisedly. A photograph of one of the Parker & Wakelin tureens (Fig. 58) survives in the albums of Mr Thomas Lumley and proves conclusively that they were certainly not made to Kent's design. The workmanship is superb, but this is true of all silver emanating from the firm's workshop. In this case it is the design which is open to criticism, the robust lines of the original shape having been replaced by a weak oval. The only possible point of similarity lies in the handles, each in the form of a single horse's head. Robert Adam has been superimposed on William Kent producing an artistic failure that is so alien to the *œuvre* of Parker and Wakelin that one is tempted to lay the blame for it squarely on the shoulders of the second Duke of Newcastle. It should be emphasized that Kent's name is not mentioned in the entry for these items in the Newcastle account in the Ledgers.

A later entry in the large order recorded on that same day, 22 December 1775, suggests that John Parker and Edward Wakelin must have been well aware of the anomaly. The significant words 'after Kent' are clearly written against an item of some importance, 'a pair fine candlesticks and noz.' weighing 95 ozs 8 dwts and costing, at fourteen shillings per troy ounce fashioning charge, £66 15s 7d.

These two candlesticks of 1775 bring the story back full circle to the Duke of Newcastle's early predilection for the designs of William Kent. In 1757, whilst still Earl of Lincoln, he ordered from Wickes's firm a pair of 'large fine chais'd candlesticks & noz^les' weighing 88 ozs

8 dwts and charged (at 14/6 per ounce fashioning) at £64 1s. The interesting point about this order is that the very next entry covers 'doing up 2 pr fine candlesticks & nozils . . . £2 10s' and is, moreover, followed closely by 'a red leather case for six candlesticks' which presupposes that all six were probably of the same shape and size. We therefore have in 1757 three pairs of 'fine candlesticks', one made by Edward Wakelin, under the ægis of Wickes, and described as 'chais'd' and two pairs by one or more unknown makers. There is no mention of the designer. The owner of these six candlesticks, the Earl of Lincoln, becomes the second Duke of Newcastle in 1768 and, under his new title, orders from the firm in 1775 yet another pair of fine candlesticks; these are made by John Parker and Edward Wakelin and are unequivocally described in the ledger as 'after Kent'. The Clumber sale of the Duke of Newcastle's silver included eight candlesticks—the number is highly pertinent—catalogued as lots 53 and 54. Lot 53 consisted of 'four table candlesticks with octagonal stems and plinths chased with foliage and shells, Paul Crespin, 1745'. Lot 54 covered 'Four ditto—two E. Wakelin, 1757, two Wakelin and Taylor, 1775'. It is curious to find silver bearing the assay date letter for 1775—when John Parker and Edward Wakelin were still in command—attributed to their successors John Wakelin (Edward's son) and William Tayler (his correct surname) when the last two makers did not register a mark until 25 September 1776. Here again the similarity of the two sets of initials beneath the Prince of Wales's feathers was sufficiently close to the joint makers' mark of Parker and Wakelin (as Edward Wakelin's single mark had been to that of Wickes) to cause yet another error in attribution.

Since there is clear documentary proof that the two 1775 candlesticks were made to Kent's design it is surely permissible to conclude that the word 'ditto' in Lot 54 implies that the other six matched them. It will be recalled that in 1738 Wickes had copied a Crespin tureen for Sir Robert Walpole, 'byling and doing up . . . as new' the original piece which had served him as model and it is strange that history should have repeated itself. The two pairs of 'fine candlesticks & nozils' which were taken in for 'doing up' and were returned on the 6 December 1757 were almost certainly the work of Paul Crespin and, in their turn, served as models for the matching pair made by Edward Wakelin which were delivered on that precise date to the then Lord Lincoln. The moulds Crespin used in 1745 may even have survived and been hired or borrowed for the purpose.

It remains to determine which of the two Kent designs published by Vardy (Figs. 59 & 60) was used for the Newcastle 'set'. The catalogue description favours the brief column rising from a calyx of leaves which rests on four owl heads cast in high relief. Crespin was

59. Design for an owl candlestick by William Kent, engraved by Vardy. This was almost certainly the design used by Parker and Wakelin for the candlesticks ordered by the second Duke of Newcastle in 1775. They are recorded in the Ledgers as 'a pair fine candlesticks and nozs (nozzils) *after Kent* . . . 95 ozs 8 dwts @ 14/- . . . £66 15s 7d.' *Courtesy of the Victoria and Albert Museum*

60. Gothick candlestick designed by William Kent, engraved by Vardy. So far as is known, this design was never translated into silver. It may, however, have been used by Edward Wakelin for a 'fine chaised candlestick' weighing 66 ozs 13 dwts and costing £90 made for the first Lord Mountford in August 1748 and returned by him to the firm shortly afterwards. *Courtesy of the Victoria and Albert Museum*

familiar with the design—he had already used it for a set of four candlesticks made in 1741 which are now in a private collection.

So far as is known, Kent's gothick candlestick was never translated into silver, but a tantalizing reference in the Ledgers reveals that a single 'fine chaised candlestick' weighing 66 ozs 13 dwts and costing £90 was charged to none other than the first Lord Mountford in August 1748. Edward Wakelin would have fashioned it and it must have been an exceptional piece since 'the expence of the pattern' alone was £70. It will come as no surprise that three weeks later the candlestick was returned by the erratic nobleman and it duly appeared in Wickes's stock ledger on the 9 September 1748. Lord Mountford's caprice cost him dear—he had perforce to bear the £70 expended on the pattern or model and was credited with a mere £20. When Wickes entered the candlestick in his stock ledger he placed a value of £65 on it and it was presumably sold for it was not included in subsequent stock-takings. Unfortunately it has not come to light in the account of another client and the intricacies of its design must remain a mystery.

1. J. F. Hayward, 'The Pelham Gold Cup', *The Connoisseur*, July 1969.

2. J. F. Hayward, 'A 'surtoute' designed by William Kent', *The Connoisseur*, March 1959.

3. J. F. Hayward, 'Silver made from the designs of William Kent', *The Connoisseur*, June 1970.

4. The Mountford account was to be a continual source of embarrassment to the firm. In 1772 it reached a point where even Lady Mountford's marriage settlement was involved. It was not until 1776 that a balance was finally struck. The firm obviously had a lien on Mountford's plate and John Parker and Edward Wakelin forced the defaulter to sell it at auction 'by Mr Christie Feby 2^d 1776'. They appear to have been responsible for the arrangements: on the credit side of the nobleman's account the sum of £61 10s—'Commiss^n p^d Christie for selling it @ 5 pc^t'—is deducted from the £1,230 7s 6d realized by the sale. The proceeds were, however, insufficient to clear the debt and on the 29 September 1776 the partners delivered an account for the £567 4s 8d still outstanding to Messrs Chamberlayne & White: to this was added £17 1s 7d, the interest at 5% per annum on the seven months and seven days which had elapsed since the sale. Christie's copy of the catalogue makes interesting reading. The descriptions of the lots are extremely brief and devoid of any information on assay dates, weights or makers (though the latter are given for watches sold on the second and last day of the sale, Perigal, Vigne, Gratton, Delander and Fladgate being named). The weight of the silver and the price per troy ounce were later written in the margin of the catalogue by the auctioneer's clerk and, on a separate sheet, there is a note of the sums fetched and the names of the buyers. John Parker purchased 'four pincushion compotiers', 'four fan ditto', 'an epergne (the glasses and case given in)' and 'a pair of terrine sauce boats with covers'. Hemming [sic] also bid successfully for several lots. An employee of Parker and Wakelin seems to have acted on behalf of one of their clients: in the account of James Martin Esq. on the 5 February 1776 'a pair of candlesticks and branches bo^t at Christie's Sale' appear; they were sold as lot 33 which fetched £46 8s 3d—the same sum is charged him in the ledger. The price per troy ounce varies from lot to lot, the lowest being 5s 4¼d (near enough the melt down price) and the highest 6s 10½d.

I am indebted to Mr Anthony Phillips of Christie's, now in New York, for giving me access to this information.

XI The Clients

The records of the clients who patronized Wickes are to be found in the books he called his Gentlemen's Ledgers. The first such ledger in the Garrard Collection was started when he moved to Panton Street in June 1735—no others prior to that date have survived. Only one client (the elder of his wife's sisters) can be linked with an earlier ledger and it is almost as though Wickes managed to persuade his customers to settle their accounts just before the move so that he could start with a clean slate. It is, however, inconceivable that they were so obliging and it is obvious that he took with him from Norris Street an earlier ledger now missing—the 'Long Book' from which his sister-in-law's account was carried forward—which he used concurrently with the brand new ledger started in Panton Street in June 1735.

It would be tempting to imagine that the 268 names in the index of the new volume were fresh accounts stemming from his appointment as goldsmith to Frederick, Prince of Wales, but this is belied by the presence of his wife's siblings and a number of friends and relatives— mostly from Suffolk, Bristol and Worcestershire and recognizable from family documents—who would have supported him long before the granting of the royal warrant. Without his 'Long Book' it is neither possible to make an accurate assessment of the volume of new business nor to estimate the extent of the trade which Wickes had built up since his beginnings in Threadneedle Street in 1722.

By singling out those accounts in which the dates coincide with the move (omitting friends and kinsmen) the number of apparently new clients totals thirty-nine in the period 25 June–31 August 1735. The nobility at the outset was conspicuous by its absence. Not all the new custom came from fashionable society: Ludby, the mason employed by Wickes on renovations to the premises, was one of the first patrons of the new shop with a purchase of a pair of silver buckles costing fifteen shillings on the 30 June. He later invested in an engraved sauceboat of some quality judging by the eight shillings per troy ounce fashioning charge. The Ludbys were still being employed by the firm in 1768 when a payment to 'Ludby ye bricklayer' appears in John Parker's accounts. The mason

61. One of a pair of soup tureens, width 13 in (32 cm), George Wickes, 1737. These exceptional pieces were made for the Earl of Malton. Wickes has skilfully incorporated the client's heraldic gryphon into the design. The tureens were originally accompanied by two soup ladles and two 'shape dishes'. The tureens alone weighed 345 ozs 15 dwts and cost the Earl of Malton £181 10s. Since under dishes could also be used for serving food, they frequently become separated from the tureens for which they were originally made. *Courtesy of Christie's*

was joined by Cobbett the glazier, possibly the Richard Cobbet, glazier, whose name appears in the Duchy of Cornwall accounts for the Prince of Wales in 1748. Briggs the painter—or Mr Briggs, as he is now styled—bought six pairs of buckles between August and October 1735 as well as six teaspoons, three table spoons and, in December, a tobacco box costing five guineas; he paid for the most part in kind, bills for painting being recorded on the contra side of the page; Wickes debited him with three shillings paid to one 'Moor for a ladder' and from time to time advanced him sums in cash.

The men who worked on his house in Panton Street were charged the same prices as Wickes's aristocratic clients and there was no question of an 'abatement' or trade discount. Their purchases suggest that the possession of wrought plate and jewels was by no means confined to the higher strata of eighteenth-century society. These clients were probably the masters of thriving small businesses which prospered in the building boom of the time.

A further nineteen 'new' names appear between 1 September and 31 December 1735, including a duke, a lord and a knight. They were followed by another twenty-nine between 1 January 1735/6 and 30 June 1736: of these nine were titled and a tenth no less a personage than Frederick, Prince of Wales. For the twelve months up to the end of June 1737 fifty-six clients are listed in the index, twelve of them with titles. Wickes could look back on the first two years in Panton Street with some satisfaction. The Prince of Wales apart, he had secured the patronage of two dukes (Chandos and Devonshire), two duchesses (Gordon and Norfolk), one marquis (Caernarvon), two earls (Inchiquin and Malton) (Fig. 61), two viscounts (Duncannon and Galway), eight lords, eleven assorted titled ladies and twelve knights. With each year that passed thereafter the clientèle became more and more illustrious.

In the first few months, however, the large order entered on the 25 September 1735 for Everard Fawkener must have been extremely gratifying. Fawkener was appointed ambassador to the Grand Signior in August of that year. *The Gentleman's Magazine* described him as 'a Turky Merchant' and he must have been trading in the Levant for some time.

An interesting item—the eighth entry—in the long and impressive list of his purchases as detailed in Wickes's Ledger (Fig. 62) is a set of

62. Page from Wickes's ledger—account of Everard Fawkener. This photograph shews only the left-hand, debtor page on which Wickes recorded the objects delivered to the client. The right-hand page—the creditor or contra side—was reserved for the settlements made in cash or by old plate traded in. *Courtesy of Garrard & Co. Ltd.*

twelve coffee spoons. Unfortunately they are grouped with twelve teaspoons, two pairs of sugar tongs and two strainers, the whole weighing 16 ozs 14 dwts. The average weight of the other items at that date would have been 8 ozs which suggests that these particular coffee spoons weighed approximately $14\frac{1}{2}$ dwts per spoon and were therefore slightly heavier and possibly larger than the teaspoons of the period. References to coffee spoons as such are rare in Wickes's Ledgers: a set of six in 1741, two sets of twelve in 1754 and a set of twelve shell coffee spoons in 1755, the average weight per spoon being over $18\frac{1}{2}$ dwts. The rarity suggests that few people went to the trouble of buying spoons specifically for coffee and the majority was content to use teaspoons for tea, coffee and other beverages.

The writing candlestick ordered by the Ambassador must have been a handsome object. A considerable weight at 98 ozs, it cost £39 4s 6d. Snuffers were supplied with it as well as a silk blind on steel springs.

The order begins with an item apparently separate from the plate actually fashioned by Wickes. Fawkener is debited with 'cash paid Bridr. Churchill for a cup & salver' weighing 189 ozs 5 dwts and costing £70 19s. This calls to mind a taunt made by Lord Lovat at his trial in March 1747 after the failure of the Jacobite Rebellion of 1745. Fawkener was one of the chief witnesses against him, having himself served as Secretary to the Duke of Cumberland, the Butcher of Culloden, during the campaign against the Young Pretender. The old Scot, immortalized by Hogarth in 1746, knew himself to be doomed and declined to examine Fawkener, choosing instead to discountenance him in open court by wishing him joy of his young wife. A month previously Fawkener, then aged fifty-three, had married Harriet the twenty-one year old natural daughter of General Charles Churchill, the man whose name appears at the head of Wickes's first order from Fawkener.

Fawkener is remembered today for his friendship with Voltaire. From 1726–1729 Voltaire was sheltered by Fawkener at his home in Wandsworth and they later entered into a correspondence covering a period of twenty years. Carlyle described him 'as a man highly unmemorable now were it not for the young Frenchman he was hospitable to'.[1] Wickes would have regarded Fawkener in a different light. His order amounted to 4,774 ozs 11 dwts of silver and cost £1,756 2s $0\frac{1}{2}d$. This large bill was settled with a promptitude which must have delighted the goldsmith. Between 22 August and 2 October 1735 four cash payments are recorded amounting to £1,710 12s $6\frac{1}{2}d$. The balance of £45 9s 6d was covered by the trading in of plate, a practice common at the time. In this case the objects were probably damaged or out of fashion: they weighed 160 ozs

63. One of a pair of sauceboats, Edward Wakelin, 1757. These sauceboats were made for the Countess of Exeter and appear in the Ledgers as 'a pair leaf sauceboats . . . 48 ozs 1 dwt @ 10/6d . . . £25 4s 6d.' They echo the current vogue for naturalism which was also widely adopted by the manufacturers of porcelain—Wakelin's design would have been described by them as 'silver shape'. *Courtesy of Christie's*

64. Coffee jug, Edward Wakelin, 1753. The design of this jug is of French derivation. A similar one was made by the French goldsmith Antoine Bailly in 1753. The same shape was used by the porcelain manufacturers: a Chelsea coffee jug in the Collection of Colonial Williamsburg closely resembles Wakelin's except for the oriental inspired decoration which is replaced with swirling strawberry leaves. *Courtesy of H. S. Wellby Ltd.*

10 dwts and, being silver-gilt, were valued by Wickes at 5s 8d per ounce, slightly higher than the standard price for sterling silver, and he would have melted them down for refashioning or refurbished them to sell second-hand. The discrepancy of 1s 4d on the transaction may have been pointed out by Fawkener—an abatement of 2s was conceded by Wickes on the final cash payment. An enigmatic entry follows this settlement: 'gave Mr Porter a brillt. [diamond] ring £6 6s'. The recipient may have been a partner in the firm of John and James Porter, exporters of Token Hoop Yard, which had an account with Wickes; he was possibly responsible for recommending Wickes to Everard Fawkener and the goldsmith counted the order well worth a diamond ring.

Fawkener emerges from the chronicles of his time as something less than a whole person. He was, however, a man of varied interests, but doomed by his inadequacy to play his part on the periphery of events. It has recently been revealed by Mr Eric Benton ('Payments by Sir Everard Fawkener to Nicholas Sprimont', *English Ceramic Circle Transactions* Vol. 10 Part 1 1976 pp. 54–59) that Fawkener was closely involved in the Chelsea Porcelain Manufactory and may have lent certain houses in Lawrence Street Chelsea to Nicholas Sprimont to which the Liègois repaired when he finally decided to forsake the mystery of the goldsmith to devote his energies to the production of porcelain.[2]

It is interesting to note that a sale catalogue of Chelsea porcelain sold by a Mr Ford on the 10 March 1755 contained thirty-eight lots

described as 'silver shape' (Figs. 63, 64). There are no references to the Chelsea Manufactory in Wickes's ledgers, although an entry made in 1753 records 'cash p^d at the Bow china warehouse ... £3 11s'; unfortunately the objects purchased are not specified.[3]

Wickes's connections with the Diplomatic Corps did not end with Everard Fawkener. He supplied wrought silver in 1737 to the British Ambassador to Vienna and executed in March 1740 a sumptuous order for 'His Excellency Mr Finch'. This latter account involved a great deal of 'pollishing and doing up as new' of existing plate, but concludes with a large number of new pieces made by Wickes and priced at £1,189 5s 2d. It is interesting to speculate on the nature of '2 masheens for dishes' weighing 109 ozs 16 dwts which must have been mechanically operated judging by the extra £4 4s charged for 'the watch work'. In this instance, as in many others, Wickes packed the silver for shipment including in his bill a charge of one guinea for a 'debenter' [debenture] and one pound for 'exspences in carriing the chest to the Custom House'.

It was no doubt owing to his wife's family connections that Wickes was able to count on the patronage of several Bristol dignitaries. The Fanes and the Scropes (Wickes spells it 'Scroop'), like the Aldworths, were closely connected with the Merchant Adventurers of Bristol. In July 1735 *The Gentleman's Magazine* announced the marriage of Henry Fane, 'nephew to Baron Scrope, to Miss Charlotte Rew, daughter of the late Poet Laureate'. Shortly before the wedding Henry Fane purchased from Wickes a quantity of household plate and several pieces of jewellery obviously intended for his bride. A gold hoop—the wedding ring—cost a modest 10s 6d and was accompanied by a diamond hoop at £14 14s. A pair of three-drop earrings set with diamonds was an expensive purchase for the bridegroom—Wickes notes that £7 10s of the £162 was 'abated by compulsion', but he presumably considered the reduction prudent in view of the importance of the Bristol connection. Henry Fane's order was not confined to new plate: he brought in a large tray for 'carving, graving and doing up', a coffee pot for 'altering, carving & graving' and a set of casters, two mugs and a ladle for similar attention. Alterations of this kind were frequently undertaken by Wickes. Experts today are wary of pieces which bear decoration in a later style, suspecting them

66. Cup and cover, height 12 in (30 cm), George Wickes, maker's mark only, *c.* 1735. Armorials of Scrope. Like the Fane family, the Scropes came from Bristol and were well known to Alder Wickes and her relatives. This richly decorated cup and cover does not appear in the Scrope accounts in Wickes's ledgers. Had this duty dodger been submitted for assay it would have been liable for a Customs tax of £2 10s 6d. *Courtesy of Christie's*

of nineteenth century meddling, but eighteenth-century goldsmiths would have thought nothing of adding a rococo touch to a plain vessel in very much the same way as Victorian goldsmiths bowed to current taste and covered the surfaces of Adam silver with busy chasing completely at variance with the original clean, neo-classical lines. The craftsmanship of Wickes and his successors was such that the same experts encountering evidence in the Ledgers of an unexpected alteration not blatantly out of period find it hard to believe even after careful reappraisal of the object.

The Fanes and Scropes were kinsmen and close enough to permit the transfer of money from one account to another in Wickes's books. Some intimacy also existed between them and his wife's family: her sister, Mary Phelpes, was involved in one such transaction, her ledger page recording a cash payment to Mr Henry Fane (Figs. 65a and b).

A more direct link with the Merchant Adventurers of Bristol was Thomas Fane who was clerk to the Society from 1726–1757, an office he gave up when he became the Earl of Westmorland. His account is interesting for the purchase of a Bristol Scabbard in three consecutive years (1740, 1741 and 1742) at an average cost of £62 6s 8d.[4] It was customary on New Year's Day for the Sheriffs of Bristol to present the retiring mayor with a silver-gilt scabbard for the State Sword, each sheriff receiving in return a pair of gold fringed gloves. Thomas Fane was not a sheriff neither was he connected with the Common Council whose accounts shew no payments to Wickes. Fane, however, would certainly have had friends on the Council and he no doubt undertook to commission the scabbards on their behalf from a reputable London goldsmith.

The Honourable John Scrope's links with Alder Wickes may have influenced her husband in defrauding the Customs and Excise of the silver duty (£2 10s 6d) on a cup and cover weighing 101 troy ounces (Fig. 66). It was not submitted for assay: Wickes's maker's mark is punched four times on the base in such a way that at first glance there appears to be a full complement of hall-marks. Its style places it in the mid 1730s, but it is significant that it was not entered in Scrope's account in Wickes's ledger. It is engraved with the armorials of the Scrope family and the engraving is contemporary. The cup was sold at Christie's on the 26 March 1975 and its appearance on the open market brought it to the notice of the Goldsmiths' Company. In accordance with current procedure, large crosses were placed over Wickes's marks in such a way that they are still distinguishable and a number assigned by the Company stamped alongside. This method has now been adopted in place of the custom which required that the marks should be obliterated and the object assayed and hall-marked with the date letter in use at the time. This is by no means the only instance of duty dodging

67a. Rococo coffee pot, height 8¾ in (22.2 cm), George Wickes, 1738. It will be seen from the detail shewing the hall-marks that Wickes intended to evade the silver duty by striking the pot four times with his maker's mark in imitation of hall-marks. A timely visit from the officers of the Customs and Excise may have induced him to change his mind and send it to Goldsmiths' Hall for assay (Fig. 67b).
The chasing extends under the body of the object to within inches of the point made by the compass when the piece was first raised, an artistic necessity due to the prominent hoof feet which lift the pot high enough to reveal the base.
The fine quality of the chasing may account for Wickes's reluctance to have hall-marks punched in the normal position at the top of the coffee pot. *Courtesy of Garrard & Co. Ltd.*

67b. Detail shewing hall-marks cancelling out Wickes's maker's mark struck four times on the base of the coffee pot. The mark left by the compass point, mentioned above, is clearly visible in the centre. *Courtesy of Garrard & Co. Ltd.*

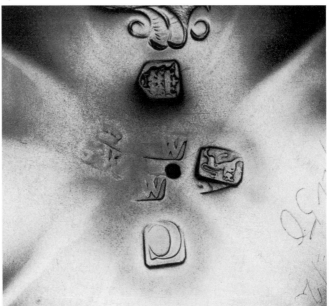

by Wickes. The coffee pot in figure 67 is a blatant example: having first stamped it with his makers' mark struck four times, he either repented or was forced to submit it for assay as the result of a visit from the Customs and Excise.

He was also not above indulging in the illegal practice of transposing marks. The fine cup and cover in figure 49a has a small round disc let in and soldered between the body and the foot ring. This was a favourite method of tax evasion in the eighteenth century. The discs were easily cut from an assayed piece brought in for melting or from a small object submitted to the Hall for assay with the deliberate intention of transposing the marks to an important piece on which the duty payable would have been considerable. The foot of a large cup or a coffee pot lent itself conveniently to this illicit practice.

It may be said in mitigation that Wickes might have felt morally justified in evading the tax when, as was frequently the case, a client had supplied for the purpose outmoded or unwanted hall-marked silver on which the full duty had been paid in the first instance. These objects, it could be argued, were returned to the original owner, albeit in a different form, and not circulated back into the trade. Such casuistry is not however advanced by the incontrovertible fact that no duty dodger bearing Wickes's mark, whether transposed or struck four times, has ever come to light in his ledgers; if the account books of Paul de Lamerie and Peter Archambo (both well known duty dodgers) had survived there would doubtless be the same singular omissions.

It has been suggested that the great makers would not have stooped to such malpractices and that, unbeknown to them, they were perpetrated by their workmen. Since the tax levied on the goldsmith was passed to the purchaser of wrought plate, the client was the person who stood to gain from duty dodging—the offending goldsmith risked a heavy fine. It is perhaps not too cynical to conjecture that they entered into a private arrangement to share the duty thus saved and, since the goldsmith was bound by law to allow the Customs and Excise officers access to his premises where his ledgers were also kept, the transaction was simply never recorded except, perhaps, in a duplicate set of books. Judging by the haphazard entries for duty in Wickes's ledgers, the risk was small and indeed the failure of the system was finally recognized in the Statute of 1757 (31 Geo. 11 c. 32) when the duty was dropped and a £2 licence substituted, payable by all those 'trading in, selling or vending gold and silver plate'.

Bristol is also represented by many of its prominent citizens (Fig. 68) in the pages of Wickes's ledgers, amongst them the Reverend Dean Creswick. Such was his passion for cock-fighting, which was extremely popular in the eighteenth century, particularly in Bristol, that when he became Dean of Bath and Wells he installed a private cockpit close to his dining room and had the windows of the room altered so that he and his guests might watch the grisly fights without having to leave the table. In 1740 he commissioned from Wickes 'a seal for the Deanery of Wells' weighing 6 ozs 18 dwts and costing £2 1s 6d. He had previously purchased flatware and no less than fifteen pieces of jewellery which included the ubiquitous gold hoop and diamond hoop rings. The total value of these acquisitions over eight years amounted to £396 15s.

The princes of the Church were slow to make their way to Panton Street. It is true that we find accounts for the Bishops of Norwich and Ely, but they are one and the same person, the somewhat notorious Robert Butts.

Born in Suffolk in 1684, the son of the Reverend William Butts, rector of Hartest, the Bishop was first cousin to Wickes's mother and the kinship was to prove important to the goldsmith. The rise of Robert Butts from modest beginnings as curate of the little village of Thurlow in Suffolk was achieved largely through the patronage of the first Earl of Bristol who appointed him, on the 19 June 1719, to the rich family living of Ickworth, near Bury St Edmunds. His meteoric preferment thereafter was attributed to the zealous political services he rendered the son on whom the Earl doted, John Lord Hervey the memoirist, who was later to become Lord Privy Seal in Walpole's administration. A satirical party squib—the 'Political Will and Testa-

68. Square coffee pot, George Wickes, 1745. This must have seemed a very old-fashioned piece to Wickes when he made it for his Bristol client Mrs Elton in 1745. It bears the arms of Sir Abraham Elton, Bart., who was Sheriff of Bristol in 1728 and Mayor of that city in 1742. He was unmarried and the coffee pot may have been a gift from a sister-in-law or an unmarried sister (Mrs being an eighteenth century courtesy title). The shape was sufficiently unusual at this date for Wickes to enter it in his ledger as 'a square coffee pot'. It weighed 21 ozs 8 dwts, the fashioning charge was 8s 3d per troy ounce and the total cost £8 16s. *Courtesy of Thomas Lumley Ltd.*

ment' of Sir Robert Walpole—published after his death in 1745, links him with the Bishop of Ely and leaves no doubt that the godliness of Robert Butts had long been a matter of question.

His worldliness was never in dispute and some proof of it can be found in the books kept by Wickes. His august cousin was still Bishop of Norwich in 1735 and as such heads the second page in the new ledger started in June of that year. The account is notable for the inclusion amongst the wrought plate and jewellery of items of a personal nature completely unconnected with silver. Such entries are often an indication that the client is something more than a business acquaintance. Wickes supplied the Fanes with cider from time to time (possibly sent down from his wife's family estate in Worcestershire) and in the case of Bishop Butts he happily settles a porterage charge 'of bacon etc from Salop'; the 'trancefer of 1000 S.S. anuits' (identified in his will as 'one thousand pounds capitall old South Sea annuitys stock'); pays the brewer; meets a bill for five pounds for a large carpet from one Lamb; arranges for Pierce, a cabinet maker, to receive three guineas for unspecified furniture and buys two pounds of 'dry sweat meats' costing eight shillings.

The Bishop's first wife was Elizabeth Pitches, sister of the Suffolk-born goldsmith who worked in London and was at one time the partner of John Edwards. She died in August 1734, aged forty-four, having borne the Bishop eleven children. Sixteen months later her widower took a new wife twenty-eight years his junior and the jewellery supplied by Wickes on the 8 December 1735 was undoubtedly destined for the new Mrs Butts.

The chased watch and chain coupled with an 'eqmareen seall transparent' were probably appendages to the then fashionable châtelaine (Mrs Henry Fane preferred 'a gold ettwee [étui] with a blood stone eg & a lapis lez. bottell'). 'Brilliant [diamond] night earrings' costing eighteen pounds were among the Bishop's purchases at this time: night earrings were usually simple gold sleepers but in this case they were obviously intended for evening wear. Her other jewels included four rings—'a neat rose ring' (twelve shillings); 'a fancey ring w^t a emrold' (one guinea); 'a splitt shank ring w^t a hart ruby' (eighteen shillings); 'a sapher splitt ring' (one guinea). These were certainly the pieces mentioned in the Bishop's will (dated 11 January 1745 and proved on the 1 February 1747/8)—'to my said dear wife the gold watch chain seals equipage and jewells with the other ornaments of her person'. She also received a 'silver kettle lamp stand and waiter thereto belonging and all other the plate spoons tongs and other equipage belonging to the tea table with one dozen of silver handle knives and forks and one dozen common silver spoons and also one pair of my silver candlesticks'. All these objects are to be found in the

Bishop's accounts in Wickes's ledgers, though without the assay dates and weights it is obviously impossible to identify them with absolute certainty.

The Reverend Eyton Butts, his eldest son, was left 'my largest silver salver waiter or teatable with my arms and the arms of the see of Norwich engraven thereon and one dozen silver handled knives and forks'. The Bishop was apparently in a quandary regarding the current name for the piece and in giving all three possibilities he raises a nice point.

Judging by his ledger entries, a salver, as Wickes understood it, was a plateau resting on a single central foot. Unless of very strong construction and perfectly balanced it must have been at times an unstable object. The waiter, however, resting squarely on three or four small feet, was a far more practical piece, albeit less elegant. Wickes's clients were quick to appreciate this advantage: salvers were brought in for conversion into waiters and a typical entry in 1743 reads: 'To altering 2 salvers into waiters and putting on feet ... 15s od'; the customer was credited with 'silver taken off the salvers ... 9 ozs 8 dwts'.

From 1735 (possibly before) Wickes was concentrating on supplying waiters of all shapes, sizes and weights (Figs. 69–73). In 112 accounts in the period 1735–40 which were analysed for this purpose he sold 118 waiters as opposed to four 'smale solvers' and four tables or trays. All four salvers were ordered by one customer in

69. Circular salver, diameter 23½ in (59.7 cm), George Wickes, 1744. The pierced and chased border is particularly fine. Bacchanalian masks alternate with large vine leaves resting on shells. Threaded through the spaces between are trailing vine tendrils, grapes and foliage. *Courtesy of Christie's*

70. Square waiter, 20 × 20 in (50.8 × 50.8 cm), George Wickes, 1744. *Courtesy of Christie's*

71. Waiter, width 29½ in (75 cm), Edward Wakelin, 1749. The design for the engraved border is the same as that used on the tray in figure 73. Although handsome, this piece appears ponderous when compared with the tray made five years later: not only is the border heavier, but the cartouche engraved in the centre lacks the inspiration of the delicate country motif which decorates the tray. *Courtesy of Christie's*

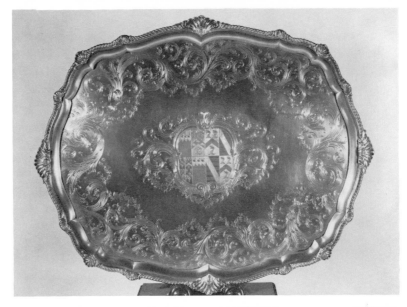

72. Tea tray, length 30 in (76.2 cm); width 24 in (61 cm), Edward Wakelin, 1754. This must rank amongst the finest trays made in the eighteenth century. The border alone is a masterpiece of the goldsmith's art. Had Wickes's Workmens' Ledgers survived it would have been possible to identify the artist who engraved the superb rococo cartouche. Little is known of the engravers and signed work of this kind is extremely rare. The cost to the client was small, often less than the wooden case sometimes supplied to transport the piece. *Courtesy of Brand Inglis Ltd.*

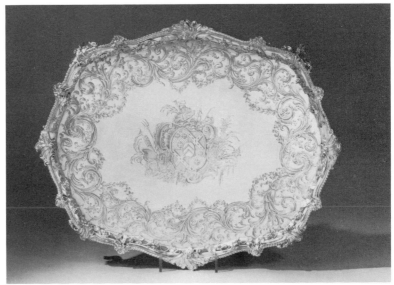

1739 and weighed in toto 47 ozs 19 dwts. One of the four tables or trays was exceptionally heavy at 177 ozs 8 dwts; the average weight of the other three was 87 ozs 16 dwts. The individual weights of the 118 waiters vary considerably, the average being 21 ozs 7 dwts. Wickes never records the dimensions and seldom gives any indication of style. The heaviest, 'a fine large graved waiter' in 1736, weighed 72 ozs 16 dwts, the lightest at 6 ozs 18 dwts is described as 'a hand waiter' and was made in 1740[6]. The 'heart cornered waiters' entered in 1747, 1751 and 1752 must have been attractive objects.

A 'table' or 'tea table'—both terms are used by Wickes—was much larger and heavier and would be catalogued today as a tea tray. It was used to hold the 'equipage' for making tea and designed to rest on a flat solid surface. Wickes occasionally supplied mahogany stands: one ordered *en suite* with a tea tray in 1736 must have been sturdy since the tray alone weighed 93 ozs 17 dwts ('a fine pierced table' costing £42 2s); the stand was priced at £1 6s. The equipage normally consisted of a silver kettle and lamp resting on its own small waiter (often triangular in shape in the 1730s), a teapot, sugar basin (Fig. 74) tongs and teaspoons. One of the rare known contemporary paintings of tea parties (Fig. 44) shews an oval fluted boat to hold teaspoons, but only one of these boats is recorded in Wickes's ledgers and that in 1735. Cream jugs, invariably called 'boats' by Wickes, were in general use (Fig. 75) and 'slop basons' (Fig. 76) were ordered from him occasionally. The tea was kept in canisters (Fig. 77), not caddies at this period (Parker and Wakelin, in later ledgers, described them as tea tubs): two were normally supplied complete with a matching 'sugar dish' (Figs. 78, 79) and often accompanied by a case, shagreen in one instance. The beverage was drunk from small porcelain cups without handles—saucers occasion-

73. One of a pair of hexagonal waiters, diameter 13 in (33 cm), George Wickes, 1745. *Courtesy of Christie's*

74a. Slop basin, diameter 6½ in
(16.5 cm), George Wickes, 1744.
Courtesy of Christie's

74b. Interior of the slop basin in
figure 74a. *Courtesy of Christie's*

75. Cream boat, George Wickes,
1742. *Courtesy of Christie's*

ally appear in the paintings of the period: Wickes supplied eight such
cups complete with saucers to his sister-in-law Mrs Dorothy Wale in
1741 at a cost of eight shillings.

'Wooden tea & chocolate cups lyn'd wᵗ silver' are mentioned in the
account of the Earl of Kildare: as late as 1745 he ordered fourteen of
them with silver saucers to match. Wooden cups lined with silver are
usually confined to chocolate in the ledgers. Six chocolate frames
weighing 44 ozs are mentioned in a 1725 inventory of royal plate—
Wickes was still supplying them in 1758, as well as repairing them,
but whether they were designed to hold the silver lined wooden cups
is not known. Two such frames or trembleuse stands by David
Tanqueray and Paul de Lamerie, dated respectively 1718 and 1713,
have come to light. The first was fitted with porcelain cups (the
second was incomplete), but without firm evidence it is impossible to

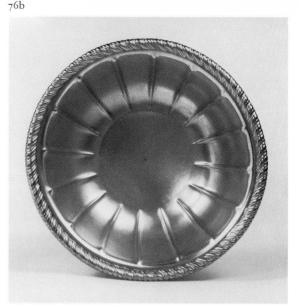

say whether the cups were those originally intended for the frames. By 1778 chocolate frames were quite outmoded and were being 'exchanged for new silver' by John Wakelin and William Tayler.

Not all Wickes's clients were preoccupied with silver. The purchases of Mrs Horton, an actress who enjoyed a modest success in minor parts at Covent Garden in 1747 and played with Garrick at Drury Lane in 1751, were heavily biased towards jewellery. The pieces become more and more ornate as we follow her progress through the Ledgers. From time to time she was forced to pawn them, leaving them with Wickes as security for the loans he advanced to her. The account is remarkable for her somewhat unorthodox method of payment: she frequently settled her debts with theatre tickets—53 for the pit, valued at £7 19s, in February 1735/6 and a further 131, in unspecified parts of the house, over the next three years. Whilst it is possible that these were silver tokens accepted at melt value, no weights are ever entered against them. Living so close to the fashionable theatres of the day Wickes and the members of his household may have kept these for their own use. It was unusual for a play to be staged for more than a few nights and fifty-three tickets would have been easily used in the space of a season.

Of far more interest than Mrs Horton's baubles is an entry in her account dated 3 August 1737. It covers 'warnings at the Hall 11s 6d and advertising 3 days 17s 6d'. In the archives of the Goldsmiths' Company there is a *Walk Book for Warning Carriers* which contains the names and addresses of persons who were to be alerted when a theft of plate or jewellery was reported. A thief would often try to sell the

76a. Slop basin, diameter 6¼ in (15.9 cm), George Wickes, 1732. *Courtesy of Christie's*

76b. Interior of the slop basin in figure 76a. *Courtesy of Christie's*

stolen goods to an unsuspecting goldsmith and the Hall distributed descriptions of the pieces and the miscreants in the hope of apprehending the criminals and restoring the objects to their rightful owners. The newspapers of the period are full of offers of rewards by goldsmiths for the recovery of stolen wares and Wickes had obviously inserted three advertisements on behalf of Mrs Horton. Occasional entries in Wickes's ledgers record the success of these measures: one such in December 1753 refers to a sum of £2 6s paid 'for the reward & advertising a seal'.

The royal appointment no doubt influenced many personal friends of the Prince of Wales to patronize Wickes. The Earl of Scarbrough, Lord North (Fig. 80) and Colonel Pelham were joined by the Earl of Egmont and the Marquis of Caernarvon. Lady Archibald Hamilton spent part of her salary on modest purchases which included a mysterious object described as 'six square boxes w^t joynts ye squadge': the overall weight was 31 ozs 10 dwts, the cost £16 15s. At first glance the word 'squadge' is completely incomprehensible, but bearing in mind that Wickes's spelling is often tortuous and based largely on his own Suffolk pronunciation, it is possible to hazard a guess that in this instance he was referring to a 'swage', the name for an ornamental moulding, border or mount. He seems to have had difficulty with words ending in 'age' and 'equipage' is frequently written 'equepadge.[7]

The name of Colonel Schutz, Frederick's Privy Purse, also appears. In 1753 he was credited with 'old plate foreign silver', possibly brought over from Hanover; it was below British sterling standards for Wickes allowed him only 4s 8d per ounce for it whilst in an entry immediately below the Colonel received 5s 8d per ounce for a quantity of English old plate.

Humbler members of the Prince's household had personal accounts in the Gentlemen's Ledgers including Mr Holzman, Page of the Bedchamber, and Mr Groves, the Clerk of the Kitchen. Denoyer, the faithful dancing master who took part in the bizarre flight from Hampton Court the night Augusta's first child was born, bought in 1738 a set of twelve knives, forks and spoons and a soup ladle, complete with case, as well as two 'little waiters', followed in May 1739 with a pocket case at £2. He seems to have had some difficulty in meeting the bill which totalled £33 18s 6d: £20 in cash materialized five months after delivery; twenty-two pit tickets brought in another £3 6s and the £10 12s 6d still outstanding was not received by Wickes until 16 May 1744.

George Cure, the Prince's upholsterer, became a client of Wickes. Entered in the ledger index as 'Mr Ceuer upholdster in y^e Hay Market', he bought in January 1738/9 a 'gold etwe [étui] a chain

77. Tea canister, Edward Wakelin, 1752. Tea was an expensive luxury in the eighteenth century and canisters were frequently fitted with locks. *Courtesy of Thomas Lumley Ltd.*

and blew egg' for £21 7s and a silver tea kettle and lamp weighing 78 ozs 10 dwts and costing £30 1s 10d, foregoing the small three-cornered waiter which usually accompanied these pieces. Wickes does, however, record the 'carving' of a large waiter for him, presumably a plain piece of an earlier period already in Cure's possession which Wickes was required to embellish in the latest fashion. The goldsmith graciously gave his fellow craftsman an 'abatement' or discount of 9s 10d. Frequent payments to George Cure are recorded in the accounts of the Earl of Scarbrough, Frederick's treasurer, and the upholsterer's itemized bills in the Archives of the Duchy of Cornwall reveal that much of the Prince's furniture was in fact hired from Cure.

Benjamin Goodison, one of the great cabinet makers of the eighteenth century, was also employed by Frederick, but his name does not appear in Wickes's ledgers.

That the Prince's friends, officers and employees should patronize Wickes is natural enough, but it is somewhat surprising to find them joined by George II's chief minister Sir Robert Walpole. His name appears for the first time on the 1 December 1737 a mere four months after the expulsion of Frederick to Kew following the scandal attendant on the birth of his first child. The King, with his insensitivity to all things artistic, would scarcely have concerned himself with his minister's choice of goldsmith: Walpole's patronage of a man appointed by her detested son might not have escaped the keen eye and cultivated mind of Queen Caroline, Walpole's great ally, but she had died some ten days previously.

Walpole had hitherto spread his patronage: Crespin and Lukin both made silver for him and the commission for his famous salver made from the Great Seal in 1728 went to Paul de Lamerie. In opening an account with Wickes in 1737 he did not necessarily cease to deal with other goldsmiths, but the ledgers record a steady flow of purchases and repairs. Interspersed with occasional important pieces of silver are motto rings to commemorate family obsequies, buckles for 'Master Walpole', a 'tip and foot for a coco shell' (much favoured in the eighteenth century and often found in Wickes's ledgers), 'a cover and foot to a ivory tankard' (31 ozs 8 dwts of silver), the 'boyling and doing up a philligrey hamper and an india tea kettle', one silver handle made to take a hair brush (twelve replacement hairbrushes were supplied with this holder) and '2 large drawings of a lustre for the house at Houghton'. The artist who supplied these drawings is unfortunately not named and the sketches themselves have not been found at Houghton.

Created Earl of Orford in 1741, Walpole continued to commission silver from Wickes until his death in 1745. His account was finally closed in 1747 by his son, the new Earl, and 'a note or reciept' recording the settlement was pasted into the ledger (Fig. 81). It was

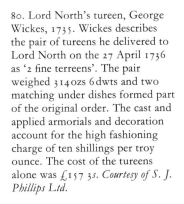

80. Lord North's tureen, George Wickes, 1735. Wickes describes the pair of tureens he delivered to Lord North on the 27 April 1736 as '2 fine terreens'. The pair weighed 314 ozs 6 dwts and two matching under dishes formed part of the original order. The cast and applied armorials and decoration account for the high fashioning charge of ten shillings per troy ounce. The cost of the tureens alone was £157 3s. *Courtesy of S. J. Phillips Ltd.*

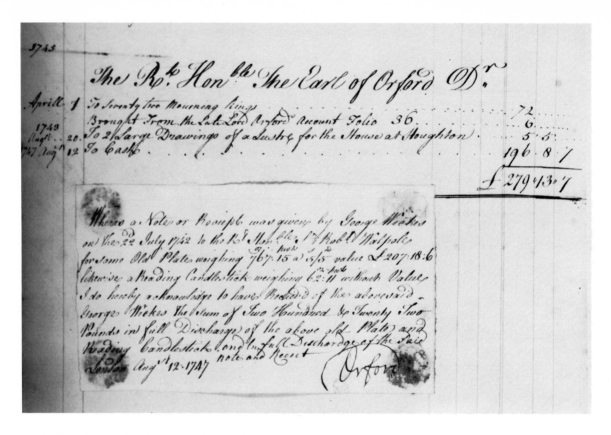

perfectly adequately drawn up by Netherton, but Wickes was not satisfied and added in his own handwriting a further ten words to make absolutely sure that there could be no possible misunderstanding regarding the discharge of his debt to his old client.

Whilst Walpole's decision to patronize Wickes may have stemmed solely from an appreciation of his high standard of workmanship, it is possible that it could have been influenced by his close family links with East Anglia. His mother was Mary, daughter and heiress of Sir Geoffrey Burwell of Rougham Hall, Rougham. When the time came for Wickes to retire to his native Suffolk he made his home in the neighbouring village of Thurston and owned a parcel of land in Rougham itself. It is more likely, however, that Wickes was brought to the notice of Walpole by Bishop Butts who knew that in spite of his coarse manners and uncouth speech the first minister of the land was a shrewd judge of a skilled goldsmith. The time was opportune. As we shall see later Wickes was still smarting from the damage done to his purse and his pride by the cancellation of a large order placed by the Prince of Wales. Walpole's patronage must have been particularly reassuring to Wickes at that time.

Wickes was to number the foremost political figures of the day

81. Settlement of account of the Earl of Orford. Sir Robert Walpole was created Earl of Orford in 1741. He died in 1745 and his account was closed in 1747 by his son, the new Earl. The note pasted into the ledger refers to old plate traded in by Walpole against future orders for which Wickes appears to have given him a receipt on the 22 July 1742. No new commissions were placed by the new Earl who elected to be reimbursed in cash rather than wrought silver. The last ten words are in Wickes's handwriting—the receipt was drawn up by Netherton. *Courtesy of Garrard & Co. Ltd.*

amongst his clients, but high ranking naval officers were few and far between. Admiral Vernon was on home leave in February 1742/3 and found time to visit Panton Street and spend £291 13s 5d on a large number of objects. One was a 'festoon sauceboat', similar to that shown in figure 82, engraved with his arms, which came on to the market in recent years. The Admiral was still buying silver from Wickes in 1754, three years before his death.

Vernon's capture of Porto Bello in 1739, though in itself a minor achievement, had made him something of a national hero. Not surprisingly, 'the Scourge of Spain' met part of his bill with 97 ounces of foreign silver: Wickes does not describe it as Spanish silver, but the 5s 5d per ounce credited to the Admiral corresponds exactly to the sum paid for 'peces of eight' in another client's account in 1737.

Admiral Vernon is celebrated today not so much for his exploits at sea as for the lasting contribution he made to naval discipline in 1740. Drunkenness had become a serious problem and on Vernon's orders the sailors' traditional daily ration of half a pint of neat rum was diluted with one quart of water. It was known as 'grog', derived it is said from the nickname bestowed on the Admiral on account of the grogram (grosgrain) boat-cloak he habitually wore.

Cloaks seem to lend themselves to legends. The large silver bowl with an indented rim (often removable) which was introduced into England as a wine glass cooler in the 1680s and known as a monteith is said to have been named after an eccentric Scot who affected a cloak with a scalloped hem. Whilst this story has always been somewhat suspect, there is a ring of truth in the Navy's version of the origin of grog.

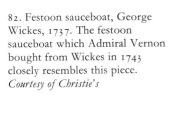

82. Festoon sauceboat, George Wickes, 1737. The festoon sauceboat which Admiral Vernon bought from Wickes in 1743 closely resembles this piece. *Courtesy of Christie's*

Vernon may have recommended Wickes to John Byng who was appointed rear-admiral under his command in August 1745. His account was opened in 1749 and in twelve months he spent £1,163 13s 7d. It ends in 1756, the year he abandoned Minorca to the French. He was found negligent by a court-martial and sentenced to death; George II refused to countenance a strong recommendation for mercy and Byng was ignominiously shot on the quarter deck of H.M.S. Monarque on the 14 March 1757.

It is to be hoped that George II was less unbending with his goldsmith, Thomas Minors, whose name appears not only at the head of an individual account but also in those of some of Wickes's most illustrious clients. Although described as a goldsmith and banker working from Lombard Street in the City of London, Minors was more banker than goldsmith and depended on the leading exponents of the day for the wrought plate required to meet the needs of the King and the royal household. Paul de Lamerie, Paul Crespin, David Willaume, Frederick Kandler, John Le Sage and his son Simon were, like Wickes, among those favoured with commissions from the King's goldsmith.

The first order placed by Minors—at least as far as the extant ledgers are concerned—was dated 15 September 1736 and consisted of twelve dish covers weighing 824 ozs 12 dwts, Minors supplying

83. Cup and cover, height 13½ in (34.3 cm), George Wickes, 1738. *Courtesy of Christie's*

84a. Cup and cover, height 14½ in (36.8 cm), George Wickes, 1740. Two years separate this ornate cup and cover from the one shewn in figure 83. The rococo extravagance of this magnificent piece is in sharp contrast with the simplicity of the other. The two demonstrate the versatility of Wickes who was equally at home in both styles. *Private Collection*

600 ounces of the silver. Wickes's charge for fashioning was 10*d* per ounce and his total profit on the order amounted to £34 6*s* 8*d*. The duty payable on the silver came to £20 12*s* and was meticulously added to the bill.

Twelve years passed before another commission materialized—at least as far as the personal account of Minors is concerned—and this time the object was of some importance. The firm was required to fashion a gold cup weighing 92 ozs 16½ dwts. The cost of making was £100, a high figure. Minors supplied 100 ozs 6¾ dwts of 'standard' gold valued at £3 18*s* per ounce, but in fact a slightly higher quality was used costing £3 19*s* 6*d* per ounce, Minors paying the difference in cash. Although the cup was engraved at a charge of 6*s*, no mention is made of the King's armorials which invariably appeared on a royal gift. The gold cup may in fact have been intended for the personal use of Thomas Minors. There is, however, an unusual feature in the provision made for 7 ozs 3½ dwts of gold which were left over from the 100 ozs allocated by Minors. Entered by Netherton, it reads as follows:

> To the remainder of the gold carried
> to the account of the R^t Honble
> Ar: Onslow Esqr towards the expence
> of fashion & gilding of the model of
> the above cup made in silver 7 ozs 3½ dwts

The date written against the entry of the gold cup is 5 December 1748 and one week later in the account of the Right Honourable Arthur Onslow, the Speaker of the House of Commons, a parallel entry appears:

1748

Dec 12	To a cup & cover	61 ozs 18 dwts	6/-	£18	11*s*	6*d*
	To making			£26	5*s*	0*d*
	To gilding the inside and pollishing the cup			£4	14*s*	6*d*
	To graving 2 coats				3*s*	0*d*
	To a case				12*s*	0*d*

Such cups were common enough (Figs. 83, 84) and this purchase by the Speaker would have been of little significance had his account not been credited on the contra side on the same date with 'gold taken off a cup at £3 19*s* 6*d* per oz . . . 7 ozs 4 dwts . . . £28 12*s* 0*d*'. This then was the silver model of the gold cup made for Thomas Minors though there is no mention of a cover in the gold version. Netherton used the word 'model' which implies that the design was first tried out in silver and this in itself suggests a very intricate vessel of some importance.

The gold cup is not mentioned by scholars and appears never to have been catalogued: if the silver version were to be traced some idea of the design would emerge which might link it to a known sketch or engraving.

An examination at the Public Record Office of a number of royal accounts relating not only to goldsmiths but also to the Monarch's gifts of wrought plate has failed to bring the gold cup to light and it may well be that Minors was acting for a private client. Although he purchased the silver replica, Arthur Onslow's connection with the gold cup itself seems to have begun and ended with the surplus gold transferred to his account 'towards the expence of fashion & gilding of the silver model'. Had the gold cup been presented to the Speaker in recognition of his outstanding services, some mention of it would have been made in 1748 or have come to light subsequently in the researches made on his life and career.

Until 1752 when he moved to Falconbergh House, a town mansion in Soho Square, Arthur Onslow lived in Leicester Street, a narrow lane leading into Leicester Fields. Panton Street was within a few minutes walking distance and it is just possible, like many collectors today, that from time to time he paused at 'The King's Arms & Feathers' to see the latest creations wrought in the workshop. He may have chanced by when the design of the cup was under discussion and, learning that it was proposed to make a preliminary model in silver, evinced an interest in acquiring it. He had possibly been privy to the commission from an early stage and may even have been instrumental in guiding it into the hands of Minors with a recommendation that his own goldsmith, Wickes, should be entrusted with the fashioning of it. Such was Onslow's reputation for probity, however, that it is highly unlikely that the gold would have been accepted by him as a gift from Minors.[8]

Both versions of the cup were probably made by Wakelin but Wickes may have risen to the challenge and taken up the hammer

84b. Ledger entry for the cup and cover in figure 84a. *Courtesy of Garrard & Co. Ltd.*

once more to prove to himself and the workshop that he was still the Master.

Thomas Minors was inevitably involved when pieces of wrought plate were required by the Monarch as christening gifts for his godchildren. Whilst the choice of a goldsmith would normally be left to Minors, it would appear from the Ledgers that the arrangements were frequently left to the fathers with Minors supplying the quantity of silver allocated. Some of these royal presents are recorded in the Lord Chamberlain's accounts at the Public Record Office and are doubly interesting because the goldsmiths' signatures occasionally appear against the entries.

Netherton signed one on the 28 March 1759 on behalf of the Earl of Coventry, a client of the firm, which reads:

> Delivered to the R^t Honble the Earl
> of Coventry as a gift from His Majesty
> at the christening of his child:
> a large gilt cup and cover w^t 130 oz

No doubt the Earl expressed surprise and delight at this signal honour, but it is apparent from the following entry in the Coventry account in Wickes's ledger that it was in fact a very business like transaction.

1759

Jany 1	To a fine cup & cover 66 ozs 14 dwts 5/10		£19	19s	0d
	To making		£26	5s	0d
	To graving the King's arms				
	supporters etc			12s	0d
	To gilding ye cup @ 3/- p^r oz			10s	0d
Mar 28	To cash p^d at the Treasury		£2	2s	0d
	To d^o at the Jewell Office		£6	15s	0d
			£56	3s	0d

On the contra side the Earl was credited on the 31 March 1759 with the sum of £54 14s described as 'cash allow^d for ye cup & cover by Mr Minors'. It would seem that the design chosen by Lord Coventry cost more than the amount of money (in lieu of silver) allocated by Minors and the difference had therefore to be borne by the Earl.

It is difficult to reconcile the weight entered in the ledger— 66 ozs 14 dwts—with the 130 ozs attested by Netherton at the Jewel Office (the gilding would not have added more than a few ounces at most). Since there is, however, no actual evidence of chicanery (no bill from Minors to the King having come to light), it is possible that the figure of 130 ounces of silver entered in the statement signed by Netherton on behalf of the Earl of Coventry was a clerical error which

85. Bread basket, width 14¼ in
(36.2 cm), George Wickes, 1737.
Arms of Cavendish with Hoskins
in pretence. Wickes made two of
these baskets for the Duke of
Devonshire. They were part of a
large order entered in the ledger
on the 22 June 1737. Although
frequently catalogued today as
'cake baskets' Wickes invariably
described them as 'bread basketts'.
The pair made for the Duke of
Devonshire weighed 166 ozs
6 dwts and cost £79. The intricate
geometrical piercing no doubt
accounted for the high fashioning
charge of 9s 6d per troy ounce.

The inclusion of armorials in
pretence indicates a marriage with
an heiress: in 1718 the Duke
married Catherine, only daughter
and heiress of John Hoskins.
Courtesy of Christie's

went unnoticed by Samuel or was added after his departure. The cup
and cover was no doubt a splendid piece, but of far more interest from
the point of view of design is the 'gothick inkstand with glasses
compleat . . . 11 oz 3 dwts . . . £7 17s 6d' ordered by Lord Coventry
in 1760.

The rents from their great estates enabled the noblemen of the
eighteenth century to embellish their homes with a wealth of fine
wrought plate. According to the journal of the poet Thomas Gray, the
fourth Duke of Devonshire enjoyed a rent roll in 1764 of £44,000. His
father's account in the Ledgers dates from 1 January 1735/6. His
purchases for the first eighteen months amounted to a meagre £4 14s 6d
but in June 1737 a larger order worth £550 3s 6d is recorded. It
included a considerable amount of new silver flatware and a pair of
pierced bread baskets which cost £79 0s 6d (Fig. 85). One hundred
'tinn plates' at 16s consort oddly with the ducal plate.

Wickes was also required to refurbish a large quantity of silver
owned by the Duke. Amongst the entries for these pieces is one 'to
refreshing the guilding of 2 bottles 2 ise payles 1 large dish & ewer
and a sett of casters . . . £12', another for 'boyling up and burnishing a
sertute compleat 12 festoon solts 6 festoon boats 4 candle sticks a
tankard a cup & cover a little sestern . . . £8 10s' whilst two others,
possibly the most interesting, allude to '6 plates alterd to godroons'
(which, with the additional silver, came to £9) and 'taken out yᵉ arms
and graving 4 crest & mottoˢ of the wrought candlesticks . . . 8s'.

The Duke of Devonshire's account, like many another in the
Ledgers, is remarkable for the number of repairs. It is apparent from

such entries as the mending of 'about 40 holes in a bowle' and the removal of 'breuses' from eighteen dish covers that servants in the eighteenth century had scant regard for their masters' plate and subjected it to the sort of treatment that would horrify collectors today.

Such misuse must partly account for the pieces missing today from the magnificent matching dinner services made by Wickes and his fellow goldsmiths, though the foundering of vast fortunes and the harsh exigencies of today's death duties have taken a greater toll. When large family collections have to be sold it is rare that buyers can be found with sufficient means to acquire them intact and they are, perforce, split up into lots by the auction houses or sold piecemeal by their owners.

One fine matching dinner service made by Wickes has survived almost complete and is now in private hands. Though known now as the Leinster Service, it was in fact commissioned when the Duke of Leinster was still the Earl of Kildare. It would be impossible to do justice to this exceptional service within the confines of a general chapter and a detailed description, together with photographs of some of the objects and the appropriate pages of Wickes's ledger, will be found in Appendix II.

Although many of Wickes's clients must have passed through the Inns of Court, only three lawyers of any distinction emerge from the Ledgers. The most illustrious was Philip Yorke, first Earl of Hardwicke and Lord Chancellor of England. Wickes, as baffled as most laymen are today by legal titles, engagingly calls him 'Honble Justice York' from 1750–54 and thereafter 'Ld Chief Justice Yorke' whereas he had been Chief Justice for only four years prior to 1737 when he became Lord Chancellor. It is, of course, possible that he was a client of Wickes long before the move to Panton Street and that his early accounts are lost with the missing ledgers.

Sir Dudley Ryder, sometime Attorney General, appears briefly in 1735 under the guise of 'Solicitor Ryder'. 'Foster Esqr', with Bristol noted against his name in the index, is identified as Michael Foster of the Middle Temple from his order for 324 gold 'serjents rings' in June 1736. A lawyer who was created a serjeant (often a stepping stone to a judicial appointment) was required to present gold rings to a large number of royal, legal and ecclesiastical dignitaries, the weight of the ring corresponding to the importance of the recipient. The rings were severely simple in design and engraved with the motto chosen for the call.[9] Fourteen serjeants were called with Michael Foster and between them they presented a total of 1,409 rings bearing the legend 'Numquam libertas gratior'. The 324 ordered from Wickes at a cost of £150 12s 6d weighed just over 35 ounces and would have been those

86. Pair of sauceboats, Edward Wakelin, 1749. These handsome sauceboats were made by Wakelin two years after he joined Wickes. Both are engraved with a crest and one with a coronet. *Courtesy of Christie's*

87. Set of four candlesticks, height 8¾ in (22.3 cm), George Wickes, c. 1745. Marked only on nozzles. It is not unusual to find candlesticks marked only on the nozzles. The crests engraved on the bases suggest that Wickes's client came from a landed family. *Courtesy of Christie's*

88. One of a pair of chamber candlesticks, Edward Wakelin, 1748. The slot in the short stem was designed to take a pair of snuffers which were frequently made of steel. The nozzles are detachable. Engraved crest. *Courtesy of Christie's*

which Serjeant Foster distributed privately, over and above the hundred or so rings he was bound to give 'as of duty'.[10] This onerous custom was abolished in 1875. Very few serjeants' rings have survived. The recipients were blind to their historical importance and treated them as bullion. Wickes accepted them for their melt value from clients such as the Honourable John Scrope in part payment for wrought silver. In 1866 Queen Victoria put some of her serjeants' rings to a strange use: a gold cross was made from them and set with deers' teeth.[11]

Wickes's contacts with lawyers were not always so trouble free. He found himself forced to call on the services of 'Mr Fra: Parry the attorney' on several occasions, notably in the case of two of his clients, Lady Lombe and Sir Robert Clifton, who were joined in a long and tedious law suit. The transcript of the proceedings does not mention Wickes, but his ledgers record the monies he expended in his efforts to recover the sums he was owed. Apart from her insolvency, Lady Lombe is of interest in being the only client in the first ledger to buy silver toys from Wickes. A 'little milk man' at five shillings is entered on the 21 January 1739/40 followed by 'To mending a parcel of children's toys'. Such references to miniatures are rare— only seven others have been noted—but in three cases the toys are described: '6 philligree chairs a tea kettle & candlestick . . . 4 ozs 2 dwts . . . £2' in 1753, 'a new joynt to a child's coffeepot . . . 3s' in 1754 and 'To mending a child's chocolate pot' in 1756. These tiny replicas would not have been made in Wickes's workshop unless he set an apprentice to the task as an exercise: it is more likely that he sent one of them out to buy the toys from a specialist maker.

Wickes and his associates had weightier matters to consider. The ledger for the years 1750–54 contains the accounts of forty-five rich and influential nobles above the rank of knight or baronet and a further thirty-three were added in the period 1756–60 (Fig. 86). The members of the nobility were not necessarily the most lavish spenders. Much of Wickes's business came from the middle and upper classes who were not exposed to the temptations of court life where high fashion in dress and high stakes at cards whittled away many a fortune (Fig. 87). Prosperous merchants (Fig. 88) who thrived in that opportunist age found themselves able to compete in monetary terms with their social superiors who, equally opportunist, were quick to realize that marriage alliances with the bourgeoisie could bring them a share in the fruits of shrewd trading. The goldsmiths were among the first to benefit from this mingling of greed, wealth and social aspiration. The satirists of the day were merciless in ridiculing such pretensions: the underlying truth of their cartoons and parodies is borne out by many an entry in Wickes's ledgers which contains the stipulation that the object ordered should be 'like Lord X's'.

Wickes's aristocratic clients figure frequently in the letters and memoirs of the period. The references are for the most part concerned with the political, social and sexual exploits of the protagonists: wrought plate is sadly absent from these often startling and scurrilous accounts. Paradoxically, the much vaunted respect for reason and proportion which is associated with this golden age was strictly intellectual: the splendid buildings, silver, paintings and furniture of the eighteenth century are somewhat at variance with the people and their mores. Seldom has an age displayed more greed and aggression. Wickes and his associates were part and parcel of it: their livelihoods depended on the whims of their clients and in order to survive in a world far removed from the serenity with which today it is often imbued, they had to be not only good goldsmiths but businessmen as acute as their masters. They lived in fact for the day when they could emulate them, exchanging the role of tradesman for that of landed gentleman. By 1760 both Wickes and Netherton were in a position to make the transition.

Notes for chapter XI

1. Thomas Carlyle, *Frederick the Great*, ii, pp. 586–587.

2. I am indebted to Mr John Mallet not only for drawing my attention to Sir Everard Fawkener's involvement with Nicholas Sprimont, but also for his advice on other matters pertaining to porcelain.

3. From time to time Wickes was required to fit silver sockets, handles, grates, chains and even spouts to 'chine' teapots: up to about 1750 the teapots would have been Chinese, though some may possibly have been Meissen or French. The pair of 'china sauceboats' bought from him in 1753 at a cost of £1 16s was, however, almost certainly of English manufacture whilst the material used for the cover of a snuffbox made 'in imitation of Dresden' in 1758 is not specified.

4. An earlier reference to a silver-gilt scabbard for the Bristol Sword occurs in December 1735 in the joint account of David Peloquin and John Clements, both of Bristol. The scabbard, which weighed 99 ounces, was finely chased and cost £60 12s 9d. The following year one was commissioned from Wickes by Jacob Elton, a member of a well known Bristol family.

5. The Honourable John Scrope's connection with goldsmiths was not to end with his purchases from George Wickes. A letter written from Treasury Chambers on the 19 April 1749 and signed by John Scrope deals with the repayment of 'money extorted by the rebels from several victuallers etc. in their passing and repassing through several counties'.

The Jacobite Rebellion had been remarkable for the absence of pillaging and foraging, the Young Pretender having provided for his followers by the simple expedient of collecting Custom and Excise monies which, he maintained, were due to his father as the rightful monarch. The rebellion quashed, the tradesmen clamoured for the return of the sums 'extorted' from them. Two goldsmiths' names appear: John Oliver of Manchester and Arthur Smith of Preston who had been relieved of 13s 4d and 4s 4½d respectively. It is unlikely that Wickes, dependent on Hanoverian favours, would have harboured any Jacobite sympathies. His family was certainly anti-Stuart judging by the list of subscribers in Bury St Edmunds and Neighbourhood to the Forty-Five National Defence Fund which contains the names of no less than ten of Wickes's kinsmen. In London, however, likenesses of Charles I were offered openly for sale in the newspapers. In the Masters/Apprentices Register, where it was the custom to record royal anniversaries, one can still see an entry made in 1746 which reads 'Fryday Jan^ry ye 30th King Char^s Martyr'.

6. Although many of the large waiters made by the firm were often accompanied by pairs of small matching ones, intended almost certainly for the purpose of hob-nob drinking (an individual waiter being used for each drinker's glass), they were not actually called 'hob-nob' waiters in the Ledgers until the 1770s. The meaning of the phrase had altered slightly since Shakespeare's time and by the 1750s it was being applied to two people drinking to each other, hence the expression 'to hob-nob with' (Arthur Grimwade, *Rococo Silver*, page 39).

7. My thanks are due to Mr Donald Slater of Buttons Green, Suffolk, for his help in resolving this problem.

8. Arthur Onslow's name is well-known in antique silver circles by a curious chance. The cast scroll ends on spoons and ladles which were introduced in the 1760s are known today as 'Onslow Pattern' and the style is widely believed to have originated with a trend set by the famous Speaker of the House of Commons. There is no evidence in the Ledgers to associate him with this design and it is far more likely, as Mr Michael Snodin has suggested (*English Silver Spoons*, page 51), that the name, like 'King's Pattern' and 'Queen's Pattern', was nothing more than a nineteenth century trade term.

9. Charles Oman, *British Rings 800–1914*, Chapter 10; Appendix 11; Pl. 95.

10. This account of Serjeant Foster's call was kindly passed to me by Dr J. H. Baker.

11. I am indebted to Mrs Shirley Bury for sharing this information with me.

XII

The Patronage of the Prince of Wales

In all respects the year 1735 was a turning point in the life of George Wickes. It brought him not only better premises and more distinguished clients, but also the patronage of the heir to the throne, Frederick Louis, Prince of Wales (Fig. 89). Curiously, Wickes did not add the title 'Goldsmith to His Royal Highness the Prince of Wales' to the advertisement he inserted in *The London Evening Post* in June of that year. The actual warrant, if indeed it was ever committed to paper, may not have reached him in time: although most of Wickes's bills are preserved in the Archives of the Duchy of Cornwall, there is no document relating to the granting of the warrant. Wickes was, however, sufficiently confident that it would materialize to have a new shop sign painted, changing 'The King's Arms' to 'The King's Arms and Feathers': the cost was duly recorded in the ledger account dated 25 June 1735 headed proudly 'My House'.

In 1735 Frederick Louis was twenty-eight years of age and, unlike his father and grandfather, deeply interested in all aspects of the Arts. Seldom can a prince have had such a choice of skilled goldsmiths— Wickes apart, Paul de Lamerie, Paul Crespin, Frederick Kandler, David Willaume II, John Le Sage, Peter Archambo I, John Edwards, Lewis Pantin I and Benjamin Godfrey were all working in London at the time. David Willaume's name appears briefly in the Prince's household accounts in late March 1735 (an order for thirteen silver badges amounting to £102 18s 8d),[1] but when the time came for the Prince to appoint a goldsmith his choice fell on Wickes. The decision may have been made purely on æsthetic grounds, but Wickes must first have been brought to the notice of the Prince by persons of influence and standing in his entourage.

The name of Pauncefort appears not only in Wickes's ledgers but also in legal documents relating to the first Panton Street house. Robert Pauncefort, the Attorney General to the Prince of Wales, was a member of this family. He was one of the co-executors and the only surviving trustee of the will of Edward Pauncefort, gentleman, of Witham-on-the-Hill in Lincolnshire, late of the parish of St James Westminster. A considerable number of copyholds and freeholds, including certain houses in Panton Street, was bequeathed to the

89. *Portrait of Frederick, Prince of Wales*, 1738. Broadley's *Annals of the Haymarket.*
Courtesy of the Archives Department, Westminster City Libraries

testator's great-nephew Tracey Pauncefort, but, he dying young, they passed to 'his heirs in entail male'. There were, inevitably, legal delays before the eventual beneficiary, another Edward Pauncefort, was able to enjoy his inheritance. A settlement was finally reached on the 23 April 1737 and amongst the parties to it were Robert Pauncefort 'of the Inner Temple Esquire Attorney General to the Prince of Wales' and John Hedges 'of Finchley Esquire Treasurer to the Prince of Wales'.

The only registration of a deed for Wickes's house in Panton Street which has come to light is one dated 1767: George Pauncefort (Edward's son) and John Parker are named in this indenture and it refers to the house as being 'heretofore in the occupation of George Wickes Goldsmith'. When the lease was assigned to Wickes in 1735 the legal ownership of the freehold had not been finally settled and his right of tenure was, therefore, by no means certain. Wickes could well have had misgivings which were allayed by the lawyer, Robert Pauncefort. If this was indeed the case, Wickes's trust in Pauncefort was rewarded since it is highly likely that it led to the goldsmith being recommended to the Prince not only by his Attorney General, but also by his then Treasurer, John Hedges.

Wickes's most influential champion may in fact have been Lord North and Guilford, Frederick's Gentleman of the Bedchamber since 1730, who, according to Lord Hervey, was described by George II as 'a very good poor creature, but a very weak man'. Lord North patronized Wickes long before his appointment as goldsmith to the Prince. The heir to the throne would possibly have seen and admired the magnificent candelabra which Lord North bought from Wickes in 1731 (Fig. 90).[2] They are the earliest known examples of objects which were not made for the Prince but for high officers in his household on which the royal crest and motto 'Ich Dien' were engraved presumably to commemorate the appointment, a practice favoured by members of Frederick's court within a court.

An endorsement of Lord North's recommendation by Pauncefort and Hedges may have served to tip the scales in favour of Wickes when the time came for Frederick to choose a goldsmith from the veritable galaxy of talent available.

Robert Pauncefort may well have been a client of Wickes prior to 1735, but his name does not appear in the Ledgers which date only from June of that year. There is, however, an account for his kinsman Edward which was opened, significantly, four days after the settlement. His purchases are less interesting than the charge of fifteen shillings debited him on the 2 August 1737 and described by Wickes as 'cash paid the Com[ssrs] of Sewers' which appears later on the credit side as 'cash allow[d] in rent for the seuers [sic] 15*s*'. Edward

90. Candlestick, one of a pair made for Lord North, George Wickes, 1731. Engraved with the crest of Frederick, Prince of Wales, and his motto 'Ich Dien' to commemorate Lord North's appointment in the Prince's household.

This candlestick is part of the magnificent candelabrum shewn opposite page 1.

Candelabra were usually fashioned in such a way that the branches could be easily removed and the candlesticks used on their own, as in this illustration.

Had Wickes used the conventional method for Lord North's candelabra he would have made the shaft of the branches so that it slipped into the body of the candlestick. Instead he adopted a device which is virtually unique. The whole of the upper part of the candlestick above the masks unscrews and is replaced by the branches which are so designed that they appear to be integral with the base.

The branches became separated from the candlesticks: an account of the remarkable circumstances in which they were reunited will be found in Note 2 at the end of this chapter.
Private Collection

Pauncefort may have been a reasonable landlord, but he was a difficult client judging by an entry in his account which reads:

By abatement in the carving
which he would not pay ... £12 17s

In June 1735, however, all was set fair. If Wickes was counting on a large order following hard on the heels of the royal warrant he was sadly mistaken. The first commission, received some ten months after his appointment, must have been something of a shock: he was required to furnish the royal household with a black ebony handle for a tea kettle and a 'button for a teapott'. This is the first entry in the account which Wickes headed with a flourish—and an obvious effort of calligraphy—'His Royall Hyghness The Prince of Wales'. It is dated 24 March 1735/6, the last day of the Church year according to the Julian Calendar which obtained in England until 1752 when it was replaced by the Gregorian Calendar. The sum of 3s 6d was entered against these items, but Wickes must have thought it politic not to charge for them and changed the figures to noughts.

In April 1736 Frederick married Augusta of Saxe-Gotha. A large quantity of splendid wrought plate might well have been required for the new royal establishment, but George II was determined not to furnish the money and, impatient to set off on one of his prolonged visits to Hanover (which he considered in every way superior to his British realms), he refused to increase his son's meagre allowance or countenance the setting up of the separate household which Frederick so sorely needed. Himself the son of a harsh father, George II saw no reason to shew any lenience to his own heir: not only did he openly declare his loathing of his elder son (which was echoed by Queen Caroline and their daughters), but he was determined to keep him short of money. Frederick had some cause to feel himself ill-used. His father when Prince of Wales had enjoyed an annual income of £100,000 whilst his son had to wait until 1733 before his slender resources were supplemented by the revenues of the Duchy of Cornwall, bringing the total to £38,000 per annum. Frederick was by this time twenty-six years of age. Sir Robert Walpole, the King's first minister, tried in vain to make his master see reason, but the monarch was obdurate and continued to keep his son so short of funds that he was forced to remain uneasily under his father's roof.

Wickes was inevitably affected by the royal parsimony. He did receive a modest commission for two items delivered on the 1 May 1736. It possibly caught him unprepared as no fashioning charges accompany the 'fine cup & cover' and the 'fine bread baskett' and he may have had recourse to the stocks of his fellow goldsmiths. The fascination with makers' marks began in the middle of the nineteenth century and whilst the weight of the objects may have been checked by the Prince's officers (each bill was carefully scrutinized and signed by at least one examinee before Frederick's Treasurer and Receiver General authorized the payment), the quality of the objects was the main concern in the eighteenth century: the assay marks and that of the maker would have been disregarded. Wickes duly received £80 for the cup and £50 for the bread basket. They were followed by a number of tedious repairs which included 'the fation and duty of a silver prong fork and half that was lost and found again of L. Norths', the charge of six shillings being again cancelled, a gesture possibly to this patron of long standing.

It is interesting to note that Wickes hired out silver plate for the Prince's more lavish entertainments, though whether he was able to supply all the items from his own stocks is open to question. Fifty-four candlesticks and twenty-six dozen knives, forks and spoons were provided at a cost of £5 5s on the 17 December 1736, the date of 'the entertainment of the Lord Mayor of London etc.' recorded in the accounts of Frederick's then Treasurer and Receiver General, Henry Arthur Herbert. It appears at the end of a long list of sundry debts incurred by the Prince in the period 30 September 1736 to 1 October 1737 which amounted to £16,218 12s. This included £189 8s 11¼d expended on entertaining the Lord Mayor of London. An entry in Wickes's ledger in August 1737 also records the hire of 'plate for yᵉ Oxford & Cambridge entertainment £6 6s'.

This constant hiring and toting of plate must have been irksome to a goldsmith eager to exercise his skill on sumptuous royal pieces. Wickes may have been slightly mollified in June 1737 when he received an order for a piece which he describes in the ledger as 'a frame wᵗ 5 plates and covers' which he wrought himself, judging by the fashioning charge of eight shillings per troy ounce. With the engraving and a case the total cost was £176 9s.

Nomenclature was never Wickes's strong suit: 'frame' may be construed as 'épergne' but 'machine' is a word which he employed with engaging but infuriating vagueness. In fact when Wickes submitted his bill for this piece he described it as 'a masheen wᵗ five covers' and that term was used for it again in July 1737 in an entry for 'a lock and knailing the case for the masheen wᵗ five dishes . . . 7s 6dᵖ' followed by 'to 2 rough cases to send them in to Clifden . . . 5s 0dᵖ'.

The considerable weight of this particular frame—434 ozs 11 dwts—suggests that it was some form of base sufficiently deep to hold hot water and designed to take four segment-shaped dishes set around a central circular one.[3] Such sets were certainly made later in the century, but they were possibly something of a novelty in England in 1737. Ceramic versions duly followed and it is interesting

91. Supper set, width 12¾ in (32.4cm), John Parker & Edward Wakelin, 1766. Set of four fan-shaped dishes, each engraved with the royal arms of George III, on a mahogany tray of shaped outline with silver cross-plates. The small vase in the centre dates from 1809. *Courtesy of Christie's*

to note the similarity between a surviving set of four fan-shaped silver dishes made by Parker and Wakelin in 1772 which were sold at Christie's in June 1974—separated, unfortunately, from their original frame and central dish—and a design in Wedgwood's first printed pattern book of 1774. An earlier set by Parker and Wakelin, made in 1766, was sold in the same rooms on the 7 May 1952: this has a mahogany base and is engraved with royal or ambassadorial arms (Fig. 91).

Wickes must have been happily awaiting further orders when the storm broke. The crises which were such a feature of Frederick's relations with his parents came to a head in July 1737. The Princess of Wales was said 'to be breeding' although both Augusta and Frederick were unforthcoming, even evasive, as to the date of her confinement. George II's instructions were clear and unequivocal: the delivery was to take place at Hampton Court in the presence of Queen Caroline. Frederick was determined to disobey his parents. On the last day of July, after a formal dinner with the Royal Family, he and Augusta had scarcely reached their own quarters when her labours began. Frederick acted with speed and, unbeknown to the King and Queen who were playing at cards, he summoned a coach. The Princess of Wales was half carried, half dragged to it. Frederick, Lady Archibald Hamilton (protesting vehemently, but to no avail), Dunoyer (the royal dancing master), an equerry and the Prince's German valet (who was also a qualified surgeon and *accoucheur*) crowded into the coach beside the wretched Augusta. The waters had already broken, but 'with an obstinacy equal to his folly, and a folly equal to his barbarity',[4] the Prince ordered the coachman to drive to St James's Square. There at 10.45 pm the Princess gave birth to 'a little rat of a girl, about the bigness of a good large toothpick case'.[5] A courier was despatched to Hampton Court and at 1.30 am the Queen was awakened with the news that the labour had started: thinking her daughter-in-law still under her roof, Caroline rose immediately only to discover that Frederick had conveyed his wife secretly to London. Accompanied by her two elder daughters, the Queen lost no time in setting out for St James's Square where she was received at 4 am by an unrepentant son who gleefully regaled her with a full account of the night's proceedings. Unmindful that history was merely repeating itself—her own husband having quarrelled furiously with George I over the birth of one of their own children at St James's Square—the Queen returned in a fury to Hampton Court to inform her spouse. The King was outraged and as soon as the Princess could safely be moved Frederick was unceremoniously turned out of St James's Square and banished to his own modest rented house at Kew. A few months later Queen Caroline was taken seriously ill: she died on the 20 November 1737, refusing to the very end to forgive her son or even receive him.

If Frederick were to be judged merely on these events, he would emerge a sorry figure. In justice to him we must glance briefly at his early years. He was born in Hanover on the 20 January 1707. No dignitaries were present, as was then customary at the birth of such a potentially important child, and the English Ambassador was not even notified. When the boy's grandfather George I succeeded to the throne of England in 1714 Frederick's parents accompanied the King to London leaving their young son alone in Hanover to be brought up by servants for the next fourteen years. His governor is alleged to have reported to the Prince's mother—who passed it on to Lord Hervey—that Frederick had 'the most vicious nature and the most false heart that ever man had'. He might have added that in spite of his atrocious upbringing the princeling was well informed, fluent in several languages and had a very real interest in the Arts. Frederick's erstwhile friend Hervey (Pope's 'painted child of dirt that stinks and stings'[6])—Queen Caroline's inseparable Vice-Chamberlain—was to add to the diatribes, but his testimony, fascinating though it may be, must of necessity be suspect. Frederick's friend Lord Egmont was more charitable in his diary in November 1731:

The character of the Pr[ince] is this: he has no reigning passion, if it be it is to pass the evening with six or seven others over a glass of wine and hear them talk of a variety of things, but he does not drink. He loves play, and plays to win, that he may supply his pleasures and generosity, which last are great, but so ill placed, that

92. Set of twelve dinner plates, diameter 9¾ in (25 cm), George Wickes, 1741. From the evidence of the numbers engraved on the base of these plates it is clear that they originally formed part of a set of at least six dozen. They bear the arms of Richard Annesley, eighth Earl of Anglesey, who succeeded in 1737 and died in 1761. The Earl does not appear to have been a client of Wickes, but there is a ledger missing for this period and his account may have been lost with it. The plates are unusually heavy, the average weight being 20 ozs 2 dwts. The quality of the workmanship is so exceptional that they could well once have been part of a royal order. Wickes recorded in the account of Frederick, Prince of Wales, that when his order was countermanded in 1737 it 'was in such forwardness . . . as amounts to more than £500'. A later entry, unfortunately undated, reveals that Wickes sold six dozen of the plates which he had made for the Prince. He could conceivably have disposed of them to a fellow goldsmith or a middleman who subsequently sold them to Lord Annesley in 1741 (this would account for the date letter—Wickes is unlikely to have submitted them for assay at the time the Prince's order was countermanded). *Courtesy of Thomas Lumley Ltd.*

he often wants wherewith to do a well-placed kindness, by giving to unworthy objects. He has had several mistresses, and now keeps one, an apothecary's daughter of Kingston; but is not nice in his choice, and talks more of feats this way than he acts. He can talk gravely according to his company, but is sometimes more childish than becomes his age. He thinks he knows business, but attends to none; likes to be flattered. He is good-natured, and if he meets with a good Ministry, may satisfy his people; he is extremely dutiful to his parents, who do not return it in love, and seem to neglect him by letting him do as he will, but they keep him short of money.

This perennial shortage of money was to be a matter of great vexation to Wickes. Banished to Kew, Frederick was reduced to living on credit and had no option but to retrench: servants were dismissed and wages reduced; he rid himself of some of his horses; even the household catering, including that of his immediate family, was farmed out. His misfortunes inevitably rebounded on Wickes who was at the time working on a sizeable order for him. His feelings are recorded in his ledger in an angry entry, alas undated but inserted on the debtor side of the royal account between 20 September 1737 and 25 November 1737:

To the damadge and loss to me in a large parcell of plate bespoke and ordered by the Prince which was in such forwardness when countermand as amounts to more then [sic] £500

The initial shock over, Wickes set about making good his loss. His efforts are best conveyed in his own words, again undated:

> The damadge on the other side [i.e. the Debtor side] being reduced by executing part of the work intended and I have now taken of taken of [sic] the whole damadge altho I have not reec^d it any other wise than by the profitt of work made . . . £450

This £450 he grudgingly entered on the credit side, balancing it against the £500 which, in his fury, he had debited the Prince's account. To this he added a further fifty pounds (thereby cancelling the debt) which is somewhat curiously described:

> Sold six dozen of plates and twelf
> dishes which I allow att six pence
> per oz 2000 ozs . . . £50

It is inconceivable that Wickes would have sold 2,000 troy ounces of wrought silver (Fig. 92) for six pence an ounce: this was in fact the prevailing rate of duty payable to the Customs & Excise, but Wickes makes no mention of duty. In happier circumstances in June of the following year twenty-four plates weighing 488 ozs 5 dwts were made for the Prince at a cost of £181 1s. One can only suppose that the £50 may have been his actual profit on the six dozen plates and twelve dishes.

As for the Prince, the scandal of his daughter's birth caused a temporary eclipse in his popularity. Though never exactly 'lov'd of the distracted multitude', the people of London, whilst disapproving of his nocturnal hooliganism—acceptable in Hanover but resented by the English—held him in some affection and had displayed sympathy in his previous vicissitudes. The City, however, remained loyal and raised £30,000 to pay his debts. The Earl of Scarbrough caused the loan to be set down by his clerk, Edward Godfrey, in a volume of the Prince's accounts which Lord Scarbrough retained as his own personal record (Fig. 93). Appointed Treasurer and Receiver General to the Prince of Wales on the 27 May 1738, he had the unenviable task of sorting out the tangle of debts left perforce unsettled by his predecessor.

The first page of this volume is headed 'Account of the Loan of £30000 to His Royal Highness on the Tin Duty'.

> June 19 1738. By His Royal Highness's own hands part of the said loan of £30000 advanced by Sir John Barnard [Lord Mayor of London] & others [Mr Richard Glover and Mr Thomas Matthew are cited in a later memorandum] in consideration of an annuity £3000 out of the tin duty granted by Privy Seal dated June 12 1738

93. Page from the Ledger of the third Earl of Scarbrough. The Earl of Scarbrough was appointed Treasurer and Receiver General to Frederick, Prince of Wales, on the 27 May 1738. Two payments to Wickes appear on this page. It will be seen that the Prince also patronized Jonas Durand & Co., pewterers, John Savigny the cutler, George Cure, upholsterer, and Benjamin Goodison, one of the finest cabinet makers of the period. *Courtesy of the Earl of Scarbrough*

His Royal Higness having retained £6000 one part thereof for his own particular use as by his signification of the same under his sign manual dated this day, returning the remainder to be applied in sundry payments for his service being . . . £24000.

The details of the Prince's income are thereafter listed under 'mony [sic] received' on the left hand side and 'money paid' on the right hand page facing it.

On the 'mony received' side an interesting entry appears:

The sundry sums of money advanced by Henry Arthur Herbert His Royal Highness's late Treasurer on account being the contents of the ballance of his account May 20 1738 . . . are brought in charge as follows viz. July 19: by cash, out of the loan, in payment of George Wickes bills for £1,678 12s 5d for table plate by warrant, in part with his note for £1000.

The sum of £1,678 12s 5d tallies exactly with the second of two consecutive entries under 'money paid' dated 19 July 1738:

To George Wickes, Silversmith, bill
for silver sconces candlesticks etc
per warrant   £392 19s 0d
To ditto bill for table plate per
warrant   £1678 12s 5d

Wickes had obviously been advised that he could safely proceed to execute the 'large parcell of plate bespoke and ordered by the Prince' and his ledger entries shew that delivery started on the 1 February 1737/8 and finished on the 27 June 1738.

Were it not for the witness of the angry notes in Wickes's ledgers, the crisis would have gone unnoticed as far as his book-keeping entries are concerned. The £1,000 first appears on the 25 September 1737 before the full effects of the King's wrath were visited on the Prince: it is entered as 'cash on account of a parcell of plate to be made'. Old plate weighing 4,184 ozs 2 dwts and valued at £1,135 4s 10d was also traded in on the 1 October 1737 followed by the sum of £216 1s described as 'cash per Mr Harbot [sic]' and dated 21 December 1737, this latter being authorized by Frederick from exile 'at Kew the twentieth day of October 1737: in the eleventh year of the reign of our Royal Father the King'.

The £1,000 non-existent 'cash' (which may have been a bill on the Prince) was carried forward from folio to folio for almost a year and it was not until the 18 July 1738 that Wickes was able to balance his books with an entry in the large cursive style affected by him on very special occasions: 'by cash . . . £1,071 11s 6d'. This brought Frederick's credit to £3,244 6s 8d, the exact sum shewn on the debtor side for wrought silver supplied to his royal patron. Wickes's satisfaction is clear in the two heavily scored broad lines (three on the debtor side) drawn with a ruler under the respective totals. The initial hold-up obviously upset him, but in the event the payment was made three weeks after Wickes had furnished the last items, delivery coinciding with the date of his ledger entry.

The order covered two pages of a folio sized ledger, but Wickes's descriptions are frustratingly brief. There is no hint as to the style apart from the bare word 'shell' in two instances and 'festoon' in a third. Since they have not survived, one can only conjecture that the two silver-gilt 'shell solt boxes' must have been of considerable interest. The word 'box' scarcely conjures up a rococo outline and

Wickes may have used it loosely, at a loss for a term which exactly conveyed the shape:[7] he does, however, use it again in January 1748/9 when the Prince's bill contains a repair to a salt box and the gilding of two salt boxes, almost certainly the pair Wickes made in June 1738. Salt and silver are incompatible and gilding prevents corrosion. Since the gold is applied thinly it soon wears off and requires renewing from time to time.

The price charged by Wickes for the Prince's shell salt boxes suggests intricate casting and chasing and some idea of their importance as objects can be gained from a comparison with the six festoon salts and two shell sauce-boats which formed part of this large order.

Object	Weight	Basic charge per oz	Making charge	Gilding	Total charge per article
Shell salt box	13 ozs 10 dwts	5s 11d	£6 6s	£1 11s 6d	£11 17s 6d
Shell sauceboat	18 ozs 9 dwts	9s 11d	Nil	—	£9 3s 0d
Festoon salt	7 ozs 17 dwts	5s 11d	£2 2s	—	£4 9s 3d

94. Gilding (the mercury process). The journeyman is applying the amalgam with a mop of chamois leather bound round the end of a stick. Detail from an illustration commissioned by the Goldsmiths' Company in 1707 (see endpapers). *Courtesy of the Worshipful Company of Goldsmiths*

The additional making charge of £2 2s each for the last item is high probably on account of the festoons which would have been cast and applied. The shell salt boxes were obviously gilded inside and out and when they left Wickes's workshop they would have passed for gold. With constant cleaning and rough handling by servants the more precious metal would gradually wear off and the objects would have to be sent back to the goldsmith for re-gilding (Fig. 94).

There are no engraving charges for any of these pieces possibly because there was no appropriate space for armorials amid the rich decoration of rococo shells and festoons.

The total cost of the Prince's 'parcel of plate'—including engraving and cases—was £3,244 6s 8d. That sum covered forty-three serving dishes (fifteen of them described as 'shape dishes' and four as 'fish plates'), eighteen dish covers, ninety-six plates, six sauceboats, eight salts, two sets of casters, three salvers, four waiters, eighty-four knives, forks and spoons, thirteen teaspoons, one soup ladle, fifteen bottle tickets or wine labels, thirty-seven candlesticks and eighteen sconces. The overall weight was 7,710 ozs 17 dwts.

In the midst of this lavish spending it is amusing to note a small economy. Wickes enters £4 2s against 'to taken out arms and doing up' forty-eight knife hafts (new steel blades at £3 were supplied, suggesting that the old ones had been badly worn by constant sharpening in a knife grinder), forty eight spoons and forks, six salts,

147

three casters and one spoon. These refurbished pieces were probably remnants of royal plate from past reigns. The garters and crests which replaced the 'taken out arms' were their only link with the new fashionable cutlery ordered by the Prince. Whereas outmoded flatware might pass unnoticed, Frederick was not taking any chances with plates: ninety-six new ones were made for him and twenty-four silver-gilt 'new star[ling]', or Britannia standard, plates were traded in. The higher Britannia standard was in force from 1697 until 1720 when it became optional so the plates could have been in the style of William and Mary, Queen Anne or George I and possibly too severe for the Prince's taste. Wickes habitually wrote 'starling' and not 'sterling' and this spelling also occurs in the Hall's registers.

Entries relating to the erasure of armorials and the engraving of new ones occur frequently in the Ledgers. Collectors and dealers fight shy of silver from which the original armorials have been removed to make way for later engraving: the erasure, even when carried out by an expert, removes a certain amount of silver. All too frequently slight traces of the former work remain or, in extreme cases, a whole skin of silver has to be removed and the piece not only loses its original patina, but can be substantially weakened: the section can often be detected by touch in hollow ware; salvers and waiters may whip or bend in the hands; spoons lose their balance. Wickes and his fellow goldsmiths may have deprecated this practice, but they had no option but to carry out their clients' instructions.

The Prince honoured Wickes's bills with reasonable speed thanks to the £30,000 raised for him by the City. The loan took rather longer to repay, but that, too, is recorded on the 5 July 1743 in the Earl of Scarbrough's personal copy of Frederick's accounts. £18,000 'in redemption & extinguishment . . . in part of the said £30,000' was paid to Sir John Barnard and Richard Glover and the remaining £12,000 on the 8 October 1743 'in full of the said £30,000 & all claims under the said Privy Seal'.

Frederick was less scrupulous in the repayment of debts to his personal friends. George Bubb Dodington, one of the least sympathetic figures of the eighteenth century, was reputed to have an annual income of £100,000: his toadying to the Prince relieved him of the £6,000 which the latter required to repay a loan advanced for the purchase of Carlton House and Frederick openly boasted of having 'fleeced' him. Dodington believed himself to be a man of taste and sensibility: some proof of his claim lies in the Ledgers for he, too, bought silver from Wickes though his choice of a goldsmith may have been influenced by the royal connection.

He was not the only member of the Prince's circle to patronize Wickes. The third Earl of Scarbrough, formerly Sir Thomas

Saunderson, made handsome purchases. It is in his accounts in the goldsmith's ledgers that we find actual evidence that the Prince's high officers commemorated their appointments by having his armorials engraved on some of their own silver. It will be recalled that the Prince of Wales's feathers surmounted by a crown and accompanied by his motto 'Ich Dien' were engraved on the candelabra made by Wickes for Lord North in 1731, but since the Garrard Collection dates only from 1735 we have no record of these pieces. Wickes's ledger account for the Earl of Scarbrough provides conclusive proof. In July 1740 the goldsmith made eighteen silver-gilt plates and eleven dishes for the Earl. Below these items appear the following entries which are of some significance:

To graving yᵉ Princes arms on yᵉ plates at 15/- each	£13 10s 0d
To graving dᵒ [ditto] on 8 dishes at £1 each	£8 0s 0d
To dᵒ on 3 dishes at £1 10s each	£4 10s 0d

When the Pelham gold cup was taken back to Wickes by Lord Lincoln in 1755 to have his own armorials engraved on it he was charged ten shillings for '2 crests coronets & garters on a gold cup & cover'. They were added discreetly, in miniature, inside the cover and at the foot of the cup thus preserving Kent's classical simplicity. The higher sums recorded fifteen years earlier for the Earl of Scarbrough's plates and dishes suggest far larger and more elaborate engraving. The Prince was charged a guinea for a 'coat and supporter' and it is clear that his full armorials were engraved on the Earl's pieces.

Silver scholars have long been puzzled by the existence, in several private collections, of ten silver-gilt dishes made by Wickes bearing the assay date letter for 1739. Made in French Régence style, they are decorated with similar borders of applied cast strapwork and foliage: the full armorials of Frederick Prince of Wales are handsomely engraved in the centre of each dish (Fig. 95). None of these ten dishes is to be found in the Prince's account in Wickes's ledgers. Those made for the Earl of Scarbrough were entered on the last day of July 1740, but they were part of a large order and could well have been made two months earlier and assayed just before the twenty-ninth day of May when the date letter was by custom changed by the Worshipful Company of Goldsmiths.

It is, of course, possible that the Earl presented the dishes to the Prince and that they passed on his death to the Dowager Princess of Wales and later found their way on to the open market. Had they been gifts from Frederick to his Treasurer they would have been recorded in the royal account in Wickes's ledger. It is far more likely that the Earl took this opportunity of publicly displaying his loyalty to the Prince at a time when many of his erstwhile friends and supporters were shunning him for fear of offending the King. One of George II's many harsh measures was the forbidding of his own court to those who frequented that of his son.

It was not unknown for Frederick to present pieces of his own plate to his officers in recognition of their services to him.[8] Three such pieces were given to his physician, Dr Matthew Lee, and were presented to Christ Church, Oxford, his old college, by his widow Sarah after Lee's death in 1755. A rococo tureen (engraved weight 127 oz 5 dwts) and an eagle-head ladle (Figs. 96 a and c), both made by Wickes, formed part of this gift: they are easily identifiable from the ledgers as part of a set of two tureens, dishes and ladles which he supplied to the Prince on the 14 April 1744 (Fig. 97) and engraved with 'coats with supporters & cor[ts]'. The third piece was a shaped oval dish with a gadrooned edge, the rim chased with rococo decoration, circa 1740 (the date letter is unfortunately rubbed) which bears the maker's mark of Peter Archambo: this, too, is engraved

95. Silver-gilt dish made for the Earl of Scarbrough, 10 ins (25.4 cm) George Wickes, 1739. The applied cast strapwork and foliage is in the French Régence taste which consorts strangely with the rococo fashion in vogue at the time. The dishes were engraved with the full armorials of the Prince of Wales in commemoration of Lord Scarbrough's appointment as Treasurer and Receiver General. Eleven such dishes made for him are recorded in Wickes's ledger. They weighed 470 ozs 15 dwts (fashioning 7s 6d per ounce) and cost £176 10s 6d. The engraving of the Prince's armorials was charged at £1 each for eight of the dishes and £1 10s each for the remaining three. The gilding at two shillings per ounce came to £87 1s. Ten of these dishes have survived and are now in private collections. *Courtesy of Christie's*

96a. Tureen (one of a pair) made for the Prince of Wales and presented by him to his physician Dr Matthew Lee, 16½ × 9 in (41.9 × 22.9 cm), George Wickes, 1743. After Dr Lee's death in 1755 the tureen (with its under-dish and ladle) was presented to Christ Church, Oxford, by his widow Mrs Sarah Lee. The tureen is engraved with the full armorials of Frederick, Prince of Wales. Wickes's bill to the Prince is reproduced in figure 97. *Courtesy of the Dean and Chapter, Christ Church, Oxford*

96b. Under-dish to the Lee Tureen, 18½ × 14¼ in (47 × 36.2 cm), Peter Archambo, *c.* 1740 (date letter illegible). This is one of a pair commissioned from Wickes by Frederick, Prince of Wales, in 1744, at the same time as the tureens. The dishes, which are recorded in Wickes's ledger, appear to have been bought by Wickes from Peter Archambo. Both were engraved with the full armorials of the Prince. The arms of the College and those of the donor were added to the Lee dish later, possibly in 1756, the date of the inscription. The location of the second tureen and dish is unknown. *Courtesy of the Dean and Chapter, Christ Church, Oxford*

with the full armorials of the Prince (Fig. 96b). Whilst it is impossible to state with absolute certainty that the dish was one of the pair made for the tureens, its engraved weight—54 ozs 18 dwts— is almost exactly half that of the two invoiced by Wickes. This suggests that he subcontracted the under-dishes to Peter Archambo or bought them from the latter's stock. The dish alone is inscribed with sufficient detail to make it clear that the plate once belonged to the Prince of Wales. Dr. Lee's long and detailed will[9] makes no mention of these

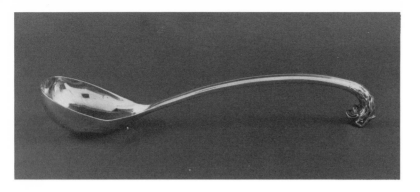

96c. Eagle-head ladle (Lee Bequest), George Wickes, *c.*1743. Although the ladle bears no date letter, it is engraved with the Prince of Wales's crest in the Garter, crowned. The Prince's order included two ladles and an identical ladle, almost certainly the pair to this one, is in the Victoria and Albert Museum. *Courtesy of the Dean and Chapter, Christ Church, Oxford*

important objects: they obviously formed part of his collection of plate which he left unconditionally to his wife.

The eagle-head ladle is of considerable interest. Engraved with the Prince's crest in the Garter, crowned, it was probably once paired with one, similarly engraved, now in the Victoria and Albert Museum. The Christ Church ladle bears Wickes's maker's mark, as does the Museum example, but there is apparently no date letter on either. English eagle-head ladles are extremely rare. Their fashioning required skill: the stems are hollow and cast longitudinally and then fitted to the fig-shaped bowl, also cast, with a lap-joint.[10] De Lamerie made similar ladles: Sidney Sussex College, Cambridge, has one probably dating from 1742. A tureen and ladle made by Wickes for Sir Lister Holte (Fig. 99) and recorded in the Ledgers on the 25 September 1742 were sold at Sotheby's in 1938. The ladle has an eagle head and though it is undated almost certainly dates from 1742 which suggests that both Wickes and de Lamerie shared the services of the same modeller. Another example by Wickes is illustrated in Eric Delieb's *Investing in Silver*: once part of the Marquess of Breadalbane's Collection, it too carries the assay date letter for 1743.

Wickes, as his appointed goldsmith, might have been expected to make all the Prince's silver himself. It was in his own interest to do so, but he was obviously not precluded, when the need arose, from turning to his fellow goldsmiths who would have supplied him at 'trade rates'. Wickes's retainer did not prevent Frederick from making an occasional purchase from other sources. An itemized bill dated 24 October 1738 in the Duchy of Cornwall Archives lists items 'bought of P. Bertrand'.[11] He was probably a middleman judging by the miscellany: 'a groupe of china figures' (£5 5s) and a pair of 'old china candlesticks'; four snuff-boxes (one of them gold); a French clock, various trinkets: '2 old white [i.e. silver] cups & silver gilt sawcers' (£10 10s), four silver salts (£13 14s) and a silver bread basket (£25 15s). The variety of his wares suggests that P. Bertrand may have specialized in curios and bric-a-brac.

97. Bill presented by Wickes to the Prince of Wales for tureens and bread baskets. One of the sets of tureens—a gift from Frederick to his physician Dr Matthew Lee—can be seen in figures 96a, b & c. The bread basket in figure 98 is one of the two invoiced by Wickes. Although his bill is dated the 14 April 1744, Wickes was not paid until the 31 May 1745 at which time he signed his name at the foot of the document. Lady Hamilton's signature shews that she endorsed the payment: Wickes noted in his ledger that the pieces were delivered to her. *Printed by permission of the Secretary and Keeper of the Records of the Duchy of Cornwall*

98. Bread basket engraved with the armorials of Frederick, Prince of Wales, width 14⅜ in (36.5 cm), George Wickes, 1743. Two bread baskets were ordered at the same time as the Lee tureen. All these pieces may have been intended as gifts to members of Frederick's household. The two baskets weighed 120 ozs 12 dwts, the fashioning charge was 9s 2d per troy ounce and the cost £55 5s 7d. See Note 8.
Donald Morrison Collection, U.S.A.

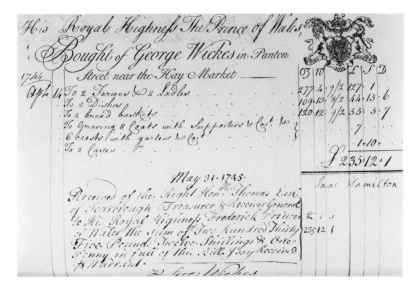

Frederick had all the time in the world to devote to curio collecting, within his limited means. Excluded from all affairs of state and expelled from the King's residences, he rented the Duke of Norfolk's house in St James's Square and continued to frequent the London scene. In 1742 he set up an establishment in Leicester House, Leicester Fields (now Leicester Square), paying £580 a year in rental plus £500 'for a bounty to the Earl of Leicester towards paying the workmen for finishing the repairs of Leicester House by

99. Soup tureen, width 19 in (48.3 cm), and eagle-head ladle, George Wickes, 1742. This tureen, made for Sir Lister Holte, is a very plain piece compared with the sumptuous one presented by the Prince to his physician Dr Lee. The same mould, however, must have been used for the eagle-head ladle. *Courtesy of Sotheby's*

29 September next'. This was the very house, so aptly described by Thomas Pennant as 'the pouting place of princes', in which George II and Queen Caroline had held brilliant court at a time when they themselves as Prince and Princess of Wales were at odds with George I.

Queen Caroline had a highly intelligent and cultivated mind and it is to be regretted that she made no attempt to reconcile father and son, choosing instead to defer to her irascible and stubborn spouse in all things. Frederick's artistic sensibility was certainly inherited from his mother: George II had nothing but scorn for 'boetry and bainting' and on one occasion when he discovered that the Queen, taking advantage of one of his prolonged sojourns in Hanover, had had numerous paintings of coarse and buxom women replaced by some of the masterpieces stored in the Royal Collection, he berated her soundly and speedily reversed her decision.

Frederick was left to his own devices and spent his days cultivating both the Opposition and the arts. As a politician he was a dismal failure, but he was to prove a serious and discriminating patron of the arts. Cliveden, which he rented as his principal country home, became the centre of musical performances, masques and amateur theatricals.[12] All the members of the Prince's immediate family joined happily in these pursuits and shared his passion for gardening and cricket. The officers of his household and his guests were also expected to participate, their enthusiasm being more tempered than that of the Prince especially when they were required to spend interminable hours digging earth and fielding cricket balls.

Cliveden and Kew gave full rein to the dilettante, but Frederick was more than that. That inveterate gossip Horace Walpole was at first disposed to dismiss him as a sham, but later changed his tune, possibly after the Prince had asked him for a copy of his *Ædes Walpoliannæ* (a catalogue of the pictures at Houghton) and invited his opinion on two paintings by Andrea del Sarto which he had recently acquired. George Vertue waxed lyrical in his praise of the Prince 'whose affection and inclination to promote art and artists is daily more and more evident, by the imployment he has given several artists and by his delight in conversations and his purchases of paintings and pictures miniatures enamells etc in a very great number'. Vertue was commissioned to prepare books of prints of Frederick's pictures and to make copies of the inventory of the paintings collected by Charles I, that great royal connoisseur whom the Prince may well have sought to emulate.

Amongst his purchases recorded in the Archives of the Duchy of Cornwall there are pictures and miniatures—three by Cooper—and a list of objects bought in France which included '1 Rainbrant—£18' and '1 Salvator Rosa—£12 12s'. William Hogarth was commissioned to paint 'six faces at 5 guineas each face' and Peter Scheemakers supplied a number of works, mostly marble busts. The signature of the Prince's architect, William Kent, appears, as examinee, on the latter's bill.[13] Michael Rysbrack the sculptor was employed by Frederick and amongst the painters who enjoyed his patronage were George Knapton, Philippe Mercier, Charles Phillips, John Wootton, Jean-Baptiste Van Loo and Barthélemy du Pan. His interest was not confined to the visual arts—he befriended and appreciated Pope, Swift, Thomson and Gay. His interest in music went further than mere attendance at concerts. He delighted in conducting orchestral concerts and from his youth had been a competent cellist. He was an enthusiastic supporter of the Italian operas presented by Bononcini and although much has been made of his boycott of Handel, his father's favourite composer, his accounts belie such pettiness: £250 was paid to 'Mr Handel for the season of operas in the Haymarket in this year 1734'; £52 10s was expended on 'Handel's entertainment' in June 1741; an entry dated 29 April 1743 reads: 'To George Frederick Handel Esq. per warrant oratorios—£73 10s'.

Entertainment of a more frivolous nature occupied much of his time. Fashionable society flocked to the pleasure gardens at Vauxhall and Ranelagh and Frederick and Augusta, studiously avoided by other members of the Royal Family, joined enthusiastically in parties and balls. Augusta, according to Horace Walpole, was easily identifiable by her jewels. Commenting on a particularly crowded masquerade, he wrote 'there were dozens of ugly Queens of Scots . . . the Princess of Wales was one, covered with diamonds'. On another occasion he described her as 'vastly bejewelled; Frankz had lent her forty thousand pounds worth, and refused to be paid for the hire, only desiring that she would tell whose they were'. A brief glance at the money spent on her jewellery is of interest: not a single piece was bought from Wickes whose unremarkable stock seems always to have been something of an afterthought. The Prince—or possibly the Princess—favoured a certain Peter Dutens, who may have been a middleman rather than a working jeweller. Considerable sums were paid to him: £4,000 in June 1741; a further £4,00 entered on the 30 September 1742 as 'To Peter Dutens principal on bond per warr'; £3,000 on the 2 January 1745 described as 'bill principal of adjusted accounts'. An Isaac Lacam is also named in the Duchy of Cornwall Archives as 'jeweller to the Princess of Wales'.

Augusta accepted her husband's marital peccadilloes as a matter of course and she and Frederick managed to create a happy family atmosphere unmarred by feuds between Frederick and his young sons. The Prince was a loving and caring parent who took his duties very seriously, particularly the question of nationality. Frederick, in his 'Instructions for my son George, drawn by my-self, for his good . . . and for that of his people', exhorted him to 'convince the nation that you are not only an Englishman born and bred, but that you are also this by inclination'.

The needs of his growing family are reflected in Wickes's pages. No papboats are recorded in the earlier accounts, but several sets of silver-gilt plate were ordered for the nursery. These included on several occasions 'a little cup & cover' and 'a little mugg'. References on the contra side—'by cash for one of the setts of guilt plate for the young princess' and 'a gilt fork for Prince George'—identify them. No knives are mentioned until December 1744 when '2 silver gilt knive handles with steel blades for Prince George & Lady Augusta' were ordered by Lady Archibald Hamilton.

The future George III was a very small boy when in January 1740 his father ordered from Wickes two silver kettle drums. According to the ledger, 123 ozs 4 dwts of silver, suitably engraved, went into their making and that—plus the 'steell work', 'covering w^t villum', '2 drum sticks' and 'two lether bags lyend w^t bays'—brought the total cost to £53 18s. That they were specially made for Prince George is clear from the wording of Wickes's bill. They must have been of sturdy construction for nineteen years passed before they were returned to Wickes for refurbishing. Augusta's account as Dowager Princess of Wales contains an entry dated 13 October 1759 for taking two kettle drums to pieces, 'poll^y ye drums & steel work refix^g d^o & furnishing 2 new drum sticks'.

In 1751, however, Frederick was busying himself with the Opposition, making no secret of his hopes of an early accession to the throne, when he was suddenly taken ill at the beginning of March. After getting wet and chilled working in his garden at Kew he had proceeded to London to attend a formal ceremony. The heavy regal robes he was required to wear left him so over-heated that on discarding them he sat in a light dressing gown by an open window to cool down. A short feverish illness followed from which he appeared to be recovering when an unexpected relapse occurred and he died on the 20 March 1750/1 fifteen days after the onset of his illness. An old injury from a cricket ball was said to have contributed to his death.

Frederick's faults were many, but at the end of the day Smollett could write of him with some truth as 'this excellent Prince ... a munificent patron of the arts, an unwearied friend to merit'. The magnificent wrought silver commissioned by him from Wickes which still survives is a fitting memorial to him.

Notes for chapter XII

1. Duchy of Cornwall Office, Household Accounts, Frederick Prince of Wales, Vol. V.
2. At some time in their history the candlesticks and the branches were separated. The candlesticks, fully hall-marked and engraved with the royal crest and the motto 'Ich Dien', were bought by Mr Thomas Lumley on the 8 May 1940 at a sale of silver belonging to the Trustees of Lord North. In order to save them from possible destruction during the bombing they were sent to Canada. Shortly after their departure Mr Lumley attended an auction of miscellaneous plated objects where he saw a pair of extremely fine branches for candelabra. Although they were unmarked, he was convinced they were silver; he was almost certain, moreover, that they matched the candlesticks made by Wickes for Lord North in 1731. He found on examining them that they too were engraved with the crest of the Prince of Wales and his motto 'Ich Dien'. He bid for them and was forced to pay dearly for the privilege since the underbidder, another dealer, believed them to be the work of Paul de Lamerie. It was six years before the candlesticks returned and Mr Lumley was able to justify his theory. The candelabra are now in a private collection in Britain.
3. This base may possibly have been the 'frame for plates' weighing 202 ounces which the Dowager Princess of Wales traded in, minus the plates (or dishes), on the 18 March 1758.
4. John, Lord Hervey, *Some Materials for the Memoirs of the Reign of George II*, ed. Romney Sedgwick.

5. Ibid. An account of the birth as described by Sarah, Duchess of Marlborough, in a letter to the Earl of Stair dated 17 August 1737, is far more charitable.

6. Alexander Pope, *Epistle to Dr Arbuthnot*, 1.309.

7. Wickes frequently used the word 'box' to describe a container, whatever its size or shape. A 'suger dish' recorded in 1740 becomes a 'sugar box' two lines later even though they are clearly one and the same object.

8. An entry in the Scarbrough Ledger dated the 31 May 1745 reads: 'To George Wickes bill for terreins & for a present . . . £235 12s 1d'. The sum in fact covered two tureens (with under dishes and ladles) and two bread baskets which had been delivered to the Prince in April 1744. This is the only reference in any of the ledgers to royal gifts. One of the bread baskets is now in the Morrison Collection, U.S.A. (see Fig. 98).

9. P.R.O.: PCC Prob 11/818–264

10. Michael Snodin, *English Silver Spoons*, pp. 10 & 46; Pl. 32.

11. Duchy of Cornwall Office, Household Accounts, Frederick Prince of Wales, Vol. VIII.

12. 'Rule Britannia' was first performed at a masque before Frederick in 1740.

13. Duchy of Cornwall Office, Household Accounts, Frederick Prince of Wales, Vol. VI.

100. Cup and salver, height of cup 14 in (35.5 cm); diameter of salver 13¾ in (35 cm). Cup unmarked, possibly George Wickes, *c*. 1738. Salver by Lewis Pantin, 1733. This exuberant rococo cup and cover, Frederick's gift to the City of Bath to commemorate his visit of 1738, has been the subject of much controversy. It is entered in Wickes's ledger, but many scholars believe it to be the work of Paul de Lamerie. *Courtesy of Bath City Council*

XIII   The Prince's Silver

Whilst most of the silver which Wickes fashioned for Frederick has long since been dispersed or melted down, many of the great pieces are still in the Royal Collection or in the care of museums and municipal authorities.

The Bath Cup is one such survivor. The commission must have come as something of a relief to Wickes. After an unending series of dreary royal repairs including 'boyling and burnishing' twenty-two pieces belonging to the drawing room in Norfolk House (£2 2s), eighteen sconces with double branches ('att 4s each') and twelve wrought candlesticks (10s 6d per pair), he records on the 27 January 1738/9 'a little strong plate box to go to Bath'. (It can hardly have been little, but the word is used to this day in Wickes's native Suffolk, invariably followed by the word 'old', when an object of interest is under discussion.) The plate box is followed on the 30 March 1739 with a one line entry:

> To a fine cup and cover and waiter guilt . . . 139 ozs 6 dwts
> . . . 15/- . . . £104 9s 6d

A case costing fifteen shillings accompanied it.

This can only refer to the 'beautiful gilt vase, richly embellished with the arms of his Royal Highness on one side and the arms of the City on the other, and his Highness's crest on the cover, all finely ornamented and interspersed with the fruit of the vine and its leaves: the handle composed of two snakes, whose tails are beautifully interwoven and twisted amidst the grapes and leaves. The waiter has also the arms of his Royal Highness on the fore part, with a border of Barroque work round it and the arms of the City on the back part, the whole of an entire new taste and much admired'. This description appeared in the *Gloucester Journal* on the 8 May 1739 following a report from Bristol dated 28 April referring to the plate which Richard [Beau] Nash had recently brought with him as a present from the Prince of Wales to commemorate his visit to Bath in 1738.[1]

The pieces (Fig. 100) are not only remarkable in themselves, but also for the controversy, decades old and still unabated, regarding the maker of the unmarked cup and cover. The salver, a somewhat strange companion piece, presents few problems: the maker's mark is clearly that of Lewis Pantin and it is hall-marked with the date letter for 1733, although the engraving of the armorials and, possibly, the intricate flat-chased inner border must have been added in 1739 and may have been the work of artists currently employed by Wickes. The salver, though supplied by Wickes, was patently not made by him. The cup, however, is generally accepted by scholars as the work of Paul de Lamerie since it invites close comparison with two similar cups made by him. But the high fashioning charge of fifteen shillings per troy ounce is entered not only against the Bath cup but also the salver, suggesting that they were both wrought by Wickes, though the salver must have been either purchased hurriedly from Pantin or have been in Wickes's stock, traded in, possibly, by a client and too finely made to melt down. The bill which Wickes sent to the Prince throws no light on the matter: in it the cup and salver are listed separately one above the other, but they are joined by a bracket and treated as a single entity for the purposes of weight, fashioning charge and price, just as they are in Wickes's ledger, though it is obvious that the fashioning of the cup must have been far more costly.

There is ample evidence that eighteenth century goldsmiths shared the services of the same modellers and may on occasion have used the same moulds. Wickes was certainly capable, technically, of making the intricately wrought Bath cup and it may well be that he did.

Its attribution to Paul de Lamerie is based on the naturalistic coiled serpents which formed the handles of a cup and cover executed by him in 1737 and now in the Collection of the Fishmongers' Company (Fig. 101). He made a slightly more elaborate copy of it in 1739 and both are conspicuous for their wealth of marine decoration: sea shells and fish scales are the principal motifs. The finial in each case is a bunch of grapes, an allusion perhaps to the original purpose of the cup as a vessel for wine.

The Bath cup has the same serpentine handles, but the realistic snakes' heads which are so striking a feature of de Lamerie's marked cups disappear behind the cast and applied armorials. There is a hint of rocaille in the chasing of the calyx, but the treatment of the foot is different, a restrained decoration replacing the shells and auricular masks of the original design. The lugubrious masks between the grapes and vine leaves at the base of the cover are obviously leonine whereas those on de Lamerie's cups are far more suggestive of sea monsters. In the sudden upsurge ending in the asymmetric and witty treatment of the stylized Prince of Wales's feathers there is, however, more than a hint of a wave breaking and were the cup itself a total failure it would be redeemed by that alone.

The case for Wickes as the maker rests uneasily on the fashioning

101. Cup and cover, silver-gilt, height 15 in (38 cm), Paul de Lamerie, 1737. This cup and cover is in the Collection of the Fishmongers' Company. An amity between the Fishmongers and the Goldsmiths dates back to mediaeval times and is preserved to this day. An almost identical serpent-handled cup and cover was made by de Lamerie in 1739. The Bath Cup, although unmarked, is so closely related that many scholars believe it to have come from the same hand. *Courtesy of the Worshipful Company of Goldsmiths*

102. Cup and cover, silver-gilt, height 18 in (45.7 cm), unmarked, c. 1740. This is the 'fine cheased gilt cup and cover' which Wickes delivered to Frederick, Prince of Wales, on the 24 January 1739/40. It has more affinity with the Bath Cup than with the two marked and dated serpentine-handled cups by de Lamerie which are remarkable for the consistency of their marine design motifs. *By gracious permission of Her Majesty the Queen*

charge entered against the piece in his ledger, which cannot be considered as conclusive since it also applied to Pantin's salver. The evidence, perversely, lies in the artistic inadequacy of the Bath cup. The incongruities, whilst not entirely uncharacteristic of de Lamerie in his more florid moments, are in sharp contrast to the calm harmony of the two marked and dated examples from his hand. These same incongruities are, for that matter, equally uncharacteristic of Wickes who was in his own way every bit as fine an artist as the Frenchman. It was, perhaps, a rushed order which left Wickes insufficient time to design and make from scratch a rococo cup which would satisfy the Prince and cause a sensation among the *haut ton* of Bath. De Lamerie could well have been fashioning a second serpent-handled cup which he was prepared to hand over, half finished, to a fellow goldsmith or he may have lent Wickes his snake moulds. Some time later he must have started work on his 1739 cup: bearing that date letter, it cannot have been ready for assay until after the 29th day of May of that year, by which time the Prince's cup had been presented to the City of Bath.

The Bath cup, coming between the 1737 and 1739 de Lamerie versions, can hardly be considered as a natural progression since for the 1739 cup de Lamerie reverted to the comparative simplicity of his original design, exercising a rare discipline which contrasts strangely with the extravagant conceit devised to flatter the City of Bath. It is perhaps not too fanciful to picture Wickes, thwarted of a proper opportunity, putting all his energies into the cover. The Prince's plumes curling over on themselves have a defiant quality quite unlike the rigid finial of the Pelham gold cup imposed upon Wickes by Kent's design in 1736.

The debate does not end here. A further 'fine cheased [chased] gilt cup and cover . . . 82 oz 4 dwts . . . 15/- [the identical fashioning charge] . . . £61 13s' is recorded in the Prince's account in Wickes's ledger against the date 24 January 1739/40. Undated and unmarked, this cup too has survived and is part of Frederick's legacy to the Royal Collection. The Prince's predilection for the rococo was well known, but it could scarcely have been carried to greater lengths than in this second cup and cover which may fairly be described as a riot of rocaille (Fig. 102).

The marine motifs begin at the finial of the high domed cover which is cast in the form of an infant Dionysus clutching a bunch of grapes and sitting athwart a rock encircled by a froth of foam. A band of chased rosettes follows and below it, round the rim, sea shells alternate with rams' heads. The entire surface of the cup itself is encrusted with marine ornament; shells of all kinds cling to both cup and cover, and miniscule limpets cling to the shells. Writhing through all this crustacea, more realistically modelled than ever before, are the serpents of Paul de Lamerie. Wreathed fantastically with the branches, stems, leaves and fruit of the vine, they form the handles and then coil around the body of the cup, one doubling back on itself to snatch at a cluster of grapes, the other emerging sinuously from a welter of sea shells.

It is with a sense of relief that the eye travels down to the rams' heads chased in high relief on the knop stem. Then the restless flow is resumed with a fluted swirl of silver which spirals up from a circular base decorated with vine leaves, shells and scrolled strapwork for good measure.

Like the Bath cup, the authorship of this exuberant piece is in dispute. It is entered in Wickes's ledgers, but generally accepted as the work of Paul de Lamerie. It is interesting to speculate whether the Prince played any part in its design, insisting in his wayward enthusiasm on the inclusion of almost every possible exotic rococo motif. Wickes might conceivably have blanched at the plethora of unrestrained ornament; de Lamerie, on the other hand, bearing in mind his tureen formerly in the Swaythling Collection, may have regarded it as an exercise in virtuosity, a challenge to his lively imagination and superior casting techniques.

It is only in recent times that Wickes has been considered as a serious rival to Paul de Lamerie. The latter was undeniably the greatest innovator of his day and to him must go the accolade for

103. Centrepiece made for Frederick, Prince of Wales, height 27 in (68.5 cm), Paul Crespin, 1741. Although marked with the punch of Paul Crespin, this centrepiece—the most important of Frederick's acquisitions—may well have been fashioned by the Liègois goldsmith Nicolas Sprimont. It has been described as 'the purest rococo creation in English silver'. *By gracious permission of Her Majesty the Queen*

having introduced the rococo taste in silver, already established in France, to the less adventurous English. Few goldsmiths have achieved his mastery of the rococo style or his fluency and inspiration and those few, for the most part, were fellow second-generation Huguenots.

The rococo pieces which bear Wickes's mark, unlike the serpent handled cups made for the Prince, have a quality which sets them apart. They lack the fantasy and sheer audacity of Huguenot work, but there is in its place a balance which would have helped to make the rococo style acceptable to the most conservative of eighteenth century collectors. He achieves, paradoxically, a harmony which does not detract from the flow and interplay which is the essence of the style; the movement is there and if it is not restless, it is always exciting. This may have evolved as a result of his early excesses, if, indeed the Prince's cups were by his hand. In spite of the need to keep pace with the Huguenots, Wickes could not deny his native instinct for a certain restraint. Notwithstanding, he was still in the van of the new style: his rivals, with the exception of de Lamerie, Crespin, Kandler and John Edwards, did not reach the height of their powers until the 1740s.

Paul Crespin's zenith was surely touched in 1741 with the superb marine centre-piece bearing his mark (Fig. 103) which has justly been described as 'the purest rococo creation in English silver'[2]. The breathtaking sublimity of its conception and the extraordinary skill which went into its execution must give it pride of place in Frederick's collection. No record of its acquisition is to be found in the Earl of Scarbrough's accounts and no bill for it survives in the Archives of the Duchy of Cornwall. The only clue lies in Wickes's ledger, but that must be regarded with the utmost reserve.

It consists of a cryptic entry in the Prince's account dated 24 June 1742—one month after the change of the assay date letter from 1741 to 1742—which reads as follows:

To a surtout compleat etc. £242 3s 6d

No fashioning charge is given nor is there any indication of its weight, the latter omission being in itself unusual. Lady Archibald Hamilton's name appears against the entry. It was rumoured that this middle-aged matron with ten children had replaced the notoriously fickle Anne Vane in Frederick's affections, but since the names of officials in the Prince's household figure constantly in his accounts, presumably as *aides-mémoire* to Wickes, the surtout is unlikely to have been destined to grace her table. In fact it was 'carried' almost immediately to the account of Frederick Ritzau (Wickes spells it 'Ritzo'), another member of the Prince's household. It appears under Ritzau's name—the only item in an account which was obviously opened for this express purpose—under the same date, 24 June 1742, and in the following terms:

To a surtout compleat etc	£242 3s 6d
To charge of shipping ye chest & bills of lading	7s 6d
	£242 11s 0d

There is no mention of the usual debenture which normally accompanied the export of wrought silver enabling the owner to recover the 6d per troy ounce duty exacted by the Excise at the time the piece was made.

The surtout, or centrepiece, was almost certainly not made by Wickes and, in the absence of any indication of its weight, the temptation to equate it with Crespin's *chef d'œuvre* must be treated with caution. An indefinable air of mystery seems to surround this *surtout à table*. It was obviously an exceptional object judging by its price, but if it was Crespin's masterpiece, to whom was it shipped and how did it find its way back to the Royal Collection?

There is a possibility that it was indeed the Poseidon centrepiece and that it was designed and made not by Crespin but by Nicholas Sprimont—then working in Liège—and smuggled into England to be punched with the maker's mark of Sprimont's friend Paul Crespin (already registered with the Goldsmiths' Company). After it had been assayed and hall-marked, meeting the requirements for sterling silver which were higher than those in most continental countries, it was shipped to Sprimont in Liège for finishing prior to being brought back again when he emigrated to England in 1742 and settled near Crespin in London. The theory that such an arrangement existed between Sprimont and Crespin was advanced by Mr Charles Oman as early as 1954,[3] based on the Liègois character of the centrepiece and its similarity in style to the hall-marked Sprimont sauce-boats of 1743 which are also in Frederick's collection and bear the maker's mark which Sprimont registered with the Goldsmiths' Company on the 25 January 1742/3. The possibility of this sponsorship of Sprimont by Crespin was further explored by Mr Arthur Grimwade in an article entitled 'Crespin or Sprimont? An unsolved problem of Rococo silver' (*Apollo*, August 1969). In the absence of designs bearing the signature of either or both makers, which could still come to light, the theory remains unproven and may yet provide ground for future research.

The appearance of the anonymous 'surtout compleat etc.' in Wickes's ledger, debited at first to the Prince then carried to the account of his servant Ritzau for immediate shipment abroad, implies complicity on the part of Frederick, Wickes and Ritzau in the machinations of Sprimont and Crespin. The whole affair may have been somewhat galling for Wickes. As a liveryman of the Worshipful Company of Goldsmiths, he must have been well aware that he was flouting the Hall's regulations. Although by 1742 the Huguenots were well established, resentment against the 'intrusion of foreigners' still smouldered and as late as February 1737 the General Committee of the Goldsmiths' Company was investigating whether foreigners might 'be excluded from the touch; and if not how they may be further charged in diet or money, for the touching of their plate'. As the Prince's appointed goldsmith, Wickes may have bemoaned the fact that Frederick had not set him to making such a piece, but more likely he accepted philosophically that the royal patronage could not be confined to Panton Street.

There is, unfortunately, no corroborative evidence in the Duchy of Cornwall Archives or in the Scarbrough Ledger. Ritzau settled Wickes's bill with two cash payments—one for £100, the other for £142—and both appear under the date 21 July 1742, though the second, judging by the ink, may have been made later. It would have been interesting had these two sums been recorded by the Earl's clerk as payments made by the Prince to Ritzau, but although the latter's name occurs constantly in the Treasurer General's accounts (linked almost invariably with the 'Secretaries Office'), the sums paid to him were blanket payments. If Frederick was involved, he may well have paid Ritzau privately out of his own pocket.[4]

It is worth noting that since the King had made it clear to foreign ambassadors that he desired them to have no contact with the Prince's court, Frederick is unlikely to have sent the surtout as a present abroad and no such gifts are recorded in his accounts. His links with Hanover were slight; his determination to become accepted as a Briton, even at the cost of severing all German connections, was well known; Hanover, moreover, was regarded by George II as his private pleasure ground. It is also doubtful whether Ritzau, who was from 1734 to 1745 Clerk to the Prince's Secretary, would have been in a position to indulge in such purchases in a private capacity. Had this been the case, the surtout would have been entered in his account from the outset and not transferred from that of the Prince.

The true authorship of the Poseidon centrepiece may be in doubt, but one thing is certain—Frederick's acquisition of 1742 far excelled his previous purchases. It behove Wickes to look to his laurels.

In June 1742, three days before the surtout was entered, a gilt basin and ewer costing £61 5s 6d appear in the Prince's account in Wickes's ledger joined by a bracket to the surtout: here again no weight is given and no fashioning charge shewn. Lady Archibald Hamilton's name is written against the joint order. Noting the price, these pieces could tally with the 'plate at Epsom Races—£63' recorded in the Earl of Scarbrough's ledger on the 24 May 1742, the slight increase in cost having been incurred by the engraving of a suitable inscription. There is no mention of Wickes in this transaction and the payment was in fact made to one William Hoskin, a minor member of the Prince's establishment whose name occurs in connection with the upkeep of horses and disbursements to coachmen. The Prince's settlement for the gilt basin and ewer purchased from Wickes appears in the royal account, in Netherton's handwriting, 6 July 1742, as 'cash per Lady Arch^d Hamilton'. The Earl of Scarbrough's meticulous clerk omitted this transaction, but, here again, it may have been concealed in one of the blanket payments regularly made to Lady Hamilton as an important salaried official in Frederick's household.

104. Christening basin and ewer made for Frederick, Prince of Wales, unmarked, *c.* 1735. Length of basin 18¼ in (46.5 cm), height of ewer 18½ in (47 cm). An inscription on the ewer attests that it was used at the christening of George III in 1738 and presented by Frederick to his wife Augusta. The inscription was added when the pieces were used for the baptism of Prince Alfred, son of George III, in 1780. *By gracious permission of Her Majesty the Queen*

An unmarked gilt basin and ewer (Fig. 104) have survived in the Collection of Her Majesty the Queen which could conceivably be those recorded by Wickes in 1742. An inscription engraved later in the century attests that 'this basin and ewer was used at the christening of George the Third at Norfolk House June 21st in the year 1738. Was presented on that occasion by his father Frederick Prince of Wales to the Princess of Wales and on the 17th of October 1780 was used at the christening of H.R.H. Prince Alfred son of George the Third'. It is unlikely that Wickes would have failed to enter such important royal pieces in his ledger for 1738, nor would he have waited four years before sending the Prince his bill. The absence of weight[5] and fashioning charge suggests that it was a special commission or a purchase from another goldsmith. Since it is clearly joined with a bracket to the 'surtout compleat', it is perhaps not unreasonable to postulate that the basin and ewer were from the same hand. The style of the objects places them nearer 1735 than 1742, but the demi-figure of Heracles slaying the Hydra which decorates the handle of the ewer is finely modelled: the Liègois favoured the gods of antiquity; could these have been early pieces by Sprimont which found favour with the Prince?

The legend that the ewer and basin had been given by Frederick to his wife on the occasion of the baptism of their first son[6] may have originated with Augusta (in an attempt to establish her ownership of the pieces) and perpetuated by George III who was very close to his mother. She died in February 1772, eight years before the birth of her grandson Alfred whose baptism is commemorated on the ewer.

George III's final rejection of Lord Bute—popularly regarded as the lover of the Dowager Princess—clouded her later years, but in 1780 the euphoria of a royal christening may have moved the sentimental king to record the history of the pieces as it was known to him. The inscription cannot predate that event and George III's armorials, cast and applied to both objects, were probably added at the same time.

By 1745 Frederick's financial position had improved and he ordered another gilt basin and ewer from Wickes which were delivered to him early in May. This time the weight—78 ozs 4 dwts—is recorded; the fashioning charge was 14s 2d; the total cost, including the engraving of armorials and a case, came to £58 15s. These pieces, surely high rococo by 1745, no longer apparently exist—they must have been given away or consigned to the melting pot by later princes. Their loss is the more regrettable because Wickes must have been then at the height of his powers and he had, moreover, to meet the standard imposed by the Crespin/Sprimont centrepiece.

The next commission was an important one consisting of three table pieces, all in silver gilt. Wickes recorded them, as a group, in the royal account on the 11 November 1745, the date presumably of their delivery since it coincides with that entered on the two bills submitted to the Prince.

The first bill lists the costs incurred in the making of the famous *épergne*, made to the design of William Kent, which after the Poseidon centrepiece is widely considered to be Frederick's most important contribution to the Royal Collection. The second bill covers two tureens complete with liners, under-dishes and ladles weighing in all 633 ozs 15 dwts and costing £456 14s 1d. The overall fashioning charge, including the gilding, was 14s 2d per troy ounce as opposed to 15s 8d for the *épergne*. Netherton was either nervous or careless when he made out the bill for the tureens, omitting the under dishes: he had included them in his ledger entry and since the total weights and the cost are identical it was obviously an oversight. This error may have been partly to blame for the lapse of eleven months between delivery and payment, but it is more likely that Frederick's habitual extravagance had outstripped his resources.

Unlike the *épergne*, the tureens have not survived. There is a possibility that they were intended to be displayed *en suite* with a centrepiece—perhaps the Poseidon one—in the manner of the celebrated integral set designed (and partly executed) by the great French *maître-orfèvre* Juste Aurèle Meissonnier for the Duke of Kingston (Fig. 105).

Whilst Meissonnier's original design was conceived in 1735, engravings of the Kingston ensemble do not seem to have been generally available until 1742. Frederick must surely have known,

105. Pair of Louis XV soup tureens made for the Duke of Kingston, Juste-Aurèle Meissonnier, Paris, 1734/36. These masterpieces of rocaille appear in a Meissonnier design which the great French goldsmith described as a 'Projet de sculpture en argent d'un grand surtout de table et les deux terrines qui ont eté executée pour le Millord Duc de Kinston [sic] en 1735'. The surtout does not appear to have been fashioned, a more modest one replacing it. Meissonnier published many other silver designs and his influence spread to England where the main exponents of the genre were the Huguenot goldsmiths. The Duke of Kingston was also a patron of George Wickes. *Courtesy of Christie's, Geneva*

however, of the existence of this masterpiece of rocaille, possibly as early as 1740 by which time the tureens had certainly been delivered to the Duke; the proud owner would have explained to him, moreover, that they were designed to flank a magnificent centrepiece, each object depending on the others for the ultimate effect.[7] Meissonnier's '*sculpture en argent*' was long in the making, and this may have deterred Frederick from going to the fountain head of eighteenth century rococo inspiration.

It may also have been the reason why the Duke of Kingston decided in April 1741 to transfer his patronage to Wickes. This decision cannot be attributed to the influence of the Duke's mistress Elizabeth Hervey through her appointment as maid of honour to Augusta, Princess of Wales, since this was made in 1743 and their notorious liaison did not begin until 1751. The Kingston account in Wickes's ledgers is disappointing: it contains no spectacular rococo pieces and consists mostly of repairs and purchases of a mundane nature. The only items of any interest are the chalice and cover entered in August 1746, one of the rare instances of church plate in the Ledgers.

The 1741 Poseidon centrepiece and the pair of Sprimont rocaille salts, hall-marked 1742, together with the same maker's set of four sauce-boats which bear the date letter for 1743, were possibly acquired in imitation of the Duke of Kingston's pieces. There is no record of these later objects in Wickes's ledger. The silver-gilt tureens which he himself made for the Prince in November 1745 may well have been rococo in style and destined to complement these pieces. They were, it is true, delivered at the same time as the Kent *épergne*, but the separate bills suggest that the three objects may not have been made as a set and the *épergne* was intended for quite another role.

It is difficult to reconcile the Kent *épergne* (Fig. 106), even without the later accretions, with the prevailing taste in 1745. As Horace

106. Centrepiece made for Frederick, Prince of Wales, width $29\frac{1}{8}$ in (74cm), George Wickes, 1745 (additions by John Bridge, 1829, and Robert Garrard, 1847). Wickes's original ethereal interpretation of Kent's design has almost vanished under the later accretions. Nothing, however, can detract from the superb engraving of the plateau. It is probable that Wickes was working on the piece before Vardy's engravings of Kent's designs were published (see Fig. 107). *By gracious permission of Her Majesty the Queen*

Walpole remarked, 'Kent's genius was not universal' and even the most ardent admirer of the great architect would be forced to admit that the design for the *épergne* with its uneasy alliance of baroque and quasi-rococo elements is not entirely felicitous. It is in fact redeemed by the brilliance of its execution, Wickes having achieved an ethereal effect with his delicate trellis work and small butterfly-winged terms, creatures from *A Midsummer Night's Dream* far removed from the stilted figures in the Vardy engraving (Fig. 107). The general lightheartedness of the fashioned object supports the theory advanced by Mr Arthur Grimwade[8] that the *épergne* with its 'arbour-like' canopy and lantern casters may well have graced the Prince's pavilion at Vauxhall, a conversation piece for the guests who attended his supper parties.

The *épergne* was not recognized as one of the Kent designs published by Vardy in 1744 until 1959 when Dr John Hayward identified it.[9] Unlike Colonel Pelham's gold cup and Lord Mountford's tureen, the centrepiece was obviously not designed by Kent for a specific client. Frederick may have been shewn the preliminary coloured drawing, now in the possession of the Royal Institute of British Architects, which was unpublished until Mr Charles Oman carried the investigation a step further[10] and posed some pertinent questions regarding the evolution of the piece. The Prince's architect could also have shewn the final design to the

Prince's goldsmith before Vardy's book went to press: both may have been instrumental in persuading him to commission the *épergne*, reinforcing their argument with the suggestion that the precariously perched tureen of the original design be replaced by the plume crest of the Prince of Wales.

Wickes must have spent several months working on this commission since the receipt of £300 'By cash on acc^t of the epargne' is recorded on the 23 August 1745. It was delivered—and entered in Wickes's ledger—on the 11 November 1745 and the balance owing, £395 14*s* 4*d*, was paid seventeen days later. The ledger description reads:

To a silver epargne a table
4 saucers 4 casters 8 branch
lights & 8 pegs 849 ozs 9 dwts   15/8   £662 5*s* 4*d*
To graving the table 4 saucers & casters   £26 16*s* 0*d*
To 6 glass saucers   £3 3*s* 0*d*
To 2 wainscott cases   £6 10*s* 0*d*

This tallies with the itemized bill presented to the Prince's Treasurer and Receiver General with the exception that the '8 branch lights' appear as '8 branches for candles'. Whereas an overall fashioning charge is entered in the ledger, this is broken down in the bill into 6*s* 2*d* for basic fashioning plus an extra 6*s* 6*d* for the intricate making and a further 3s for gilding, in all a total of 15s 8d per troy ounce.

It is strange that no contemporary allusions to the *épergne* have emerged from the letters exchanged between the gossips of the period. By any standards it is an exceptional piece of wrought silver and even the 'improvements' of George IV and Victoria cannot detract from the superb work of the unknown engraver on the base plate.

The *épergne* in its original elegant form was apparently no match for the grandiose pieces made for George IV by Rundell, Bridge and Rundell. In 1829 John Bridge was authorized to carry out extensive alterations, effectively destroying the symmetry and restraint achieved by Wickes. A lion and unicorn accompanied by two tritons plus four extra dishes and two candle branches were added to the plateau. The elaborate neo-rococo swags and festoons applied in 1847 were the work of Robert Garrard when the firm founded by Wickes succeeded Rundell, Bridge and Rundell as Royal Goldsmiths and Crown Jewellers between 1840 and 1842.

After making the silver-gilt tureens and the Kent *épergne*, Wickes went back to humdrum repairs and the 'boyling and burnishing' of the Prince's plate, interspersed with small domestic items such as the re-engraving and 'blacking ye letters' on eleven bottle tickets or wine lables. Pannakins, papboats and rattles marked the arrival of each new baby and orders were placed for a silver 'eye cup [bath]', stay hooks for the Princess and collars for innumerable royal dogs.

In the autumn of 1748 Frederick decided to augment his silver-gilt dinner service and Wickes was required to make twenty-eight dishes, six sauce boats and six 'saucespoons [small ladles],' six salts and spoons plus twelve salt glasses and twelve salad dishes. Twenty silver-gilt 'bells' were included in the order, each weighing $52\frac{1}{2}$ ounces, the English equivalent of the French *cloche* or domed dish cover. Pewter covers also appear in Wickes's ledgers: 34 in July 1752 were bought for a client direct from the pewterers at a cost of £21 8s.

Accustomed by now to erratic payment, Wickes may have requested an advance for Frederick signed an 'imprest warrant', addressed to his 'trusty and right welbeloved cousin Thomas Earl of Scarbrough', stating 'our will and pleasure is that you pay or cause to be paid without fee or deduction unto Mr George Wickes silversmith the sum of one thousand pounds by imprest on account in part for gilt plate to be made for our service'. It will be noticed that whilst he has always before been referred to as 'George Wickes silversmith', the prefix 'Mr' is now used. This was not customary even with craftsmen of Wickes's standing and it suggests that he had attained a position which commanded a certain amount of respect.

108. Last trade-card of Wickes and Netherton, 1751. When Wickes and Netherton printed their first joint trade-card in November 1750 they proudly proclaimed themselves goldsmiths to the Prince of Wales. His untimely death in March 1751 caused them to issue a new one adding the name of the Princess Dowager of Wales to that of her young son, the future George III. *Courtesy of the Archives Department, Westminster City Libraries*

109. First trade-card of John Parker and Edward Wakelin, 1760. This trade-card differs only very slightly from the one used by Wickes and Netherton from 1751 to 1760. *Courtesy of the Trustees of the British Museum*

The plate was delivered on the 14 February 1748/9. The silver weighed 5,098 ozs 8 dwts; the gilding added a further 453 ozs 6 dwts; the total cost was £1,532 3s 6d. Wickes's bill of the same date included a further £124 14s 6d for the 'setting to rights' and regilding of a parcel of plate which he had supplied on a previous occasion. One thousand pounds had already been paid by imprest, but Wickes had to wait seven months before receiving the £656 18s which was still outstanding.

After this order for silver-gilt the demands on Wickes dwindled, the only sizeable items being a 'table' (tray), a waiter and a bread basket in October 1750. Two red leather cases were supplied with this order.

On the 7 March 1750/1 Wickes delivered to the Prince a marrow spoon. It was to be the last piece he would make for Frederick who died thirteen days later.

The dismay in Panton Street at the unexpected death of the Prince must have been considerable. Wickes and his associates Netherton and Wakelin could reasonably have expected an appointment as Goldsmiths to the King when Frederick succeeded George II and their hopes had now to be pinned on the new heir to the throne, Prince George, then a mere boy of thirteen. The young Prince of Wales was reputed to be a backward child of poor physique, very much under the influence of his mother, now the Dowager Princess. She continued to patronize Wickes and his new partner Netherton as shewn by the entries dated 11 July 1751 for a silver pannakin, papboat and rattle for the Princess Caroline Matilda, who was born after Frederick's death. Anticipating the baby's teething troubles, a coral was also ordered: the age-old belief in the magic properties of colour still obtained: smooth red coral for inflamed gums as red flannel is used as a specific for sore throats.

The future George III assumed responsibility for the needs of his siblings and his name was added to that of his father in the alphabetical index at the front of the ledger so that two Princes of Wales are entered on that page.

At this point Wickes and Netherton changed their trade card, replacing the one they had had printed in November 1750. This, their last card (Fig. 108), describes them as 'Goldsmiths & Jewellers, Silversmiths to their Royal Highnesses the Prince and Princess Dowager of Wales'. Sprays of flowers were introduced into the new design which was still dominated by the royal arms, prominent in their first joint card. Mr Charles Oman has attributed this design to the unknown artist who engraved the plateau of the Kent *épergne* as well as the armorials on the punchbowl made for the Prince in 1750 and now in the possession of the Victoria and Albert Museum.

The new royal account started promisingly with 'a terrine and cover', accompanied by a ladle, delivered on the 31 May 1751. This was followed by nine 'nerl'd [gadrooned] dishes'. Thereafter it deteriorated into engraved plates for dog collars and spurs, buckles and buttons for the Prince and his brothers. Wickes was frequently required to mend and 'colour' a 'gold George'[11] for each of them and there is mention of 'an onyx George'. The only items of interest were a tea kettle (with a lamp but without a waiter on which to stand it), an agate box mounted in gold for Prince Edward and a gadrooned inkstand, all delivered between May and September 1752.

The next eight years brought only trifling purchases and mundane repairs, including '2 sponges fix'd to ye handles of tonguescrapers'. The account petered out, the last entry being dated 30 May 1760. The Clients' Ledger for the following five years is missing from the Garrard Collection, but it is unlikely that the Prince on his accession to the throne as George III on the 25 October 1760 continued to patronize the firm.

Parker and Wakelin had clearly not anticipated the death of George II and their first trade card (Fig. 109) must have been ready to circulate as soon as they took over the business on 11 October 1760. Almost identical to the second card issued by Wickes and Netherton after the death of Frederick Louis in March 1751, it proudly

110. Second trade-card of John Parker and Edward Wakelin, 1761. The death of George II and the accession of his grandson removed from the firm the royal patronage enjoyed since 1735. Parker and Wakelin were forced to abandon their first trade-card; its successor is very different in design. *Courtesy of the Archives Department, Westminster City Libraries*

proclaimed them too as 'Silversmiths to their Royal Highnesses the Prince and Princess Dowager of Wales': like the first joint card of their predecessors it must have had a short life. The coveted warrant as goldsmith to the King was bestowed on Thomas Heming (at 'The King's Arms' in Bond Street) and Parker and Wakelin were forced to redesign their card. They retained the King's Arms, which had always been their shop sign, framing them and the text in heavily fringed drapes ending in tassels (Fig. 110). There is no mention of a royal appointment, even to the Dowager Princess of Wales. Eighty years were to pass before the royal warrant returned to the firm founded by Wickes, by which time it was in the hands of Robert Garrard.

Notes for chapter XIII

1. Llewellyn Jewitt and W. H. St John Hope, *The Corporation Plate and Insignia of Office of the Cities and Towns of England and Wales*, Vol. 11, page 296.
2. Arthur Grimwade, *Rococo Silver*, page 30.
3. Charles Oman, *Catalogue of an Exhibition of Royal Plate from Buckingham Palace and Windsor Castle 1954*.
4. The Earl of Scarbrough's Ledger records from time to time large payments 'To His Royal Highness own hands per signification being to discharge some debts formerly contracted for money lent'. The payment of Ritzau may well have been one of these unspecified debts.
5. The present weight of these pieces—ewer 78 ozs and basin 83 ozs—inevitably includes the cast and applied armorials which were added later. On the hypothesis that they may in fact be the pieces entered in Wickes's ledger in 1742, it is possible, by dividing the sum entered (£61 5s 6d) by the weights given above, to conjecture that the fashioning charge would have been approximately 7s 8d per troy ounce overall, i.e. half the fashioning cost of the Bath Cup and Salver. Taking the basic cost as 6s per ounce, the price for making and gilding would be £12 19s 6d, a not unreasonable sum considering that the pieces were comparatively simple.
6. There is no mention of the vessels used on this occasion in the Lord Chamberlain's Records. The plate issued to William Westphal, Yeoman of the Pantry and Ewry, for 'the christening of the young Princess' on the 29 August 1737 consisted of 'one gilt font and bason' and 'two gilt tankards'. No weight is given, but for subsequent royal christenings in 1763, 1765, 1766 and 1767 the same pieces were apparently used and in each case the weight is shewn as 913 ounces (P.R.O.: LC9/45 f. 62).
7. Henry H. Hawley, 'Meissonnier's Silver for the Duke of Kingston', *The Bulletin of the Cleveland Museum of Art*, Vol. LXV No. 10 December 1978.
8. Arthur Grimwade, *Rococo Silver*, page 32.
9. 'A 'Surtoute' designed by William Kent', *The Connoisseur*, March 1959.
10. 'Silver Designs' by William Kent, *Apollo*, January 1972.
11. The 'George' was the pendant on the Order of the Garter.

Epilogue

The eleventh day of October 1760 marked the end of an era. The firm was handed over to Parker and Wakelin and Wickes finally left London for the estate he had acquired in Thurston, Suffolk, a few miles from his birthplace, Bury St Edmunds.

Samuel Netherton chose to retire with him even though he was only thirty-seven at the time, eleven years older than his cousin John Parker and seven years younger than Edward Wakelin. As Wickes's partner since 1750, his responsibilities could well have eventually increased to such an extent that they became a burden to him. His personal feelings for George and Alder Wickes no doubt influenced his decision. Since his arrival in their household at a tender age the childless couple had treated him like a son, one, moreover, who had remained at their side for over twenty-six years. Nothing is known of Wickes's state of health in 1760, but it may have been steadily deteriorating and Netherton could have known that Wickes was a sick man with only a short time to live.

The family circle was dwindling: Wickes's last surviving sister, Mary Skurray, died at the end of March 1756 and his remaining brother James followed her a few days later. In August 1759 Alder buried her sister Mary in St Michael Bassisshaw, the parish church of the Phelpes family. The ties between them had been close and there is ample proof that she held Wickes and his relatives in some affection: theirs was an age where the extended family was accepted as natural and normal. Plans may in fact have been made for her to join her sister and brother-in-law in their retirement. She had spent two years in their household in Panton Street from September 1749 prior to her move to a rural retreat in Kensington. Whilst under her brother-in-law's roof she was charged fifteen pounds a quarter for her board, four times the sum allowed for that of an apprentice—Wickes and his immediate family fared well. He attended to all her various business affairs, collecting rents and settling bills and taxes, even paying 'a chaer woman for scouring' a house.

Wickes's choice of Thurston as his retirement home may have been made as early as 1752. In March of the previous year he had advanced the sum of £1,200 to his second cousin the Reverend Eyton Butts, the eldest son of the Bishop of Ely. The terms of the loan are set out in Wickes's handwriting (which rarely appears in the Ledgers at this period) in Eyton Butts's account in the following terms:

> twelve hundred pounds and have given up all his bond^s and notes— and I have excep^d as a securety a morgage of two farms in Suffolk and a sing [?single] bond for the said sume w^t three numbers in the Amicable Society.

The entry is dated 25 March 1751. Alder Wickes's account in the Ledgers from 1771 (the earliest available record) reveals that her contacts with the Amicable Society were maintained until her death when they were transferred to Samuel Netherton.

The mortgage accepted by Wickes as security for the loan to Eyton Butts is almost certainly the one which Bishop Butts settled on his son in a codicil to his will dated 13 November 1747 which reads:

> I do hereby give and bequeath to my son Eyton Butts the sum of nine hundred and forty-six pounds now placed out in a mortgage upon the estate of my sister Blackbourn [née Philippa Butts] in Thurston in the county of Suffolk together with the further sum of one hundred and fifty-four pounds being the sum intended by me for the purchase of the estate together with the further sum of twenty pounds to defray the charge of taking up the said estate which legacy of eleven hundred and twenty pounds or estate if I should live to compleat the purchase of the same I give my to my [sic] said son Eyton Butts.

The will was proved in the Prerogative Court of Canterbury on the 1 February 1747/8.[1]

The Hearth Tax Returns for 1674 shew that one George Blackbone owned a four hearth house in Thurston. The tax was universally resented and led to widespread concealment and falsified returns. George Blackbone, or Blackbourn, may have owned a far larger house with many more hearths than the relatively modest dwelling conjured up by the Hearth Tax Returns. In 1727 a certain George Blackbourn—the son of a father of the same name who died in 1707 and was buried at Thurston—left all his freehold and copyhold land in Thurston to his wife, formerly Philippa Butts: this then was the estate mortgaged to her brother the Bishop of Ely.

In 1750, when his name first appears in the Ledgers, the Reverend Eyton Butts, Rector of Snailwell in Cambridgeshire, was thirty-one years of age. He was clearly a man who lived above his income and he turned to Wickes for money to pay his creditors. Between 19 June and 9 August 1750 the goldsmith settled thirteen outstanding bills and accepted in return his cousin's bond for £304. Undeterred, Eyton

Butts proceeded to incur further and larger debts which by 25 March 1751 had mounted to £1,200.

One debt is of particular interest since it concerns a Peter Rogers of Bury St Edmunds, a goldsmith who was also patronized by the Earl of Bristol. Rogers was the master of George Coyte. A boyhood friend of the painter Thomas Gainsborough, Coyte had left Suffolk for London and was probably the goldsmith who is traditionally believed to have sheltered the young Gainsborough when he arrived in the metropolis.[2] Coyte's portrait by Gainsborough is now in the John G. Johnson Collection in Philadelphia. Caroline Butts, sister to the Reverend Eyton Butts, had married Gainsborough's first cousin the Reverend Henry Burrough in 1750. Like Gainsborough's mother, the wife of Eyton Butts was born Mary Burrough, but she appears to have stemmed from a different line.

Eyton Butts's brother Robert, who also entered the Church, was equally improvident. Wickes lent him money at 5% per annum interest in June 1751 and took as security 'his plate to the value of £104 13s for the principall and interest of ninty six pounds 17:6 . . . and agreed to keep it two years and then to sell it for the most I can get and after paying my self principle [sic] and intrest & exspences to repay the ballance to him or his ex^{rs} if any remains'. A further note in Wickes's handwriting refers to another transaction 'for securerty of which sume I have one brilliant diamond hoop ring and a motto ring with a single brill^t diamond valued at about fifteen pounds, which I formerly sold to Mr. Butts at £20, as appears by his acc^t in my smale ledger'. That small ledger, missing from the Collection, would no doubt have revealed many such transactions for the spendthrift sons of the Bishop of Ely.

Not content with running up debts, the Reverend Eyton Butts ran foul of the Law and Wickes notes the payment 'to the Sheriff of Suffolk' of 'a post fine on Thurston due from Mr E Butts on his passing a fine . . . 15s'. A further £10 19s is entered as being paid to a Mr Grigbey in connection with 'a bill of charges for Mr E Butts for copy hold lands to make the securety good'. A year's interest on £1,200 at 5% added another £60 bringing the total owed to Wickes to £1,271 14s. An entry dated 12 October 1752 would seem on first sight to have restored Eyton Butts to solvency and enabled him to reclaim his mortgage: he is credited with two cash payments, one for £1,200, the other for £71 14s. There is, however, the possibility that the twelve hundred pounds was paid not by Eyton Butts but by Wickes who had agreed to purchase his cousin's rights in the estate at Thurston. The entry on the contra side was necessary because the loan had in fact been made by the firm (Wickes & Netherton) and put through the firm's books. In order to balance the books Wickes would have had to reimburse the partnership. In the absence of a deed of title, this hypothesis cannot be proved, but shortly afterwards the Reverend Eyton Butts removed himself to Ireland where he became a protégé of the Bishop of Derry, apparently severing all connection with Suffolk.

Wickes, for his part, acquired at some time prior to the 22 March 1761 (the date of his will) 'freehold and copyhold estates . . . situate lying and being in Thurston and Rougham [an adjoining village] or either of them in the County of Suffolk'.

Whilst the formal transfer of the firm to Parker and Wakelin was dated 11 October 1760, Wickes may have moved to Thurston before that date. The joint makers' mark of the new partners was entered in the missing Large Plate Workers' Book which covered the period 30 September 1759–7 March 1773. Proof that it was registered some-time between 30 September 1759 and 28 May 1760 lies in the date letter for 1759/60 which was found on twelve gadrooned plates bearing their mark which were auctioned by Christie's on the 31 March 1976 (lot 104). Since this date letter covered the assay year 29 May 1759–28 May 1760, Parker and Wakelin were clearly working as partners prior to October 1760 when Wickes finally relinquished the reins.

Wickes could then have removed his household to Suffolk sometime in 1759, possibly returning to London at intervals to deal with the legal aspects of the transfer. He may have left his country house in the charge of his sister-in-law Elizabeth, the widow of his brother James: when she remarried in 1758 the licence described her as 'widow of Thurston'—the bondsman was George Wickes.

Elizabeth entered the Wickes family in 1752 when as a widow of thirty-five she married George's sixty year old widower brother James in Ely Chapel, Holborn, the church chosen by Wakelin and Netherton for their nuptials. James died on the 4 April 1756 leaving Elizabeth his business as a vintner and, for the term of her life, the land in Charsfield, Suffolk (valued at £400) bequeathed to him in 1745 by his maternal aunt Rebecca Burton. His will[3] ends on a rueful note: 'I am sorry I can't leave my wife in better circumstances she gave me her fortune'. His widow's new husband, Orbell Ray, came from an old Suffolk banking family. According to a memorial stone erected in St Mary's Church, Bury St Edmunds, he was 'one of the capital burgesses of this burgh'. He had already buried two wives and at the time of his marriage to Elizabeth Wickes he was fifty and she forty-one. No doubt they formed part of the circle which Wickes and his wife joined, with Netherton, on their retirement. So devoted was Elizabeth Wickes Ray to Netherton that on her death in 1791 she bequeathed to him the bulk of her estate.

An indication that Wickes and his wife were probably in Thurston in the summer of 1759 comes from an unexpected source, the Calendar or Index of wills proved in the Prerogative Court of Canterbury. It was customary to note the county of the testator and in the case of Mary Phelpes, Alder's sister, this is given, somewhat surprisingly, as Suffolk: her will, made in 1755, gives her domicile as Kensington in the county of Middlesex. She may have died whilst on a visit to her sister or she may have been living with them at Thurston in 1759.

Another will,[4] that of Mrs Catherine Purt [née Butts], of Bury St Edmunds, made in August 1758 names 'Mr George Wickes who I hope will be my executor'. The testator was seventy-five years old at the time and her holograph testament—which must be one of the most endearing of all time—whilst rich in human interest is lacking in essential detail: she makes no mention of Wickes's location. All the other people listed in her will lived near her in Suffolk with the possible exception of Wickes's niece Mary Skurray who is placed third after George and Alder at the head of a long muster roll of relatives and friends. An orphan since 1756, Mary may have joined Wickes's household. He as executor would have been hard put to it had he been required to settle the estate and arrange the funeral from London—'twenty pounds to be laid out . . . a sone coffin [sic] to put over my grave'—and it is possible that by 1758 he was already easing himself into retirement and dividing his time between Thurston and Panton Street. He is, moreover, referred to as 'Mr George Wickes' and not 'George Wickes, goldsmith'—the translation to country gentleman was well under way.

The old lady was his mother's first cousin and it is interesting that she should have treated him with such deference, hoping somewhat timidly that he would act as executor and diffidently offering 'Mrs Alder Wickes a ring & all my cheany [china] if worth her excepting'.

Judging by the names scattered through Catherine Purt's testament, the Wickes household was unlikely to have been short of company in an age when country dwellers counted on visits for their chief source of amusement. There were no less than six unmarried daughters of the Bishop of Ely as well as his youthful widow now remarried, albeit unhappily, to Mr George Green.

As the brother-in-law of the third baronet, the late Sir Dudley Cullum, Wickes would have had an entrée to the homes of the Cullum family in Hawstead and Hardwick. Sir Dudley's heir Sir Jasper Cullum was succeeded in 1754 by his son John who was two years younger than Wickes. Elizabeth Ray was certainly on intimate terms with the Cullum family later in the century and when she made her will in 1791 she left Lady Mary Cullum a cabinet in her parlour 'with all the china upon it' whilst her husband Sir Thomas Gery Cullum received a 'scarf hatband and gloves of the best sort' as mourning.

Without documentary evidence, the earliest tentative date for Wickes's removal to Suffolk is 1758. The actual year and the circumstances would certainly have emerged from a study of his personal and family accounts, but these were kept separate from those of his clients in the 'smale little book' which he kept in his desk. His sisters-in-law, Dorothy Wale and Mary Phelpes, were, however, treated as clients and their accounts give a clear idea of the value of the property held by the three sisters which passed in its entirety to Alder on the death of Mary in 1759.

Up until the autumn of 1759 Alder had owned a moiety or half share in the Phelpes lands in Chaceley, being with Mary 'one of the co-heiresses at law' of their late sister Dorothy Wale. On Mary's death Alder not only became the Lady of the Manor of Chaceley but also the owner of the two houses in Basinghall Street which their grandfather Samuel Phelpes I had built in the City of London after the Great Fire. In the event of Alder predeceasing her husband, Wickes was to inherit all Mary's property with the proviso that on his death the two City houses should return to the Phelpes family to be shared between the three children of her cousin. Over and above this considerable property, Mary bequeathed to her 'loving sister Alder' all her jewels (many of them bought from Wickes and itemized in his ledgers) and 'one thousand pounds which together with all interest thereof I will she may enjoy for her own sole and separate use so as not to be subject to the debts controul or engagements of her husband George Wickes'. Were it not for the generous provisions for her property to pass to Wickes should he outlive her sister and the affectionate bequests to his relatives, this clause might have suggested some antipathy to her brother-in-law. A married woman had no rights in the eighteenth century and her property usually passed automatically into the control of her husband. Wickes must have amassed a considerable fortune from his business as a goldsmith, but he may have kept a tight hold on the purse strings. Since a large amount of Phelpes and Aldworth money must have gone into his coffers, the sisters may have derived a certain amusement from reminding him occasionally of his indebtedness. As a wealthy spinster, Mary enjoyed far greater freedom than her sister and a thousand pounds for her own exclusive use restored the balance a little and was no doubt appreciated by Alder. Netherton, who, with James Wickes, was one of the trustees named, was left £50. Wickes's sister Mary Skurray also received £50 and her two daughters, Mary and Alder Rachael, 'ten pounds each to be laid out in cloathes for them as soon as they shall

111. Inkstand, width $11\frac{1}{2}$ in (29.2 cm), Edward Wakelin, 1755. This inkstand is engraved with the arms of Martin impaling Jackson. John Martin of Overbury represented the Borough of Tewkesbury in Parliament. He was married to Katherine, née Jackson, a Bristol cousin of Alder Wickes. *Courtesy of Christie's*

come out of their apprenticeships'.[5] She made generous provision for her personal maid and left 'five pounds each for mourning' to 'all the men and maid servants who may be then living with my said sister Wickes'. A further ten pounds was set aside for the Poor of Chaceley and her cousin Mrs Catherine Martin of Overbury[6] (Fig. 111) was left a cabinet inlaid with mother of pearl.

Mary Phelpes's will was dated 2 March 1755 (a codicil of the 23 January 1758 was witnessed by Netherton) and proved by Alder Wickes, the sole executrix, in the Prerogative Court of Canterbury on the 12 December 1759, some four months after Mary's burial.[7] If Alder was at that time living in Thurston the obtaining of administration would have necessitated a visit to London and it is perhaps significant that the last entry made in Wickes's handwriting in the Ledgers is dated 14 December 1759, proof that he was certainly in Panton Street on that particular day.

All was set fair for a peaceful retirement for Wickes away from the stress and strain of Panton Street. His wealth would have ensured his material comfort. The Thurston property was described in 1751 as consisting of two farms: the larger of the two farm houses was probably used as their dwelling and the two farms amalgamated into a home farm to supply them with dairy produce. His wife was there to act as hostess to a large circle of friends and relatives and, moreover, enjoyed some status in her own right. The faithful Netherton was still at his side and his two young nieces no doubt enlivened the household from time to time.

Wickes was not to enjoy this enviable state of affairs for long. Some idea of the state of his health and the date of the onset of the disease which killed him might have been gleaned from payments to apothecaries had the first clients' ledger of Parker and Wakelin survived. Accounts for Alder Wickes and Netherton were kept in later ledgers and there must have been one for Wickes himself up to the time of his death, if only to keep a record of the rent paid to him by the new partners as well as the interest payments on his loan. He possibly knew the end was near in March 1761 when he summoned John Parker to witness his will. Parker may have brought him the news of the appointment of Thomas Heming as goldsmith to the King. This must have been a bitter blow to Wickes. Had his old patron Frederick Louis succeeded to the throne, Parker and Wakelin would have been the natural choice. They had, moreover, served the youthful George III for nine years when he was Prince of Wales with very little reward and might reasonably have hoped for future preferment. The new monarch had little feeling for the Arts and, unlike his father, may not have regarded the choice of a goldsmith as a matter requiring serious deliberation.

Parker was accompanied by his sister Ann whose signature, almost as elegant as that of her brother, appears beneath his at the foot of Wickes's last will and testament. Ann had left Longdon in order to be with her brother in London; he did not marry until 1766 and Ann probably kept house for him and was by this time the new châtelaine of Panton Street.

Wickes's will[8] which bears the date 22 March 1761, is a cold document. It begins, perfunctorily, with the customary 'In the Name of God Amen' and proceeds to proclaim that it is the last will and testament of George Wickes of Thurston in the County of Suffolk, Gentleman.

Wickes tells us nothing about himself—he even disdains to make the usual assurance that he was of sound mind. The will, which was obviously drawn up by a lawyer's clerk, is concerned only with his property and possessions and not a hint of human warmth shines through the legal jargon of the time.

After the payment of his just debts and funeral expenses, he devised all the land he owned to his 'loving wife Alder Wickes' for the term of her natural life; after her death it was to pass to his niece Mary Skurray and 'her heirs and assigns for ever'. Mary was required to pay out of this inheritance two annuities, one of thirty pounds to her sister Alder Rachael and another of forty pounds to her uncle's 'worthy friend Samuel Netherton'. Both nieces were to receive five hundred pounds each, but here again not until Alder Wickes had died (they had to wait thirteen years before enjoying their inheritance and by that time Alder Rachael Skurray was dead). The will concludes: 'all the rest residue and remainder of my estate and effects not herein otherwise by me given or disposed of as well real as personal which I shall dye seized or possessed of or anywise entitled to of what nature kind or quality soever the same shall or may consist I give devise and bequeath unto my said dear wife whom I do hereby make ordain constitute and appoint sole executrix'.

The rest, residue and remainder was probably considerable. It would have included dividends from shares, the rent from Panton Street and the 5% interest per annum on the £1,800 which Wickes lent to Parker and Wakelin in 1760 as well as the capital (which was repaid in June 1772). The contents of the house were thereby bequeathed to Alder and, more importantly, the silver. Wickes must have possessed a quantity of plate, some surely from his own hand, but no pieces bearing his mark and engraved with his assumed armorials have come to light. Paintings are mentioned in Alder's will: the 'eight pictures as they are now hanging in the back parlor in my dwellinghouse'—they were probably family portraits collected by Wickes—were left to her husband's niece Mary, whilst the remainder (in the front parlour and the other rooms in the house, presumably) were bequeathed to Netherton.

Apart from the annuity to Netherton, payable after Alder's death, Wickes left nothing to his erstwhile apprentices. There were no remembrances for old friends, no mourning for relatives, no mourning rings. Servants were unrequited and the poor of the parish ignored. There may have been an understanding between Wickes and his wife that she should repair these omissions, but lacking such provisions the will emerges as starkly materialistic, in sharp contrast to those of Edward Wakelin and William Tayler who remembered with affection their old companions from Panton Street. John Parker left no will, but the note he made in his own handwriting five months before he died left clear instructions to his son (including bequests to his successors in the firm) and gives the impression of a warm human being.

Wickes may have made an undertaking to his wife that in return for the capital she had poured into his business he would amply recompense her should she outlive him—if so, he kept his promise.

George Wickes died at Thurston on the 31 August 1761 and was buried in St Peter's, the parish church, seven days later. An obituary notice was eventually published in *The Gentleman's Magazine*: 'Monday, Aug. 31st. Geo. Wickes, Esq. of Therston, Suffolk'. It is perhaps a commentary on the eighteenth century that no one saw fit to mention that he had been one of the greatest goldsmiths of his day.

Alder must have found life in Suffolk congenial for she continued to live in Thurston for the next thirteen years with Netherton in constant attendance. Her manor in Worcestershire held little attraction for her: she appears to have entrusted its management to John Parker's elder brother Thomas whose family estate was adjacent to her own. He farmed his own lands *in absentia*, preferring to live in the City of Worcester where he practised as an attorney. She received £90 a year in rents from Chaceley, less £23 6s 6d deducted for unspecified taxes.

Since the ledger containing the early accounts of Alder Wickes and Netherton is missing, there is no documentation until 1771. Netherton might have been expected to take over the handling of their affairs, but in fact this was done by the firm in London. As a result it is possible to learn a little about the life they led in Thurston. Certain delicacies were obviously unobtainable locally and 'cordial confection' and bottles of Hungary Water and Usquebaugh (whiskey) were frequently sent down to Thurston. Alder Wickes is debited with regular sums paid to Pontet for rolls of tobacco (4/- per pound) and to Teale for snuff. Netherton's account contains payments to grocers and cheese merchants as well as one to 'Twinings for 2 lbs tea & cannisters . . . £1 13s' in August 1772. He appears, like Samuel Pepys, to have been particular about the candles he used, patronizing 'Vere yᵉ Tallow Chandler' for certain items and Barret for 'mortar wax lights'. One dozen packs of playing cards cost him 18/- in 1772 suggesting interminable hours spent at Thurston in card games.

Whilst these provisions were being despatched to Suffolk, supplies from there were sent back to Parker and Wakelin in London, possibly the produce of Alder's home farm. Both men received regular consignments of butter, presumably well salted as it was bought by the firkin (56 lbs to the firkin as each noted in his account) at a cost of £1 13s per firkin.

It is impossible to pinpoint the date when Elizabeth Meade Smith, spinster, joined the household at Thurston. The first apparent reference to her occurs in May 1770 when an entry in Wakelin's personal account concerns 'a gold box locket wᵗʰ diamᵈˢ & rubys (was Miss Meads) . . . £1 16s'. She is more positively identified in November 1771 when Netherton's account is credited with £78 3s 2d 'by cash pʳ Mr Thoˢ Parker on acct of Miss Elizabeth Meade Smith'.

A memorandum found in John Parker's personal papers lists the birth dates of members of his family circle. Samuel Netherton is placed immediately after Ann Parker and under his name appears that of 'John Smith (brotherlaw) [sic]' followed by 'Mrs Netherton (Eliz Mead Smith)' born on the 12 July 1730. John Smith, of the City of Worcester, married Parker's sister Mary in 1751. Whilst the juxtaposition of two people with the same surname may be nothing more than a coincidence, the supposition that Elizabeth was the sister of John Smith is perhaps not entirely unreasonable, particularly as a lease of land in the City of Worcester made to her in 1762 had formerly been held by a John Smith; it was transferred to Netherton after her marriage.

Whatever her origins, she was described as 'of Thurston' in the parish register when she married 'Samuel Netherton, Esq. Wdr.' by licence at St Peter's Church on the 23 July 1772. Alder Wickes was by this time an old woman. Had she been born, like Wickes, in 1698, she would have been seventy-four in 1772, but it is possible that she was his elder by several years. Elizabeth Meade Netherton may have been invited to Thurston for a visit and stayed on as companion to Alder to be entrusted later with the running of the house and the supervision of the servants. Samuel Netherton would scarcely have married a menial housekeeper and the union may well have been a match arranged by Alder—perhaps with the aid of John and Thomas Parker. Knowing her years were numbered, she would have been anxious to ensure Samuel's comfort and wellbeing, particularly since he would have to vacate Thurston on her death and make a new life for himself in Worcestershire. Elizabeth's roots were in that county and she must have seemed an ideal candidate. George Wickes had made it clear in his will that his property at Thurston was devised to Alder for the term of her life only, passing after her death to his niece, now Mrs George Fleming. It may have long been understood between them that Samuel's inheritance and ultimate reward would be Hill End House at Chaceley and the manor lands, together with all that was left of the 'rest residue and remainder' of Wickes's estate which had been left unconditionally to his widow.

When it became apparent to Alder that her death and Samuel's consequent removal to Worcestershire were close, she may have exerted pressure on him to marry Elizabeth Meade Smith. The bride was forty-two and the groom almost forty-nine; he had been a widower for seventeen years. Four months after their marriage Alder had a new will[9] drawn up revoking all previous ones. Dated 30 November 1772, it was made on the day after Samuel's birthday. All her estate, real and personal, was bequeathed to Netherton, 'his heirs and assigns for ever', with the exception of the eight paintings already mentioned and all her 'wearing apparel cloathes and wearing linnen' which she left to Elizabeth Meade Netherton. Like her husband before her, she made no bequests to friends or servants and left nothing to the Poor of Chaceley or Thurston. Netherton was named sole executor.

Alder Wickes died on the 4 June 1774 and was buried six days later beside her husband in St Peter's Church. A handsome black memorial flagstone was placed over their grave (Fig. 112). According to Darby's Church Notes, this appears to have been situated originally in the nave—the armorials, carved in high relief, are described as 'ermine three battleaxes Wickes on an escutcheon of pretence a lion rampant. Helmet, mantle crest an arm in armour

112. Memorial flagstone to George and Alder Wickes. Originally in the nave of St Peter's Church, Thurston, Suffolk, the stone now lies beneath the tower. It was probably moved there when the church was restored following the collapse of the fourteenth century tower in 1860. The small brass plaque bearing their names and the dates of their deaths may have been added to the memorial at the same time.

holding in ye hand a battleaxe'. They were accompanied by a legend which has since disappeared: Wickes's age is given but that of Alder is omitted—Netherton may have realized that it was a sensitive subject and respected her reticence even after her death. As noted by Darby, it reads as follows:

Here lieth the body of
Mr George Wickes
who departed this life
The 31 August 1761
Aged 63 years
also
In memory of
Alder Wickes his wife
who died the 4 June
1774[10)]

For reasons unknown the memorial slab was later moved to a position beneath the tower where it still lies. It is identifiable by the armorials and a small brass plaque which has been fixed to the top right hand corner. A large crack runs across the stone from the top left hand corner to the centre of the base. This damage may have been sustained in 1860 when the fourteenth century tower collapsed. The plaque bearing the names of George and Alder Wickes and the dates of their deaths was almost certainly added when the church was repaired and restored.

The College of Arms has recently ruled that George Wickes had not established his right to the arms carved on the memorial stone. Those of Alder are shewn on an escutcheon of pretence as befitted an heiress, but she too had no entitlement though there may have been some tradition of a descent from a family entered in the records of the College of Arms whose right had been recognized. An imaginary crest appears on the tombstone; original arms had no crest (old arms very seldom did), but people in later days thought there ought to be one and added it. Netherton was almost certainly the culprit—after years of supervising the engraving of heraldic devices on silver he was perfectly capable of designing one for George Wickes.

The Nethertons moved from one close family circle to another with Parker kinsfolk replacing those of Wickes. Samuel was returning to the county of his forebears as a wealthy landed gentleman. There would have been no problem in setting up house in Chaceley: it was simply a matter of removing the furniture from Thurston and installing it in Hill End House. 'Plate jewells monies securities for money household goods furniture and household linnen and pictures', 'whatsoever and wheresoever and of what nature sort or quality soever the same may be', all now belonged to Netherton and there must have been a quantity of fine silver, china and linen.

The jewellery Alder had amassed in her lifetime must have been considerable and she had, moreover, inherited all the pieces which had belonged to her two sisters; Mary's purchases from George Wickes were by no means negligible judging by his entries in her ledger account (four diamond stay buckles alone cost her £181 10s). All these jewels Netherton no doubt passed to his wife. He himself bought wedding jewellery for her from Parker and Wakelin amounting to £136: Elizabeth appears to have had a penchant for diamonds which were set in drop earrings (two pairs), stay hooks and, above all, star pins (John Parker enters them in the firm's account as 'star pin', 'another star pin' and '2 more star pins').

Netherton was still young enough to play an active part in local affairs and in 1777 he was appointed High Sheriff of Worcester (Parker's brother-in-law Samuel West had preceded him in the office in 1775). *The Heraldry of Worcestershire* written by H. Sydney Grazebrook and published in 1873 devotes a paragraph to the armorials of 'Netherton, of Hill End House, Chasely; as borne by Samuel Netherton, High Sheriff in 1777.—Argent, a fesse dancetté between three goat's heads erased . . . (Nash).'. His duties as High Sheriff would have taken him frequently to Worcester. By 1777 John Parker had retired and was living in that city, a short walk from the house of his brother Thomas. There exists to this day in Worcester on the actual City Wall a passage known as Netherton Lane.

Netherton continued to keep in close touch with the firm in London. Edward Wakelin had retired at the same time as Parker and was succeeded by his son John Wakelin in partnership with William Tayler. John Wakelin had been apprenticed to his father and Tayler to John Parker: the continuity of Wickes's firm was assured.

According to Nash's *History of Worcestershire*, Netherton was in possession of the Manor of Chaceley until 1782, the descent of the estate being thereafter untraced. In Elizabeth Wickes Ray's will[11] made in 1791 he was 'of the City of Worcester'. His own will[12] is disappointingly brief. It was made from Chaceley in May 1775—he gave, devised and bequeathed all and every his real and personal estate and estates to his dearly beloved wife Elizabeth Mead [sic] Netherton who was named sole executrix. There are no bequests to any friends or erstwhile colleagues in London, Suffolk or Worcestershire though many of them were alive at the time. His godson, Thomas Netherton Parker, is not mentioned though he was remembered in the will of Elizabeth Ray. In 1775 the child was only three years of age and had yet to survive the notoriously unhealthy conditions of London to which his two sisters had fallen victim in infancy. Netherton must, however, have known his godson in Worcester from 1776 onwards and followed his career through Eton and Oriel College, Oxford. Every luxury available to the doting parents was lavished on their only surviving child and Netherton may have felt no compulsion to draw up a new will making provision for him. Elizabeth Meade Netherton must have shared his views for in her will[13] dated 27 June 1803 Thomas is not named: by this time he had inherited his parents' fortunes and married a young heiress.

Netherton died in February 1803 at the age of eighty. Middlesex is the county noted in the Index of Wills proved in the Prerogative Court of Canterbury and it is possible that he was in London at the time of his death. Elizabeth survived him a bare eight months: in her case, conversely, Worcester is the county written in the margin of the Index although in the will itself she clearly states that she was of Great Eaton Street Pimlico in the county of Middlesex. Her estate was divided between her own two nieces Susanna and Eleanor. Susanna, née Sansom, was married to the Reverend John Harward of Hartlebury, a member of an old landed Worcestershire family. Netherton's name was thereafter added to their own. John Harward's sister Susan married Thomas Gainsborough's nephew Edward Richard Gardiner.[14] Their daughter Charlotte Gardiner married her first cousin Thomas Netherton Harward, the son of Elizabeth Meade Netherton's niece and co-heiress, Susanna. It is fitting that the combined fortunes of George Wickes, Alder Wickes and Samuel Netherton finally found their way into a family with roots in both Suffolk and Worcestershire.

Although he figures frequently as a beneficiary in innumerable testaments, few details have emerged on Netherton the man. He must have made an indelible impression on one of the firm's clients, John Fannen, 'gentleman of Parson's Yard Kensington'. His will,[15] made in 1771, is remarkable because it is rare for a testator to name the goldsmiths who are to be entrusted with the making of a piece of memorial jewellery. In this case it concerned a 'diamond ring or any other diamond trinket' . . . 'and I shall be glad to have it made by Messrs Wakelin and Parker in Panton Street (Goldsmiths and Jewellers) near the Haymarket London'.

The words of his bequest to Netherton are an eloquent reminder of Samuel's qualities:

I give and bequeath to my dear friend Samuel Netherton Esqr of Thurston near Bury in Suffolk the sum of twenty-one pounds to buy a ring if he pleases in token of my love for him which ever was very great.

Notes for chapter XIV

1. P.R.O.: PCC Prob 11/759–46
2. Elaine Barr, 'Gainsborough and the Silversmith', *The Burlington Magazine*, February 1977.
3. P.R.O.: PCC Prob 11/822–127
4. Arch. Sudbury, Dalton 111, 120
5. They had probably been sent to live with a relative in order to learn housewifery: such apprenticeships are known in Suffolk in the eighteenth century.
6. The Martin connection is of some interest. Katherine, née Jackson of Snead Park Bristol, was married to John Martin of Overbury Court near Tewkesbury, a few miles from Chaceley. Formerly an eminent banker in Lombard Street, London, John Martin had acquired a fine estate at Overbury and represented the Borough of Tewkesbury in Parliament. An inkstand engraved with the arms of Martin impaling Jackson was made by Edward Wakelin in 1755 and sold at Christie's in November 1957 (Fig. 111).
7. P.R.O.: PCC Prob 11/851–410
8. P.R.O.: PCC Prob 11/869–334
9. P.R.O.: PCC Prob 11/999
10. This accords with a reference to the church in *A Concise Description of Bury St Edmunds and its Environs within the Distance of Ten Miles* written by an anonymous author and published in 1827.
11. P.R.O.: PCC Prob 11/1232–283
12. P.R.O.: PCC Prob 11/1387–132
13. P.R.O.: PCC Prob 11/1401–912
14. Gainsborough's brother-in-law Richard Gardiner is mentioned only briefly by the artist's biographers, but it is not inconceivable that he might have been related to the Edmund Gardiner who married Dorothy Butts—an aunt of the Bishop of Ely and a great-aunt of Henry Burrough's wife Caroline—at Stoke Ash in December 1691. George Wickes was first cousin once removed to Bishop Butts and it is obvious from the will of George's maternal aunt Rebecca Burton that the Gardiners were close kin: her legatees included her 'cousin Gardner and godson Gardner'.
15. P.R.O.: PCC Prob 11/966–158

Appendix I   Duty and Drawback

On the 1 June 1720, some two weeks before Wickes was made free of the Worshipful Company of Goldsmiths, an Act of Parliament came into force containing two important provisions. Goldsmiths were once more permitted to work in the old sterling standard (proscribed by the Statute of 1696/7 8 William III c. 8. in an attempt to prevent the debasement of the coinage) whilst the higher Britannia silver, the only kind Wickes would have fashioned during his apprenticeship, was retained as an alternative.

The new Statute—1719 6 George I c. 11—also made provision for the levying of a duty on all wrought silver (gold was excepted). This duty, in the words of the Statute, was by 'His Majesty's most dutiful and loyal subjects, the said Commons of Great Britain in Parliament assembled . . . cheerfully and unanimously granted'. Similar words are used to this day in certain Statutes.

The duty so cheerfully granted was sixpence per troy ounce on 'all Silver Plate to be made or wrought in Great Britain, or to be imported or brought into the same'. Since it was further enacted that the duty was 'to be paid by the Makers or Workers thereof', the goldsmiths were burdened not only with the calculation of the dues, but also the payment of them to the Customs and Excise. Furthermore, all goldsmiths were required to give notice in writing by the 1 of June 1720 of their 'Names and Places of Abode, and of the Houses or Places by them respectively made use of for the working or making of Silver Plate . . . upon pain to forfeit the Sum of twenty Pounds'. They had, moreover, to make each month an 'Entry in Writing . . . for the Said Duties of all the Silver Plate . . . wrought within such Month respectively; which Entry shall contain the Weight and Kinds of all the Silver Plate and Manufactures mentioned therein, and how much thereof respectively was made in each Week, on pain to forfeit for every neglect of Entry the sum of one hundred Pounds'. These monthly returns were to be made on the oath of the manufacturer or his chief workman: no fee was to be exacted by the officers appointed to take the oaths.

Within six weeks of making each entry the goldsmith had to pay the duty owed: if he failed to do so he was fined 'double the Sum of the said Duty'. The Customs and Excise officers were empowered to enter the goldsmiths' premises 'at all Times in the Day-time' to make a list of pieces liable to duty, 'leaving a true Copy thereof (if demanded) with the Maker'. Officers refusing to leave such copies were to be fined forty shillings, but the forfeit for any goldsmith who hindered or obstructed their searches was forty pounds.

Before the Bill became law the goldsmiths put forward cogent arguments against the proposed silver duty in a broadsheet entitled 'The Case of the Working Goldsmiths' (in which they also advocated the retention of the finer Britannia standard).

None of their arguments against the imposition of duty prevailed and they were forced to comply. They thereupon set their minds to inventing ways of evading the tax and, as we have seen, Wickes was of their mind. Objects were spirited to clients without being hall-marked; makers' marks were struck in imitation of hall-marks; small pieces were submitted for assay and once hall-marked subsequently incorporated in larger ones or the vital marks were actually cut out and the discs soldered into more substantial objects; the dies and marks used by the Assay Office were counterfeited.

Wickes must have kept some kind of record of his monthly Customs returns, but it has not survived. By 1735, the date of the first of the Garrard Ledgers, the enforcement of the law and the collection of the dues had clearly become impracticable and the Act was more honoured in the breach than in the observance. In the first Clients' Ledger references to duty are rare and the sums involved negligible. Thomas Minors, the King's goldsmith, was, it is true, meticulously charged duty amounting to £20 12s on 824 ozs 12 dwts in September 1736, but in the same year Lord North's account was debited the duty for sixty ounces when the weight of the pieces he purchased was 671 ozs 7 dwts whilst the Earl of Malton paid only £1 1s 6d—on forty-three ounces of silver used for four large scroll feet 'putt a sertuit table'—and no duty at all on candle sticks, sauce boats and waiters weighing some 1,051 ozs.

Wickes seems to have arrived at a strange compromise in later ledgers: he concentrated on gadrooning and time after time clients were charged the 'duty of ye nerls'. The Custom and Excise thus derived some small benefit from the change in style which required the addition of gadrooned borders to plates and dishes which had hitherto been plain.

There appears to have been—at least from 1755 onwards—some tacit acceptance on the part of the Customs and Excise of a rebate of duty on wrought silver traded in to Wickes. On the contra side of the account of the Countess of Exeter on the 22 March 1755 Wickes entered in his own handwriting 'By the duty of 12 plates & 2 old dishes taken of and allow^d for . . . 280 oz . . . *6d* . . . £7', The following year Lord Berkley was credited with £3 10*s*, the 'Duty allow^d on the 8 old dishes . . . 140 ozs'. The word 'old' seemingly applied to any piece made after 1720, the year in which the duty was first introduced. It must be presumed that the clients—or Wickes—were able to prove that the duty had been paid in the first instance. No provision for rebates of this kind was made in the Statute.

Duty payments are recorded in the annual reckonings in the Associates' Ledger, but the figures bear no relation to the weights entered in the Clients' Ledgers which are far in excess. A total for the year is usually shewn without explanation except in the period 1747–8. Here a second set of figures has been entered, in a different handwriting, in the column set aside for weights; it adds up to 1,770 ozs 1 dwt—considerably less than the original estimates—and against this total the words 'no duty' have been written. According to the Associates' Ledger duty was apparently paid on 15,743 ozs in 1749; the figure for the following year was 20,616 ozs 5 dwts; in 1755 it had fallen to 13,491 ozs.

The visits of the Customs and Excise men must have ceased to be a threat even before 1745 when Netherton openly credited the account of Wickes's sister-in-law Mary Phelpes with a quantity of silver objects traded in which included 'small pieces of coin': the practice of clipping the coinage and so debasing it was apparently still condoned.

Although the difficulty of enforcing the 1720 law must have been obvious, no attempt was made to change it. Instead, in a febrile effort to recoup lost revenue, yet another Act was passed. The Statute 29 George II c. 14 is little known and seldom quoted: it imposed a duty on all 'Persons and Bodies Politick or Corporate . . . who shall own, use, have or keep any Quantity of Silver Plate'. Declarations of such holdings had to be made in writing at the 'Chief Office of Excise' from the 5 of July 1756 and yearly thereafter. The basic rate of the duty was five shillings for every one hundred troy ounces. Holdings of 4,000 ozs and upwards were taxed at £10. The Customs officers were ordered to give receipts and enter the details in special registers.

The goldsmiths were exempted as far as their stock in trade was concerned, but all silver plate used by them and their families was subject to the tax.

It is impossible to assess the number of Wickes's clients who complied and duly presented themselves at the chief office of the Excise. Some law abiding customers relied upon him to make declarations on their behalf and several accounts in July 1756 are debited with 'Cash p^d at ye Excise Office' and 'Cash p^d for his Plate Tax'. The sums vary: a Miss Thruppe paid ten shillings in July 1758 for two hundred ounces whilst Lord Robert Manners was charged the maximum duty—ten pounds—on four thousand troy ounces. For three years running Sir Kenrick Clayton declared 2,100 ounces on which £5 5s was levied annually.

The collection of this new duty was no more successful than that of its predecessor and the Act was repealed in 1777 by the Statute 17 George III, c. 39.

It should be emphasized that the tax on the possession of wrought silver plate did not replace the duty of six pence per ounce exacted from the goldsmiths who manufactured it. That remained until it was cancelled by the Statute of 1757 31 George II, c. 32 whereby a system of licences was introduced requiring all persons 'trading in, selling or vending gold or silver plate' to pay two pounds per annum (increased to five pounds in July 1759).

This Act was not confined to licences for goldsmiths. The counterfeiting of dies and marks used at the assay offices and the fraudulent transposing of genuine marks—for which the penalty had previously been a fine of one hundred pounds—was now declared a felony punishable by death (commuted in 1773 to transportation for fourteen years).

The Ledgers yield no information on the actual methods adopted by the Customs and Excise for the collection of duty in Wickes's day. The Revenue officers' return books no longer survive: they were kept for two years and then sold 'to the King's best advantage'. It is possible that a procedure was agreed with the Assay Office similar to that adopted when Pitt reintroduced the duty of six pence per ounce on wrought silver (eight shillings for gold) in the Statute of 1784 24 George III, c. 53. Under that Act each goldsmith was compelled to send the amount of the duty with his wrought plate for assay together with a note specifying his name, address, the number and nature of the objects, total weight of the parcel and the amount of duty payable. The assay officer on receipt of the duty and the note was required to give a receipt for the money, file the note and enter the particulars in books kept for the purpose. These books had to be made available for inspection by the Revenue officers at all times; the responsibility for accounting and paying over the duty to the Commissioners of Stamps was, however, placed on the Assay Office which was allowed poundage for collection. Proof that this system was followed came to light recently when restoration of a papier-mâché terrestrial globe of the last quarter of the eighteenth century disclosed an inner lining of narrow strips of paper bearing the printed names of goldsmiths, amongst them that of Richard Crossley. It was discovered on examination that the slips were in fact lists of pieces of wrought silver submitted for assay; furthermore, the weights and duty payable were shewn at the bottom of the slips. The paper slips, measuring approximately 2 in. wide by 6 in. long, were exactly the right size for the purpose of lining the globes and the manufacturers, Wright–Ferguson, whose workshop was situated in the vicinity of the Hall, had obviously come to an arrangement with the Goldsmiths' Company to buy the discarded slips once they had served their purpose.

Pitt's tax of 1784 was relatively successful, due possibly to the efficient arrangements made for its collection. The system in force from 1720–1757 must have been far less stringent.

DRAWBACK   Although the sixpence per ounce duty imposed in 1720 applied equally to imported wrought silver, provision was made for the refund of this money when plate was exported. The exporters were required to 'make Proof upon Oath . . . that the same Silver Plate or Manufactures were actually made or marked as aforesaid, after the said first day of June one thousand seven hundred and twenty'. A certified debenture 'expressing the true Kinds and Qualities' was then handed to the Collector of the Duty on Plate who 'shall forthwith pay a Draw-back or Allowance after the Rate of six Pence for every Ounce'.

The wording of the Statute—'in case any Person or Persons whatsoever shall . . . export by way of Merchandize for any foreign Parts' could be taken to mean that the drawback applied to wrought silver intended for overseas customers or markets. This, however, was not the interpretation placed upon it by Wickes and his clients who, acting as private individuals, frequently took their silver plate abroad with them.

Sir Joshua Vanneck's ledger account was credited with a drawback of £5 12s 6d on an *épergne* weighing 225 ozs exported in November 1754. He was charged £1 7s by Wickes to cover the 'debenture and expence of shipping'. The *épergne* also appears on the debtor side priced at £142 16s 6d.: no entry for duty follows it and it must be inferred that this was covered in the overall price charged by Wickes for the *épergne* which would have been included in his monthly return to the Excise.

It is inconceivable that the Customs and Excise officials at the ports would have refunded the silver duty without some kind of receipt shewing that it had indeed been paid. The 1720 Act made provision for exporters 'to make Proof upon Oath', but they were not, apparently, required to support their sworn statements with any document other than the debenture. It is possible that a receipt had to be produced before the debenture was issued in the first place, but this is not mentioned in the Statute.

'Sufficient Security' that the plate exported should 'not be relanded or brought again into Great Britain' had to be given before shipping. Few noblemen embarking on an extended tour of the Continent would have ventured abroad without some kind of domestic and toilet silver and it is unlikely that they would have been prepared to leave it behind on their return to Britain.

In the early 1750s entries in the Ledgers for 'the expense of a debenture, carriage to Chester & shipping to Dublin' occur with surprising frequency. Some of the clients concerned may well have been domiciled in Ireland. However, the lives of certain of these men have been well documented and when, in those cases, no connection with Ireland is apparent, it is difficult to dispel the suspicion that not all these shipments were bona fide exports. The cost involved was usually considerably less than the amount recovered on the drawback of the silver duty and it is even possible that the plate never left the country, the 'shipment' being merely a paper transaction carried out with the connivance of a dishonest revenue official.

113. The Leinster Service as it appears in the account of the Earl of Kildare in Wickes's ledger. *Courtesy of the Victoria and Albert Museum*

Appendix II   The Leinster Dinner Service

The superb matched service made by Wickes for the Duke of Leinster between 1745 and 1747 (Fig. 114) is one of the few that has survived. With the exception of a relatively small number of objects, it is still intact and some 170 pieces are now in a private collection. It is also remarkable from the point of view of design. The influence of French forms is clearly visible and it will be recalled that this was the client who commissioned replicas of a Thomas Germain candelabrum from Wickes in 1745 and whose account at that time included 'a book of drawings'.

When Wickes began work on the dinner service his client was still the Earl of Kildare and his account in the Ledgers uses that title. He was not created Duke of Leinster until 1766, but somewhat confusingly a viscountcy—Leinster of Taplow—was added to his titles in 1746 on the occasion of his marriage to Emilia Mary, daughter of Charles Lennox, second Duke of Richmond, and god-daughter of George II, Horace Walpole, with more truth than he could have imagined, commented that the bride's parents 'have not given her a shilling, but the King endows her by making Lord Kildare a Viscount sterling'. Wicke's client is hereafter referred to as the Duke of Leinster for convenience.

114. Part of the Leinster Service. An idea of the comparative dimensions of the main pieces may be gained from this illustration. The four condiment urns and the sugar bowls have been placed on the plateau of the *épergne. Courtesy of Sotheby Parke Bernet Inc. New York*

Seen in its entirety the Leinster Service gives an insight into the grandeur of life in the great houses of the eighteenth century. The full magnificence of the service in its present state can be judged from the list below. The original service was slightly larger as will be seen from the Earl of Kildare's account in Wickes's ledger (Fig. 113). For ease of comparison, the numbers entered in the ledger have been placed in brackets after the objects, accompanied where necessary by Wickes's own description of the pieces.

19	oval serving dishes	(30 dishes)
59	dinner plates	(7 dozⁿ ½ of
18	soup plates	plates)
8	sauce boats	(10 sauceboats
4	sauce ladles	& spoons)
2	mazarines complete with dishes	(4 fish plates)
1	large waiter (21½ ins)	(1 large &
8	small waiters (in graduated sizes from 7½ ins)	10 smaller waiters)
4	candlesticks (2 pairs)	(4 pairs)
22	dish covers	(22)
2	soup tureens complete with under dishes & ladles	(2 tarrines 2 dishes & 2 ladles)
2	oval covered bowls	(2 ovill and four
4	pyriform containers	round boxes)
2	cruets	(2 cruet boxes)
1	epergne (less silver basket)	(a fine epergne & basket
1	plateau	& table)
1	wooden base	(a mahogany board & brass casters silverᵈ for the table)

Apart from the omissions shewn above—and the flatware—only a few of the major pieces are missing: two bread baskets, 'a machine dish ring', six 'escallopᵈ shells' and eight salts with their spoons.

A dish ring ensuite with the service would not be difficult to picture were it not for the word 'machine'. No 'watch work' is mentioned—indicating some kind of mechanical contrivance—and it may be another instance of Wickes's old habit of falling back on the term 'machine' when at a loss for an exact description of a piece.

On the evidence of the Ledgers, the scallop dishes would have been used for oysters. The shells ordered by the Duke of Leinster weighed 3 ozs 14 dwts each: the heaviest made by Wickes was 5 ozs 5 dwts. At this weight they would have been unsuitable dishes for unopened oysters in any quantity and it can only be assumed that the molluscs were removed from their shells and served in silver counterparts. Oysters baked in natural scallop shells with bread crumbs, cream and butter were popular delicacies in the eighteenth century. Whilst these silver scallop shells make ideal dishes for butter served in the elegant curls favoured today, basins appear to have been used for butter in Wickes's time and two such were traded in by a client in 1738. Whilst they are clearly described as butter basins, this is the only mention of them in the Ledgers: they may have gone out of fashion, but it is possible that the sugar basins purchased in such quantities served a dual purpose. The orders for scallop dishes are too rare to suggest that it had become *à la mode* to serve pats of butter in slender silver shells. No butter knives as such are entered though spades appear later in the century and in 1798 butter ladles suddenly became the vogue, used possibly for pouring melted butter over vegetables.

Since bread baskets were important items in a dinner service it is reasonable to suppose that those made for the Duke of Leinster were elaborately wrought in the manner of the tureens. In the same collection there is coincidentally a fine bread basket made by John Luff and hallmarked 1744 which bears a marked resemblance to certain pieces in the Leinster Service. It, too, shews the influence of French design: the engraved armorials are not, however, those of the Earl of Kildare.

The eight salts must have been handsome objects, each weighing over nine ounces: this also covered the matching spoon, the weight of the two together being nearly three times that of the oyster scallops. Glass containers made to fit inside the salts were provided to protect the silver from corrosion. These glasses had to be taken out each time the salts were used in order to remove any grains which might have slipped behind them: breakages were inevitable and eight replacements were ordered, to be followed later in the account by a further twenty-four.

These, then, are the few objects which are missing from the service. Those which have survived are now the prime concern. The smallest pieces are of particular interest. The pyriform containers (Fig. 115) described by Wickes as '4 round boxes' are in fact the earliest documented condiment urns, so different in shape from the casters which preceded them that, until they were identified by Mr Michael Snodin ('Silver Vases and their purpose', *The Connoisseur*, January

115

116

117

118a

118b

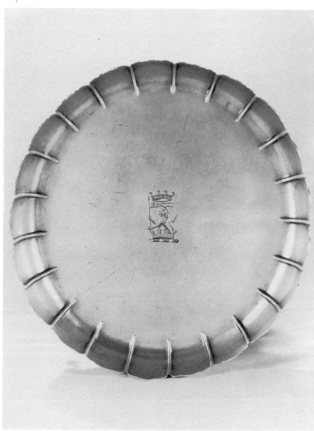

1977), they were universally mistaken for tea and sugar vases. The pieces which resemble small covered tureens (Fig. 115) are Wickes's two 'ovill' boxes which were intended to hold sugar, one of the ingredients for making a salad dressing. The purpose of these six 'boxes' is underlined by the entries which immediately follow them:

> To 2 suger spoons 2 pepper 2 musterd spoons
> To 24 salt glasses and 12 musterd and pepper glasses

The intricately pierced cruets (Fig. 116) held oil and vinegar and here again '8 cut [glass] cruets' were delivered, allowing four spare bottles to replace any that were broken or chipped. Wickes's four silver cruet tops, complete with '4 tips for yᵉ cruets', would have been interchangeable.

No dinner service at this period would have been complete without special serving dishes for the salad. Green vegetables were not always available throughout the year in the eighteenth century and salads made of fresh herbs were frequently substituted. Twelve 'sallet dishes' were included in the silver-gilt service made by Wickes's firm for the Prince of Wales in 1748/9, but eight were sufficient for the Duke of Leinster: this was the number usually ordered by clients. These small fluted dishes, circular in shape, are reminiscent of the so-called strawberry dishes of Caroline times. The incurved edges, which were scalloped in the 1740s, were bordered with gadrooning in the 1750s. They had long been taken for dessert or *épergne* dishes and were not accurately identified until 1965 when a pair engraved with the arms of Lord Mountford came up for auction at Christie's (Fig. 117). On recourse to the Ledgers Mr Arthur Grimwade found that they had formed part of a set of eight salad dishes made by Wickes in 1744. The Mountford salad dishes have a timeless simple charm. The set of eight in the Leinster Service would have been far more ornate.

The distinctive feature of the salad dish at this date is that it rests on small feet (Fig. 118a). Wickes was occasionally required to add feet to existing pieces and make them into salad dishes: one such conversion is recorded by him in 1744: 'To silver feet put on 8 sallad dishes' and 'making & doing' them up 'as new'.

The motif which unites all the pieces in the Leinster Service is most prominent in the waiters (Fig. 119), serving dishes and plates (Fig. 120) where it is unobscured by additional decoration. It takes the form of a serpentine threaded border which is bound at intervals with beaded strapwork and interspersed with shells of two types which interrupt the flow of the reeding. The same shells are used on the bases of the baluster candlesticks (Fig. 121). In the condiment

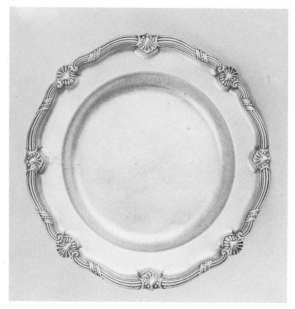

urns and sugar bowls foliage is also introduced accompanied by scrolling strapwork.

The imposing soup tureens (Fig. 122) are slightly bombé and set on pierced socle and scroll feet. The massive ornament in the French taste is at first glance almost overwhelming. Closer inspection reveals the brilliance of the fashioning and the technical virtuosity of these extraordinary pieces. An unusual feature of the design is the bold piercing, like the slashes in a Renaissance sleeve, to reveal the silver liner inside. The piercing is emphasized by alternating leaf scrolls and tendrils which radiate from a large rococo shell. The rest of the body of the tureen is completely covered with elaborate chasing. The handles, set in cast and applied scrolls, bring a note of simplicity, as does the border which is decorated with the familiar threadwork which distinguishes every piece in the service. Not content to echo in the lid the conceits used with such effect on the body of the tureen, designer and goldsmith turn to an entirely different concept. Two streams of silver, part wave, part drape, flow from an ornate threaded handle and spread across the surface of the lid stopping short with an inward curl at the very edge of the cover. A plain band with restrained shell and tongue decoration intervenes between the lid and the body of the tureen.

Edward Wakelin was to fashion an almost identical handle for the cover of the superb soup tureens (Fig. 123) which he made for the ninth Earl of Exeter eight years later in 1755, echoing not only the thread border but also the unusual quilting effect which Wickes

119. Waiter from the Leinster Service, diameter 21½ in (54.6 cm). This is the large waiter made for the Leinster Service. Wickes also made ten smaller matching waiters (eight of which have survived) in graduated sizes from 7½ in. *Courtesy of Sotheby Parke Bernet Inc. New York*

120. Plate from the Leinster Service. *Photograph courtesy of Australian Consolidated Press Limited*

121. Two pairs of candlesticks from the Leinster Service. *Photograph courtesy of Australian Consolidated Press Ltd.*

122. Soup tureen, under dish & ladle from the Leinster Service. *Photograph courtesy of Australian Consolidated Press Limited*

introduced in the feet of the sauce boats which he made for the Duke of Leinster (Fig. 125).

The same handle, in a simpler form and set into a disc bordered with thread work, surmounts the dish covers (Fig. 127) in the Leinster Service. These domed covers are striking for the comparative simplicity and economy of the scrolling strapwork which decorates them, strange precursors of the art nouveau style still a century and a half away.

It will be noted that no mazarines are recorded in the Earl's account. The term was never employed by Wickes though it was used freely by his successors Parker and Wakelin to describe a pierced flat plate inserted in a dish for draining certain types of food.

Cardinal Mazarin (or possibly his niece, the Duchesse de Mazarin, who was renowned for the refinement of her table) is popularly

203

supposed to have given the strainer plate its name. Neither the word nor the object is known in that sense in France and it is far more likely that it has an English derivation and is in fact a diminutive of 'mazer', a type of bowl. After exhaustive research this was the conclusion reached by Dr N. M. Penzer ('What is a Mazerine?' *Apollo*, April 1955). He discloses, inter alia, on the authority of the poet Andrew Marvell in 1673 and of John Kersey, the lexicographer, in 1708, that mazarins or mazarines appear originally to have been small dishes for ragoûts and fricassées which were arranged on a large flat dish. The practice may have been abandoned by 1735 for no such sets, whether described as mazers, mazarins or mazarines, appear in the Ledgers in Wickes's day.

Wickes was notoriously indifferent to exact terminology and many of the objects he made would be difficult to identify were it not for the information set out in accompanying entries which relate to their fashioning. As far as Wickes was concerned, a mazarine was a fish plate and when one is recorded in the Ledgers it is invariably accompanied by a charge for 'making and piercing' though this detail was omitted in the account of the Duke of Leinster, covered no doubt

123. One of a pair of two tureens under dishes & ladles made for the Earl of Exeter, Edward Wakelin, 1755. The Ledger entry reads:

To 2 terrines & dishes
500 ozs 14 dwts 11/1   £277   9s   6d

To 2 soup ladles
23 ozs 18 dwts 9/1   £10   17s   0d

To graving 2 coats & supporters
& 6 crests & cor^ts   £2   8s   0d
Courtesy of Sotheby's

124. *Epergne* and plateau from the Leinster Service (the basket is missing from the Collection). *Photograph courtesy of Australian Consolidated Press Limited*

125. Two pairs of sauce boats from the Leinster Service. *Photograph courtesy of Australian Consolidated Press Limited*

by the high fashioning cost of 9*s* 7*d* per troy ounce. These mazarines took their long oval lines from the shape of fish such as salmon or pike which were served whole. Their original purpose was strictly functional and the strainer was constructed so that it rested on an inside rim of a serving dish of appropriate size and shape. The piercing became more and more elaborate: whilst geometric patterns were usually chosen, other more delicate designs are occasionally found, one of the most remarkable being the fishes struggling in a net which decorates a magnificent pair of silver-gilt mazarines, made by George Hunter in 1762, in the Collection of Her Majesty the Queen.

Wickes describes the oval centrepiece (Fig. 124) not as a surtout à table, but as 'a fine epargne & basket & table'. With the basket (now missing) it weighed 427 ozs 16 dwts and cost the Duke £360 11*s*. The influence of William Kent can be seen in the trellis canopy which Wickes had used with such felicity in the *épergne* he made for the Prince of Wales in 1745. The Leinster centrepiece is, however, conceived on a smaller scale, its weight and cost being half those of the royal piece. The plateau or table on which the canopy rests achieves a marvellous balance. Its base, set on scrolled and foliated feet, is richly ornamented with cast and applied foliage, shells and cornucopia which in no way detract from the restrained elegance of the engraving (Fig. 126). The same bound threadwork border—the integral motif of the Leinster Service—appears on the plateau.

By the time the service was finished Wickes was forty-nine years old and nearing the end of his life as a working goldsmith. I like to think that he may have seen it as his swan song, pouring into it all the artistry, skill and technical knowledge he had acquired over more than a quarter of a century.

127. Dishes and covers from the Leinster Service. The dish in the centre of the photograph has feet and was probably a salad dish. *Photograph courtesy of Australian Consolidated Press Limited*

Bibliography

ALDWORTH, Richard. *A Letter to Wm. Lenthall, Esq.*, Bristol, 1643

BEAVEN, A. B. *The Aldermen of the City of London*, 2 vols, 1908

CULLUM, Sir John, Bart. *A Collection of miscellaneous cuttings from newspapers and periodicals*, 1712–1785

CULLUM, The Rev. Sir Thomas Gery, Bart., *History & Antiquities of Hawsted and Hardwick in the County of Suffolk*, London, 1813

DEFOE, Daniel. *The Complete English Tradesman*, 1726

DOWELL, Stephen. *A History of Taxation & Taxes in England*, Vol. IV, London, 1884

EGMONT, Earl of. *Memoirs*, 3 vols, ed. R. A. Roberts (Hist. Man. Comm.), 1920–23

GEORGE, M. Dorothy. *London Life in the XVIIIth Century*, 1925

GRAZEBROOK, H. Sydney. *The Heraldry of Worcestershire*, 1873

GRIMWADE, Arthur G. *The Garrard Ledgers*, Proceedings of the Society of Silver Collectors, 1961

GRIMWADE, Arthur G. *Rococo Silver, 1727–1765*, London, 1974

GRIMWADE, Arthur G. *London Goldsmiths, 1697–1837*, 1976

HARWARD, Thomas Netherton. *Hereward the Saxon Patriot*, 1896

HAYWARD, J. F. *Huguenot Silver in England*, 1688–1727, London, 1959

HEAL, Ambrose. *The London Goldsmiths, 1200–1800*, London, 1935

HERVEY, John, 1st Earl of Bristol. *Diary*, Wells, 1894

HERVEY, John, Lord. *Some Materials for the Reign of King George II*, 3 vols, ed. Romney Sedgwick, 1931

JACKSON, Sir Charles. *Illustrated History of English Plate*, London, 1911

JONES, E. Alfred. *The Gold and Silver of Windsor Castle*, London, 1911

MacINNES, C. M. & WHITTARD, W. F. (editors), *Bristol and its adjoining Counties*

OMAN, Charles. *English Domestic Silver*, 1934

PENNANT, Thomas. *Some Account of London*, 1805

POWELL, J. W. Damer. *Thomas Aldworth: Founder of British India*, (United Empire XXII—new series), 1931

PRIDEAUX, Walter S. *Memorials of the Goldsmiths' Company, 1335–1815*, 2 vols, London, 1896–7

RUDÉ, George *Hanoverian London, 1714–1808*, London, 1971

SALISBURY, Edward Elbridge *Memorials on Families of Salisbury, Aldworth–Elbridge*, 1885

SNODIN, Michael. *English Silver Spoons*, 1974

STRYPE, John *A Survey of the Cities of London and Westminster*, 1720

TAYLOR, Gerald. *Silver*, London, 1956

VULLIAMY, C. E. *The Onslow Family, 1528–1874*, 1953

WALPOLE, Horace. *Memoirs of the Reign of George II*, 1845

WALPOLE, Horace *The Letters of Horace Walpole*, 9 vols, ed. Peter Cunningham, London, 1861

YOUNG, Sir George. *Poor Fred*, London, 1937

Touching Gold & Silver—500 Years of Hallmarks—Catalogue of Exhibition at Goldsmiths' Hall, November 1978

Eighteenth Century Newspapers: *Daily Advertiser, Daily Courant, Daily Journal, Daily Post, London Evening Post* and *London Gazette*

Acknowledgements

But for the timely rescue of the Garrard Ledgers by Mr Arthur Grimwade this book would never have been written. My debt is greater for his enthusiasm and help during the writing of it, and particularly for his kindness in providing the introduction.

Few researchers can have received the encouragement and scholarly support so freely given me by Mr Claude Blair, Keeper of the Department of Metalwork at the Victoria and Albert Museum, and Mrs Shirley Bury, Deputy Keeper (to whom I owe my introduction to the Ledgers).

Mr L. H. Haydon Whitehead of Long Melford, Suffolk, placed at my disposal his deep knowledge of Suffolk genealogy and I gratefully acknowledge not only his invaluable advice but also his guidance. I should like to thank Miss Susan Hare, Librarian to the Worshipful Company of Goldsmiths, for her generous help and infinite patience.

Through the kindness of Mr Anthony Gray, Secretary and Keeper of the Records of the Duchy of Cornwall, I was able to examine the bills of George Wickes in the Household Accounts of Frederick, Prince of Wales. The assistance given to me by Dr Graham Haslam, the Librarian to the Duchy, is greatly appreciated.

I am also indebted to Mr Geoffrey de Bellaigue, Mr Ronald Lightbown, Mr John Mallet, Mr Charles Oman, Mr Anthony Phillips, Mr Basil Robinson, Mrs Jean Schofield and Mr Michael Snodin. Miss Melissa Denny, my editor at Studio Vista, deserves special thanks for her enthusiasm and concern, as does Mr Conway Lloyd Morgan for his guidance and interest.

Many of the portraits and objects illustrated in the book are in private collections and I am most grateful to their owners for permission to reproduce them.

Messrs Garrard & Co Ltd, the Crown Goldsmiths, kindly allowed me access to the two earliest ledgers of George Wickes which are still in their possession. My thanks are due to Mr Frederick Bingham, Mr Bernard Copping, Mr Brand Inglis, Mr Ronald Lee, Mr John Partridge, Mr Ian Pickford, Mr Eric J. G. Smith and—particularly—to Mr Thomas Lumley.

I have had recourse to many County Record Offices whose archivists have been unfailingly helpful. I am grateful to the late Mr M. P. Statham and to Mrs Margaret Statham, his widow, in Wickes's native county, Suffolk; to Mr E. H. Sargeant and Miss Margaret Henderson (Worcester); to Mr Brian S. Smith (Gloucester); Miss Mary C. Hill and Mrs Marion Halford (Salop); Miss Mary Williams (Bristol).

The task of assembling the illustrations was lightened by the courtesy and co-operation of Messrs Christie, Manson & Woods, Ltd and Messrs Sotheby & Co.

I should also like to thank the following photographers: Mr Peter MacDonald, Mr Stanley Eost, Mr Martin Bladon, Mr O. G. Jarman of Bury St Edmunds, Messrs A. C. Cooper Ltd, Godfrey New Photographics Ltd and John Freeman Group.

The rubbing of the Wickes memorial in St Peter's Church, Thurston was made by Mr Brian Cooper of Studio 69, Norwich.

Index of names